Nuclear Proliferation in South Asia

NUCLEAR PROLIFERATION IN SOUTH ASIA

Dr, Charu Lata Singh

NEHA PUBLISHERS & DISTRIBUTORS
DELHI

Publisher
NEHA PUBLISHERS & DISTRIBUTORS
4832/24,Prahlad Lane,S-207 Ansari
Road, Daryaganj, Delhi-110002
Ph.: 43570976, 23278261
Email: nehapubdistributors@gmail.com

Edition: 2015

ISBN: 978-93-80318-60-8

Laser Typesetting
JEE-VEE Graphics, Delhi

Price: 1195/-

Printed
Vikas Computers, Delhi

Contents

	Preface	(*vii*)
1.	Introduction	1
2.	Nuclear Weapons and Strategy	31
3.	Nuclear Proliferation	83
4.	Nuclear Command and Control in India and Pakistan	97
5.	Challenge of Nuclear Weapons	142
6.	Nuclear Non-Proliferation Treaty	193
7.	Nuclear Explosions	201
8.	Nuclear Power Growth in India	260
	Bibliography	293
	Index	295

Preface

As aforementioned, nuclear weapons development and enhancement in South Asia are intricately related to long-standing rivalries between the concerned states. However, instability does not just stem from the risk of nuclear warfare between states in the region. Non-state actors also play a significant role in the nuclear security framework, aside from their role in facilitating nuclear proliferation. First, terrorist groups (such as Jaish-e-Mohammed and Lashkar-e-Toiba) that are connected to the Pakistani religious-political establishment can provoke tensions between India and Pakistan through mass casualty attacks.

China's proposed sale of two civilian nuclear-power reactors to Pakistan hardly seems a danger sign. Pakistan already has the bomb, so it has all the nuclear secrets it needs. Next-door India has the bomb too, and has been seeking similar deals with other countries.

Yet the sale (really a gift, as Pakistan is broke) has caused shudders at the Nuclear Suppliers Group (NSG), an informal cartel of countries who want to stop their advanced nuclear technology getting into the wrong hands. They are meeting in New Zealand, for what was supposed to be a quiet and nerdish rule-tightening session. But their efforts may now fall victim to China's rivalry with America.

By any measure, Pakistan is a shocker. Its proliferation record would make the serial nuclear mischief-makers of North Korea blush. If the Chinese reactor deal goes ahead, the damage will be huge: beyond just stoking the already alarming nuclear rivalry between Pakistan and India.

This book is a modest attempt to discuss all these issues.

—Editor

1

Introduction

In recent years, experts have closely studied two main aspects of regarding South Asian nuclear issues. First, nuclear modernization in the region continues with the development of longer-range and more reliable delivery systems, as well as qualitative and quantitative increases in fissile material and warheads. Initiatives, such as the Indo-U.S. nuclear deal, have brought renewed focus on this issue due to its potential impact on proliferation in South Asia. Second, the A.Q. Khan network confirmed the entry of non-state actors into the realm of nuclear proliferation. Lingering questions regarding the network's activities suggest that its impact has not yet been fully assessed. There is still considerable demand for nuclear technology, both through horizontal proliferation from aspiring nuclear states such as Iran, and terrorist networks looking to augment their capabilities. This study will analyse these varied developments and investigate proliferation trends in the region.

This study examines proliferation trends from three perspectives. The first section looks at the doctrinal issues arising from security disputes that are the driving forces for nuclear modernization in South Asia. The second section examines proliferation linkages between South Asia and other regions, focusing on the A.Q. Khan network, among other issues. This section also highlights a key problem arising from contemporary WMD proliferation-the involvement of non-state actors. The final section addresses the potential impact of a crucial development-the Indo-U.S. nuclear cooperation agreement. Nuclear proliferation in South Asia is in part a consequence of the security dilemma existing in the subcontinent. Security dilemmas arise when a state's mechanisms for increasing its security negatively impact the security and threat perceptions of other states. As one expert stated, the South Asian nuclear security complex involves several security dilemmas, including Pakistan/India, India/China, and Russia/United States. A further security dilemma dyad is that of the United States and China, since it has an impact on attitudes in India and Pakistan, and helps shape their nuclear decisions.

It is helpful to analyse the security dilemma briefly through an example. From India's perspective, the threat from China is of prime importance, and therefore New Delhi's nuclear and missile development program is geared, in part, toward countering Beijing with a secure deterrent.

However, Beijing's primary threat perception stems from the United States' role in the Asia-Pacific region. Consequently, one must consider the possibility that Beijing may conduct nuclear tests in the coming years if Washington goes ahead with plans to construct newer, more reliable warheads. In addition, analysts have predicted that Washington is likely to abandon the Strategic Arms Reduction Treaty-I (START-I) when it goes out of force in 2009. The abandonment of START-1 would remove all obstacles for U.S. plans to counter the strategic threat from China and other potential adversaries. To deal with this threat from the United States, Beijing has proceeded with its plan to strengthen its second strike capability through the development of mobile long-range ballistic missiles, both land-based and submarine-launched, according to a May 2007 Pentagon report.

However, China's desire to catch up with the United States would oblige India to prevent an adverse strategic balance. India's need for a reliable nuclear deterrent against China involves expanding New Delhi's nuclear weapons and delivery systems capabilities. Advanced capabilities include the development of a thermonuclear weapon and second strike capabilities through long-range ballistic missiles, such as the Agni-III or submarine launched ballistic missile capabilities, within the proposed nuclear submarine project and the Sagarika missile.

This impacts on the Indo-Pakistani equation because while New Delhi has a China focus for its expanding nuclear arsenal, it naturally increases its capability vis-à-vis Islamabad as well. It is widely accepted that since its inception, Pakistan's nuclear policy has been a constant response to the perceived threat from India. Therefore, in order to maintain the strategic balance or to at least prevent from the present imbalance from widening, Pakistan further expands its own nuclear capabilities. Furthermore, India on one side, and China and Pakistan on the other, are concerned over the extent of U.S. interactions with the other side, and the long-term impact this will have on the strategic balance in South Asia. This was evidenced in the immediate period after 9/11, when the U.S.-Pakistan counter-terrorism alliance was seen as detrimental to Indian interests.

The security dilemma in the South Asian subcontinent operates as a chain reaction that includes regional and extra-regional powers with competing interests. For countries like India and China, it is important to note that while the goals of nonproliferation (especially at a time of potential WMD-related terrorism) are extremely crucial, perceived national interests are a greater factor in shaping the eventual policy direction. With this motivational framework in mind, one must examine recent proliferation-related developments in South Asia, that are likely to have far reaching consequences both regionally and in terms of the global nonproliferation regime. They include the proposed Indo-U.S. nuclear cooperation, the significance of the A.Q. Khan network, and links between South Asian and Middle East proliferation dynamics. These developments reflect, partly or in whole, the need for the weaker protagonist to correct the perceived security imbalance against the stronger threat.

NON-STATE ACTORS AND SECURITY IN SOUTH ASIA

As aforementioned, nuclear weapons development and enhancement in South Asia are intricately related to long-standing rivalries between the concerned states. However, instability does not just stem from the risk of nuclear warfare between states in the region. Non-state actors also play a significant role in the nuclear security framework, aside from their role in facilitating nuclear proliferation. First, terrorist groups (such as Jaish-e-Mohammed and Lashkar-e-Toiba) that are connected to the Pakistani religious-political establishment can provoke tensions between India and Pakistan through mass casualty attacks. This was amply demonstrated following the December 2001 attack on the Indian Parliament by Jaish-e-Mohammed militants, which led to a ten-month stand-off between the two armies.

A second danger is through a Kargil-style episode in which militants, in cooperation with official Pakistani agencies and the military, occupy territory in Kashmir. As the July 2007 siege of the Lal Masjid (Red Mosque) complex in the heart of Islamabad showed, militant groups are steadily expanding their geographical area of influence, adversely affecting the stability of Pakistan. Although the nuclear weapon complex is under military control, there might be pockets within the military that are sympathetic to fundamentalist groups. At the very least, political and religious instability in Pakistan creates uncertainty in the minds of policymakers within and outside the region.

Finally, fears have been heightened since 9/11 over the possibility of nuclear weapons technology transfers from Pakistan to terrorist networks, especially after it was revealed that some senior Pakistani nuclear scientists met with the Al Qaeda leadership prior to 9/11. A related concern in the aftermath of 9/11 is that a fundamentalist Islamic group with Taliban/Al Qaeda links could take over Pakistan and with it, possession of the country's nuclear arsenal. Thus, Indian (as well as U.S.) threat perceptions include not just bilateral nuclear stability issues between India and Pakistan, but also the consequences of nuclear technology and materials falling into the hands of militant groups.

In general, the complex nuclear weapons scenario in South Asia is shaped by two main factors. First, the intense nature of the dispute between India and Pakistan strikes at the very core of their nationhood. It involves territorial disputes and terrorist violence, and is further complicated by the desire of some terrorist groups to acquire non-conventional technology. Second, South Asia is part of a broader nuclear weapons context that includes China and the United States. Military developments by either Washington or

Beijing, which are perceived as a direct threat, also impact military policies (both conventional and non-conventional) in South Asia. At the same time, the continued strategic military collaboration between China and Pakistan (such as the joint development of the JF-17 fighter plane) is a factor that motivates India to continue nuclear and conventional modernization. Furthermore, while the territorial disputes between India and China are relatively dormant, there is no final resolution. As developments in 2006-2007 demonstrated, there is still a considerable gap between the two sides on the territorial issue. Due to this combination of factors, there are no clear incentives for either party to drastically reorient its nuclear policy.

Nuclear Policies in South Asia

Keeping the various security disputes and attitudes in mind, the next step is to consider the nuclear doctrines and policies of protagonists in the region. Both India and Pakistan strive for a minimum deterrent. The objective of India's nuclear strategy is credible minimum deterrence (CMD), meaning a secure and reliable second-strike capability after absorbing an adversary's first strike. The main potential targets of this projected deterrence capability are Pakistan and China. Pakistan's nuclear doctrine also seeks a credible deterrent, against India, and according to one senior nuclear weapons planner, its weapons are "aimed solely at India." In particular it seeks to deter New Delhi from launching a conventional military attack such as an offensive for limited war objectives, including destruction of terrorist training camps, as well as attacks on nuclear facilities.

For both India and Pakistan, key components of their attitudes in nuclear defence demonstrate the incompatibility between their mutual nuclear postures. India's offer of a no-first use pact has been rejected by Pakistan as nuclear weapons are an integral element of its (Islamabad's) defence doctrine. On the other hand, Islamabad has offered New Delhi a no-war pact, which ostensibly would reduce the prospect of full-scale conventional war and the risk of nuclear crises. However, such a proposal does not touch upon the proxy war waged by the Kashmiri militants and therefore has been rejected by New Delhi.

Thus, both India and Pakistan strive for a secure second-strike capability as an integral element of their credible minimum deterrent doctrines. Since neither side has constructed systems that are deemed completely satisfactory and reliable, nuclear modernization continues. For India, this means a survivable delivery mechanism that can conceivably strike major cities in China. At present the longest range deployed missile is believed to be the Agni-II with a range of 2,000-2,500 km, and can reach parts of western China. To have an increased range capability, the Indian Defence Research and Development Organization (DRDO) is developing the Agni III intermediate range ballistic missile, which was successfully tested for the first time in April 2007 and has a range of about 3,500 km. Nevertheless, reports have stated that the Indian military is not altogether satisfied with the nuclear capable missiles that are in its arsenal-Prithvi I (short range ballistic missiles) and the Agni I & II. Thus, India's nuclear delivery systems are deemed far from adequate and for the time being. In the opinion of the Indian Air Force, there will be considerable reliance on fighter bombers such as the Mig 27, Jaguar, and Mirage-2000 for a nuclear delivery role.

This implies that for the foreseeable future, the Indian scientific-military establishment will reinforce their commitment to adequate delivery systems, especially the Agni III and the nuclear submarine project (the Advanced Technology Vessel or ATV) that could carry a sea-based deterrent in the form of a submarine-launched cruise missile (the Sagarika-currently under development). Reports in May 2007 stated that the ATV will be commissioned in 2011-2012 and that two Russian nuclear submarines might be leased before that.

As stated earlier, Pakistan's deployed missile systems can reach most parts of India. These deployed missiles include the Ghaznavi (Hatf-3, range 290 km), Shaheen-I (Hatf-4, range 600-800 km), and the Ghauri-I (Hatf-5, range 1,500 km). Development is also taking place on the Shaheen-II (Hatf-6, range 2,000-3,000 km), which was successfully tested in February 2007. These missile developments illustrate Pakistan's desire for a more secure deterrent, once the range issue had been dealt with. In addition, Pakistan is also seeking a more secure second-strike capability through the acquisition of the Agosta 90B class submarine in late 2007. This vessel, the second to be added to Pakistan's navy, can carry the nuclear capable Harpoon cruise missiles.

Both countries have also achieved considerable progress in manufacturing another delivery system-cruise missiles. India, in partnership with Russia, has developed the BrahMos, while Pakistan has the Babur. These missiles are meant to have land, sea, and air versions, and at least in the case of the BrahMos, will also have a variant for export. In the near future, Indian defence planners hope to introduce land attack cruise missiles with the capacity to carry a nuclear warhead over 1,500 km. In addition, submarine and air force versions of the BrahMos are due to be tested in 2007. The missile is also being installed on ships and IL-38D maritime reconnaissance aircraft to give "strategic relevance" to the Indian Navy. Similarly, Pakistan has successfully tested its nuclear capable Babur (Hatf VII) cruise missile (range 700 km), most recently in March 2007.

In sum, in order to strengthen their nuclear delivery capabilities both India and Pakistan are seeking to perfect their missile arsenals, both ballistic and cruise. The dynamic nature of the pursuit of more reliable deterrence capabilities is also affected by strategic developments involving extra-regional actors, especially China and the United States.

Fissile Material Accumulation

The final factor with an impact on nuclear acquisition dynamics is fissile material production. The renewed discussion on the Fissile Material Cutoff Treaty (FMCT) in 2006 focused attention on the attitudes of India and Pakistan (among other concerned states). The argument put forward by some is that capping the production of fissile material in South Asia would be an important step toward nuclear stability in the subcontinent. However, issues arising from the South Asian security dilemma play a role in stalled FMCT negotiations.

As some analysts have stated, a key motivation for Washington's support of the FMCT is to limit China's nuclear arsenal. Beijing is unlikely to agree to the FMCT under the current circumstances without amelioration of its concerns. If Beijing does not accept the treaty, there is little chance that New Delhi would accept it either resulting in Islamabad's refusal as well. While the Chinese government considers the FMCT to be crucial, its concern also lies in progress on a framework for the Prevention of an Arms Race in Outer Space (PAROS). Beijing has effectively linked progress on the FMCT to that on PAROS. Further, while Beijing is supposed to have stopped fissile material production, there is no official confirmation of this. In addition, theoretically the Chinese government can restart production of fissile material.

The lack of progress on PAROS is said to have been one of the reasons behind China's anti-satellite test in January 2007. Certain policymakers and analysts in the United States perceived the tests as symbolic of the potential military threat from China, a view that reinforces their arguments for the need for dominance in space. In response, China needs to counter a future U.S. national missile defence (NMD), possibly by increasing its quantity of warheads through increased fissile production. China's concern is that U.S. policies under the Bush administration, such as the withdrawal from the ABM Treaty and the reinforced focus on NMD, degrade Beijing's deterrent, which relies on about two dozen intercontinental ballistic missiles (ICBMs). Also, Washington's reluctance to consider a "no first use" policy increases the threat perception of the U.S. use of nuclear weapons in a Taiwan crisis.

From the Indian perspective, Beijing's anti-satellite test refocused the attention of analysts on the considerable gap between Indian and Chinese aerospace capabilities and its consequences for the strategic balance. Indian defence scientists have stated that India would take appropriate measures to deal with this expansion of Beijing's offensive capabilities, possibly through collaboration between the Defence Research and Development Organization (DRDO) and the Indian Space Research Organization (ISRO). The test came at a time when both India and China are pushing ahead with space-based projects (especially lunar missions) and this would be the sign of a new rivalry. Thus, security perceptions in South Asia (including by extension China and the United States) contain a reinforced belief in the necessity of nuclear weapons and delivery systems development.

Even if China maintains its undeclared moratorium on fissile material production, it is unclear if India would consent to capping its fissile stock at a level much lower than that of China. This also strengthens the argument of Indian analysts who advocate more than just the minimum deterrent-related warheads stockpile and propose a thermonuclear arsenal. Furthermore, the Indian government also has a problem with the lack of verification measures in the existing FMCT proposals. Pakistan for its part has opposed any FMCT that would effectively perpetuate the fissile material asymmetry in the subcontinent, and wants negotiations to cover existing stocks as well. Pakistan's contention is that since its nuclear weapons program is a product of the threat from India, Islamabad would consent to a cap on fissile material production only as part of a bilateral moratorium.

However, since New Delhi's nuclear weapon expansion is driven by the need to construct a secure deterrent against Beijing, such a proposal is a non-starter in the present circumstances. Thus, while Pakistan may have reached the fissile material capacity to suit its credible minimum deterrent needs, this is not necessarily the case for India. Nevertheless, in the context of the proposed FMCT, some Indian analysts have stated that New Delhi has to decide whether its existing stocks are adequate for "strategic purposes," and if so, the FMCT could be beneficial for international stability.

In sum, from the South Asian perspective, there are no credible proliferation disincentives that would surmount security concerns driving India and Pakistan toward strengthening their nuclear capabilities. In essence, nuclear modernization, or vertical proliferation is likely to continue in South Asia. Next, we turn to the issue of horizontal proliferation in the South Asian context.

SECURITY DISPUTES, NUCLEAR DOCTRINES, AND PROLIFERATION TRENDS

To begin with, proliferation issues in South Asia must be understood in context of vertical and horizontal proliferation.

Vertical proliferation takes place as nuclear states modernize their nuclear arsenals with more reliable delivery systems and warheads. Countries including the United States, China, India, and Pakistan, are in the process of modernizing their arsenals through actions such as proposals for "a reliable replacement warhead" (as in the case of the United States). In the context of South Asia, nuclear modernization is mainly a function of prevailing threat perceptions arising from security dilemmas. Modernization of arsenals includes the development and testing of longer-range missiles-such as the tests of the Agni-III by India, and the Shaheen-II by Pakistan in the first half of 2007. Horizontal proliferation is the spread of nuclear weapons technology from nuclear states to other entities, including aspiring nuclear weapon states, as well as non-state actors such as terrorist groups. Horizontal proliferation generally involves a significant role for WMD supply networks that may or may not have a connection to official entities in a nuclear state. In the South Asian context, this variant of proliferation is especially pertinent, given the history of the A.Q. Khan network and its assistance to states such as North Korea and Iran. In addition, horizontal proliferation includes second-tier proliferation, where developing countries trade and barter nuclear technology with each other. While vertical and horizontal proliferation are variants of the proliferation dynamic, it is entirely possible that a nuclear state (such as Pakistan) could make use of non-state networks in the pursuit of nuclear modernization.

From the subcontinental perspective, one main question arises-given the lack of a comprehensive resolution of the disputes between India and Pakistan and India and China, how do nuclear doctrines in South Asia impact trends in the acquisition of nuclear and missile technology? The answer to this question links threat perceptions and nuclear doctrines with recent proliferation-related developments and requires a brief discussion of existing nuclear postures of India and Pakistan.

Subcontinental Rivalry

So what are the characteristics of the sub-continental rivalry that make nuclear proliferation in South Asia such a crucial security issue? Threat perceptions based on long-standing security disputes shape nuclear doctrines and proliferation dynamics. The intensity of disputes brings in security dilemmas that ensure continued dependence on nuclear weapons in South Asia. South Asia is one of the most populated regions of the world, with India and Pakistan alone accounting for about 1.35 billion people. Both countries have been bitter rivals since partition of the subcontinent in 1947 that led to the creation of independent Pakistan and independence for India. The two countries have fought two wars over Kashmir (1947, 1965), one over East Pakistan/Bangladesh (1971), one limited war and the ongoing insurgency in Kashmir (since 1989). The 2001-2002 crisis further highlighted the dangers of terrorist violence provoking a conventional conflict that could lead to a nuclear crisis. Kashmir, which lies at the heart of the dispute, is more than a simple territorial problem. The province has a Muslim majority, and for India it is a symbol of its secular credentials as well as a repudiation of the partition, which was based on religion. For Pakistan, Kashmir is crucial because it is seen as an unfinished agenda of partition, which was supposed to provide a homeland for the subcontinent's Muslim community. Thus, Kashmir is an integral part of both countries' perceived self-identities. Since the 2001-2002 crisis, Islamabad and New Delhi have conducted several rounds of peace talks aimed at bringing a lasting settlement to the Kashmir issue. This peace process has involved several confidence-building measures such as strengthening of transport links between the two countries. The two sides also signed a crucial agreement on reducing the risk of nuclear accidents in February 2007. Nevertheless, the key dispute, Kashmir, is nowhere near resolution. This implies that both New Delhi and Islamabad are more inclined toward strengthening existing military capabilities, both conventional and non-conventional, to prevent an unfavorable scenario in a future standoff.

Apart from notions of sovereignty and nationhood, Kashmir is also of considerable strategic importance. Rivers originating in the Kashmir region provide crucial water supplies for food producing areas in the heartland. Furthermore, the Siachen glacier is also a region of military significance. The glacier, to the north of Kashmir, commands a strategic overlook of the small border between Pakistan and China and can potentially be used as a point of attack on India from northwest Kashmir. The glacier became a battle ground between the two armies in April 1984 and despite repeated talks, there has been no movement toward demilitarization. The complex rivalry between India and Pakistan involves territorial disputes based on notions of national identity as well as terrorist violence. Another integral element of the subcontinental security dyad is the role of China.

The China Factor

The role of China in South Asian security issues as well as in future conflict scenarios is crucial when considering two realities- (a) the historical animosity between India and China, and (b) the long standing 'all-weather' political and military alliance between Pakistan and China. Indian analysts often cite transfer of nuclear and missile technology from Beijing to Islamabad as evidence of an encircled threat to India. Through nuclear and missile technology transfers to Pakistan, Beijing restricts India to the South Asian strategic framework, and this constrains New Delhi's stated desire to seek a more global presence. From the Chinese political establishment's perspective, the concern is over India's defence expansion, its desire and movement toward a stronger regional and global role, and its increasing strategic connections with Washington.

Thus, any examination of the South Asian proliferation framework takes into account the Sino-Indian rivalry and dispute, the lowest point of which was the 1962 border war. In recent years, Indian and Chinese leaders and special representatives have met for regular talks on the border dispute issue; the most recent session (the 10th such round), took place in April 2007. In early rounds of these talks, China granted de facto recognition of Sikkim as a province of India, while India accepted Tibet as part of China. However, serious differences remain, and strategically important areas such as the state of Arunachal Pradesh have been claimed by China, while India has claimed Aksai Chin and certain parts of Kashmir handed over by Pakistan to China.

Despite periodic meetings, little progress has been made on these issues, and from time to time, controversial statements by each side threaten to derail talks. Whether a hardening of positions or a negotiating strategy, it demonstrates that the potential for friction is ever-present. Furthermore, there is also some dispute over an earlier agreement between the two sides to not insist on territorial exchanges of areas with settled populations, reflected in Beijing's recent demands that India cede Arunachal Pradesh, especially the Tawang tract. Therefore, in the absence of a permanent settlement, both India and China have adopted a hedging strategy to guard against any future strategic disadvantages. A hedging strategy involves bolstering military-related capabilities in an ambiguous way that is not directly threatening to the adversary. At the same time, cooperative ties are encouraged without necessarily making any major concessions. In part, such an approach is chosen due to uncertainty over the adversary's future intentions and capabilities and as a way to safeguard against a downturn in future ties or in the regional or global strategic environment. Therefore, modernization of nuclear arsenals in South Asia has to be considered in this context.

Similarly, in the case of India and Pakistan, despite sustained peace talks and CBMs, the two sides continue a hedging strategy to guard against future uncertainty, such as another crisis situation like Operation Parakram in 2001-2002. This is done by developing more reliable nuclear delivery systems (especially longer range ballistic missiles), perfecting and increasing fissile material stock, and acquiring conventional weaponry in line with contemporary war-fighting doctrines.

Thus, in South Asia, underlying security disputes, based on territorial rivalry and terrorist violence, combined with a need to expand the nation's global and regional position encourages future uncertainties that shape the actors' nuclear policy decision-making. As mentioned earlier, apart from the Indo-Pakistan rivalry, strategic uncertainty, and suspicion in New Delhi is also generated by Pakistan's close military links with China. With China in the picture as a rival of India and a strategic ally of Pakistan, even if Delhi and Islamabad move towards a peaceful resolution of the Kashmir dispute, Beijing is likely to be the biggest factor in Indian threat calculations. At the same time, the present threat perceptions between India and China are not the same as between India and Pakistan, which are more immediate and based on a 'hot' territorial dispute and state-sponsored terrorism. Nevertheless, analysts in New Delhi have long pointed to Chinese military modernization as a coercive threat to India. This modernization includes missile development, such as the current deployment of the DF-21 and DF-3 missiles in Qinghai and Yunnan provinces. Furthermore, there is some suspicion among Indian analysts that though Beijing's stated policy is that of minimum deterrence, the stationing of missiles such as DF-3 and DF-21 reflects a posture of nuclear coercion, and under some conditions, does not preclude a first strike against its neighbours. It is also possible that since 1998, Beijing may have deployed nuclear weapons on the Tibetan plateau in response to a perceived Indian conventional military advantage and the May 1998 nuclear tests. Thus, despite growing trade between the two sides, there is some degree of unease in India over China's long-term intentions, more so in light of predictions of increased competition between the two countries for global energy resources. The concern in New Delhi is that if bilateral relations take a negative turn at some point in the future, China's current military modernization will give Beijing a significant advantage.

The Sino-Indian security dilemma is also a function of China's desire to establish close relationships with other countries in the Indian Ocean region (most notably Myanmar), a policy that is seen as a potential threat by India and termed as "strategic containment." For India and China, the security dilemma also arises from threat perceptions based on consequences of future nationalistic tendencies. Both sides fear that a rise in nationalism in the other could lead to more hostile attitudes. China's concerns over future expansions of the U.S. nuclear arsenal, missile defence and space dominance plans also lessen the possibility of any immediate restraint with respect to Beijing's nuclear plans. Therefore a chain reaction exists in South Asia where New Delhi, at the very least, wants to maintain its current relative capabilities vis-à-vis Beijing, if not actually improve them. The interconnected security dilemmas in the Asia-Pacific region shape defence policies and impact stability.

SOUTH ASIA AND THE MIDDLE EAST: PROLIFERATION LINKS

While an analysis of proliferation in the Middle East is outside the scope of this study, it is necessary to highlight existing and potential links between the Middle East and South Asia, apart from the A.Q. Khan network mentioned above. Khan's network provided significant know-how to Iran in the late eighties and early nineties (including centrifuge technology), though the full extent of these transfers has still not been confirmed. While nuclear links between Iran and Pakistan have ended for now, Islamabad's nuclear connection to the Middle East remains, such as through possible collaboration with Saudi Arabia.

From the South Asian proliferation perspective, the close ties between Saudi Arabia and the development of Pakistan's nuclear program is a crucial development. News reports as well as official U.S. government analyses have claimed that Riyadh provided considerable financing for Pakistan's nuclear and missile program in the past, but some reports now suggest a more proactive role by Saudi Arabia-in terms of nuclear energy development itself. This is in line with the announcement in November 2006 by six Arab states-Saudi Arabia, Morocco, Egypt, Algeria, Tunisia, and the United Arab Emirates-that they would develop civilian nuclear programs. Earlier, in 2005, Saudi Arabia applied for and was granted exemption from nuclear inspections through the IAEA's 'small quantities protocol.' Before that, a widely quoted 2003 report in The Guardian stated that Riyadh was considering three nuclear options: (a) building a nuclear deterrent, (b) allying with a nuclear power, or (c) working toward a nuclear weapon free zone in the Middle East. Recent developments suggest that a combination of the first two options might be adopted given that it is highly unlikely that Iran and Israel relinquish their nuclear programs in the near future.

This is where Pakistan's role could be significant. German news reports stated in early 2006 that Pakistani scientists assisted Saudi efforts to develop a nuclear program and that this was done under the guise of pilgrimages to Saudi Arabia between 2003 and 2005. Several high-ranking Saudi royals as well as government officials are among the few non-Pakistanis who have toured Islamabad's nuclear facilities. These include defence minister Prince Sultan (now also crown prince) who visited the Kahuta uranium enrichment facility in 1999, and a son of the current Saudi ruler, King Abdullah, who attended a test of the nuclear-capable 950-mile range Ghauri missile in 1999. These developments suggest that if Riyadh decides to acquire nuclear weapons, the spotlight could be on Pakistan as one of the sources. A factor that could prompt Saudi Arabia to pursue nuclear weapons would be if Tehran unambiguously builds it own nuclear weapon, prompting Israel to shed the opacity over its arsenal.

While disincentives for Pakistan to go along this route are considerable (most notably, U.S. opposition), there are also incentives for Islamabad to aid the Saudis in their quest-cheap oil from Saudi Arabia, and a favorable endorsement for the Musharraf regime (or a successor regime) from powerful conservative Sunni religious and political groups within Pakistan. A 2003 news report quoted an anonymous Pakistani official who claimed that Riyadh and Islamabad had concluded a secret agreement under which Pakistan would receive subsidized oil in exchange for transferring nuclear technology. In 2004, Iranian government sources also claimed that they had information that confirmed this agreement, but there was no further corroboration of this from other sources. Therefore, even if there is no immediate possibility of such a transfer, Saudi Arabia could pursue this with Pakistan in the future to hedge against nuclear developments in the Middle East.

A key incentive for Pakistan could also be to use Saudi Arabia for strategic depth purposes. Islamabad's traditional geographic buffer against Indian military campaigns was Afghanistan, but that was lost after the fall of the Taliban in 2001. Ostensibly, Pakistan requires strategic depth to protect its forces (conventional and nuclear) from an armored offensive by the Indian military, which could cut off the country similar to the 1971 war. Saudi Arabia could provide a base for stationing Pakistani nuclear devices that would be safe from the reach of Indian missiles and give Islamabad a semblance of second-strike capability. This idea of looking towards the Middle East for strategic depth is not new.

In the 1990s, former Prime Minister Benazir Bhutto, skeptical of the reliance on Afghanistan, recommended Iran as a more useful ally for purposes of strategic depth.

Apart from the Pakistan-Saudi Arabia link, concerns have also been expressed (especially in the U.S. Congress) over India's ties to Iran, at a time when the IAEA and western powers led by the United States are working toward controlling Tehran's uranium enrichment program. These concerns have arisen during the broader debate in Washington on the nuclear agreement with India. In particular, attention has focused on India's long-standing political and diplomatic relationship with Iran as well as the imposition of sanctions on two private Indian companies suspected of transferring chemicals meant for rocket fuel as well as chemical weapons. The Indian government claimed that both companies (Balaji Amines Ltd. & Prachi Poly Products) were doing legitimate business with Iranian firms. Balaji Amines insisted that they had been supplying products used for manufacturing life-saving drugs such as ampicillin and other antibiotics, but nevertheless, New Delhi ordered the company to stop all trade with Iran.

Both India and Pakistan have attempted to ensure that they are in compliance with the latest international regulations against Tehran's nuclear program. In February 2007, Pakistan froze assets of several individuals and other entities connected to Tehran's nuclear and missile projects in accordance with UN Security Council resolution 1737. In the same month, New Delhi banned exports of equipment and technologies to Iran that could be used in nuclear and missile development projects.

The Iran nuclear issue has been an important point of discussion in context of the Indo-U.S. nuclear agreement. The Hyde Act, passed by the U.S. Congress in December 2006, endorses nuclear cooperation between India and the United States, but it also states that New Delhi should assist the international community in clamping down on Iran's nuclear program. Furthermore, in May 2007, a group of U.S. senators sent a joint letter to Indian Prime Minister Manmohan Singh articulating their dissatisfaction over India's military ties with Iran, especially a 'joint defence working group' between the two countries. Nuclear ties between India and the United States are not limited to nuclear trade between the two, but also extends to discussions over restricting proliferation elsewhere.

Prime Minister Manmohan Singh has stated in the past that New Delhi does not favour another nuclear power in the neighborhood, and India voted against Iran at the IAEA in September 2005 and February 2006. However, two factors have restrained the Indian government from opposing Iran's nuclear weapons program more forcefully. First, the scramble for energy resources has made the Iran-Pakistan-India (IPI) natural gas pipeline a crucial economic issue for India. Stern Indian opposition to Iran's nuclear program would jeopardize the proposed IPI pipeline from Iran to India. The pipeline is considered to be of crucial importance to India in order to sustain high economic growth rates in the coming years. Thus, economic imperatives, specifically the need for energy sources, are an important factor in nonproliferation positions of countries such as India and China. In this context, New Delhi has reiterated that the construction of the pipeline will proceed in spite of pressures from Washington to cancel the project.

Second, for New Delhi, another variable is satisfying domestic political constituencies that are skeptical of the nuclear overtures from Washington that come at the cost of long-standing ties with Tehran. Since the Congress Party-led coalition government depends on parliamentary support from Communist parties, the government is obliged to periodically hold positions on contentious issues such as the Iranian nuclear program. The Manmohan Singh government has stated that it would be guided by India's national interest on the Iran nuclear issue, but this does not clarify to what extent India would be willing to go along with the United States on this issue. Some recent reports have also stated that New Delhi could play a more formal role in mediating the growing tensions over Iran's nuclear program in conjunction with the UN Security Council. However, it is unclear what form this would take.

In sum, nuclear issues in South Asia cannot be examined in isolation from developments elsewhere. Historically close political ties have existed between the South Asian subcontinent and the

Middle East, and therefore, regional rivalries and bilateral relations play an important role in shaping decisions that impact broader nuclear issues, including horizontal proliferation.

Indo-U.S. Nuclear Cooperation

Since July 2005, when the U.S. and Indian governments unveiled their nuclear cooperation agreement, a debate has risen over its impact on the global nonproliferation regime. This agreement will allow India to acquire nuclear technology and materials from the United States and other suppliers. In return, New Delhi will designate which of its nuclear facilities are for civilian use and which are for military use. The former list would be opened up for international inspections. Prior to implementation, New Delhi will have to conclude a safeguards agreement with the IAEA, while the Nuclear Suppliers Group (NSG) will have to effect changes in its rules to enable nuclear cooperation between its member states and India.

The Hyde Act passed by the U.S. Congress in December 2006, authorized the Bush administration to bring into place a nuclear cooperation mechanism with India, after concluding a bilateral agreement under Section 123 of the U.S. Atomic Energy Act. Negotiations on the '123' agreement began in early 2007, but as of early June, talks were stalled on a few contentious issues. The disagreement is over five main items; (i) the right to reprocess spent fuel, (ii) the conversion of a voluntary moratorium on nuclear testing into a legal commitment by India, (iii) the assured supply of fuel by the United States, (iv) the return of all equipment to the United States if India conducts a nuclear test, and (v) the level of inspections of Indian facilities.

The nuclear deal reflects an influential view in India that the nonproliferation regime embodied in the NPT is defective. According to Indian Prime Minister Manmohan Singh, the regime is ineffective and that the international community should introduce measures that restrict nuclear proliferation more effectively without suppressing peaceful uses of nuclear energy. At the same time, the contention is that India is a responsible nuclear state that has adhered to the guidelines of nonproliferation (without legally being part of the NPT regime) through strict export controls and denying nuclear assistance to other states, unlike the record of some nuclear weapon states.

A basic feature of this agreement is that by acquiring uranium from foreign sources (to free up domestic supplies) and by placing a set of nuclear facilities on the military list, India can increase its fissile material production for weaponization purposes. However, a different line of analysis examines the implications of increased uranium supplies in the context of India's fledgling nuclear submarine project. This perspective views that rather than increasing nuclear warhead production, New Delhi would use the expansion of its uranium supplies and enrichment capability to fuel its nuclear submarine project, a key element of India's desire to achieve a secure second strike capability under its credible minimum deterrence doctrine.

There are two separate lines of criticism of the deal; the first focuses on the nonproliferation objective, and the second on India's strategic needs. The first perspective is that the agreement will weaken the global nonproliferation regime by condoning India's nuclear weapons program. The argument is that by introducing India-specific changes to global as well as domestic U.S. nonproliferation laws, it will be more difficult to prevent nuclear transfers involving other countries such as China-Pakistan and Russia-Iran. A further objection is that even with 14 reactors under safeguards, 8 others will remain on the military list, free to manufacture plutonium for several nuclear weapons annually. Additionally, critics have stated that the agreement so far does not commit India to eschew nuclear testing formally, or to end fissile material production.

The second criticism comes most notably, from members of the nuclear scientific community in India, who contend that elements of the agreement would in effect cap India's nuclear program and constrain its thorium-based three stage nuclear project. They argue that while New Delhi has maintained a unilateral moratorium on nuclear testing, it does not want such a clause legalized in a bilateral treaty. The argument here is that India might have to reconsider its moratorium in the event that China or Pakistan conducts a nuclear test.

In addition, India's scientific community and government have insisted that it be explicitly granted the right to reprocess spent fuel for the three stage nuclear project that exploits the ample thorium reserves in the country (about 30% of the global supply).

The Indian government wants to retain reprocessing rights as part of an advanced nuclear fuel cycle. This would involve recycling uranium oxide fuel while the consequent plutonium would be used with thorium in fast breeder reactors. However, some Indian scientific experts have stated that even if reprocessing rights and technology are not granted under the 123 agreement, it is likely that the initial reactors bought by New Delhi will come from Russia and France, rather than the United States. It is entirely possible that trade with these two countries, especially Russia, will involve reprocessing rights and sale of reactors and fuel. On the other hand, Indian analysts criticize the reported objective of the U.S. government of insuring that India's nuclear trade with other supplier states has equally rigorous conditions attached. Finally, Indian analysts have faulted the U.S. position of not allowing assurances of fuel supplies and of prohibiting India from stockpiling nuclear fuel.

Thus, the nuclear agreement between India and the United States has been criticized on the grounds of its potential impact on the global nonproliferation regime as well as its impact on India's strategic nuclear program. It must also be noted that since the bilateral 123 agreement between India and the United States is still under negotiation, it is too early to assume the eventual direction of the nuclear agreement framework. Even if the two countries conclude the 123 agreement satisfactorily (for both sides), India still must obtain approval for nuclear trade from the NSG and has to negotiate a safeguards agreement with the IAEA.

The China Issue

Several rationales have been offered as justification for the nuclear agreement (such as economics, strategic alliance, and nonproliferation benefits), but perhaps the most intriguing is one has been left largely unstated by the two governments-that of balancing China. Both India and the United States are concerned about the future direction of Chinese foreign and security policy. For the United States, aiding India through nuclear cooperation as well as a strategic partnership, Washington would be able to balance China more effectively in the region. In the process it would divert China from its main security issue-Taiwan. For India, the agreement is a significant diplomatic and strategic addition to its capabilities vis-à-vis China, with both the possible increase in fissile material production and a strengthened strategic partnership with the United States.

One argument supportive of the Indo-U.S. agreement stresses that China has built up Pakistan as a counter to India for several decades, a policy that involved transfers of nuclear and missile technology. It must also be noted that more than a year before the Indo-U.S. nuclear agreement was first announced in July 2005, there were reports in March 2004 that China was planning to provide Islamabad with a nuclear reactor. The implication is that that the Beijing-Islamabad nuclear partnership might have continued in any case. Nevertheless, it is important to consider the current pattern of nuclear cooperation between China and Pakistan in the light of the Indo-U.S. deal. Regardless of the pros and cons of the deal, it can be used by Beijing to lay the grounds for legitimizing continued nuclear collaboration with Pakistan. A sign of this has been China's argument that any changes in the NSG rules should be criteria-based rather than country specific.

In December 2005, China began construction of the 300 MW second phase of the Chashma Nuclear Power Plant (contracted in May 2004), subsequent to the commissioning of the first phase in September 2000. Parallel to the Indo-U.S. deal, China and Pakistan also reportedly agreed to a nuclear cooperation arrangement under which as many as six nuclear reactors of at least 600 MW capacity would be provided to Islamabad. As of now, no other details are available so it is not clear what kind of safeguards will be installed, though some sources have stated that this initiative is being opposed by the NSG.

Reports of a possible Beijing-Islamabad nuclear agreement gained ground ahead of Chinese President Hu Jintao's visit to Pakistan in November 2006. However, no such deal was announced during the visit, leading to a conclusion that Beijing is possibly waiting to see the final shape of the Indo-U.S. agreement to gauge its impact on China. However, one influential Pakistani analyst stated that the lack of a public nuclear cooperation agreement between Beijing and Islamabad does not mean that such an arrangement will not come about; China can supply Pakistan with the required nuclear technology at a more politically convenient time.

Pakistan's desire for a stronger and more public nuclear relationship with China is in part because Islamabad failed to obtain a similar arrangement with the United States. Some Pakistani commentators have in fact argued that their country needs nuclear cooperation with the United States (and other suppliers, for that matter) more than India because the gap between existing energy supplies and future energy requirements is far more serious for Pakistan that it is for India. A senior Pakistani official connected to the nuclear program, stated in October 2006 that Washington's nuclear policy should be guided by a "criteria-based" approach rather than one geared toward a single country. However, U.S. government officials have stated that they have no intention of considering a similar agreement with Pakistan. It is likely that this refusal has much to do with the activities of the A.Q. Khan network as well as Islamabad's reluctance to allow a full interrogation of Khan by U.S. experts that would shed light on some unanswered questions related to the network.

Islamabad has cited the fact that Washington declined to offer Pakistan a nuclear cooperation agreement as a motivation for increased self-reliance on nuclear energy, through indigenous fuel manufacturing capabilities. In this context, government officials in Pakistan stated in April 2007 that the country would set up an installation for fuel testing for use in nuclear plants in a quest for "complete technological capability." As highlighted previously, Pakistan's overall agenda is to redress the perceived widening of the nuclear imbalance with India. Nevertheless, Pakistani experts have admitted that Islamabad's quest for increased nuclear capability is a result of the tacit rivalry between Beijing and New Delhi and the latter's desire to catch up with China. Apart from the impending nuclear technology transfers from Beijing, recent reports have also stated that the Musharraf regime has commenced construction of a 1,000 MW heavy water reactor that will potentially produce adequate plutonium for as many as 50 warheads per year. In addition, Islamabad is setting up a commercial scale nuclear reprocessing plant to allow production of weapons grade plutonium. Such activities would enable Islamabad to stockpile as much fissile material as possible before a future FMCT comes into force.

These developments suggest that Islamabad is attempting to diversify its nuclear weapons program through plutonium, as opposed to its traditional reliance on uranium as fissile material. Plutonium allows for more compact weapons and provides increased flexibility for the arsenal. For Islamabad, this is critical for developing a second strike capability against India. However, some Indian scientific experts have stated that even with the new Pakistani reactor, India will still be able to maintain an insurmountable lead in fissile material production through unsafeguarded reactors under the nuclear agreement.

Chinese support is key to Pakistan's quest for some strategic benefits vis-à-vis India, especially if the U.S.-India nuclear agreement reaches the implementation stage. In a possible attempt to reduce Chinese opposition to the nuclear deal with Washington, New Delhi has committed itself, in principle, to civilian nuclear cooperation with Beijing, a declaration announced during President Hu's visit to New Delhi in November 2006.

This could be viewed as an incentive from Beijing to dissuade India from a potential anti-China partnership with Washington. Nuclear trade between India and China is not necessarily an empty proposal; it has a precedent. In 1995, India acquired low enriched uranium from China for the Tarapur nuclear reactors. The official Chinese position is opposition to any NSG amendments that would adversely effect the non-proliferation regime, and that they would consider viable arrangements at the NSG, and not bilaterally. Beijing's response reiterates its view that any exceptions should not be India-specific and should include other states. Interestingly, Indian Foreign Minister Pranab Mukherjee stated in November

2006 that New Delhi does not have any problem with a similar nuclear agreement between Pakistan and China. If this attitude is indeed the Indian government's position, the implication could be that New Delhi is confident that the benefits it will accrue from the agreement with the United States far outweigh the possible increase in nuclear cooperation between China and Pakistan.

Commercial Issues

The Indo-U.S. nuclear agreement also demonstrates that changes in the nuclear supplier regimes will not be restricted only to bilateral nuclear trade between the United States and India. Nuclear energy firms from several countries other than India are already lining up to negotiate commercial nuclear deals with India. NSG member states such as Australia are considering approval of changes in the group's rules to permit nuclear cooperation with New Delhi. Even though Australia (a major uranium producer) has not yet agreed to revoke the prohibition of supply to India, Australian companies such as BHP Billiton are anticipating lucrative sales. Other important members of the NSG have also supported civilian nuclear cooperation with India, within the appropriate IAEA safeguards framework. French and Canadian companies have also contacted the Nuclear Power Corporation of India (one of the main government nuclear energy entities), in connection with the supply of light-water nuclear power related equipment.

Thus, nuclear energy companies are important players in the future of this agreement as well as the broader nonproliferation regime. Firms such as General Electric and Bechtel have lobbied the Bush administration in favour of the agreement. Besides deals in the nuclear energy sector, the expectation is also that such cooperation will facilitate contracts in the conventional military sector, especially with respect to the impending deal for 126 fighter aircraft for the Indian Air Force, a deal worth about $9 billion. Aerospace giants such as Lockheed Martin and Boeing are among the contenders for the contract. Therefore, the implication is that the incentives go well beyond the nuclear energy sector.

Finally, it is instructive to consider the scenario if the nuclear agreement between India and the United States is scrapped, either because of insurmountable differences over the 123 agreement or later in the implementation stage. In India, several members of the influential atomic energy scientific community have expressed reservations over the agreement as have the communist parties and the opposition Bharatiya Janata Party (BJP). In the United States as well, there has been considerable opposition from nonproliferation experts as well as sections of the political establishment. It is not certain if the reservations expressed by the Indian government towards certain clauses of the December 2006 Hyde Act will be rectified in New Delhi's favour in the bilateral 123 agreement, which again has to be approved by the U.S. Congress. Given these complicating factors, the implications of scrapping the agreement are immense; affecting broader bilateral ties between India and the United States, the nonproliferation regime in general, and the global nuclear energy market.

SOUTH ASIA AND HORIZONTAL PROLIFERATION

As a starting point, it is helpful to focus on cases of horizontal proliferation elsewhere that are connected to South Asia. This includes potential WMD supply routes as well as entities that might be involved, some of whom may be operating outside state control. In particular, the focus is on connections between entities in Pakistan and proliferation dynamics in other regions. Three major issues need to be addressed-(i) the North Korean nuclear program, and in particular the impact of the October 2006 nuclear test on South Asia; (ii) the current state of the A.Q. Khan network and its implications for WMD supply trends; and (iii) proliferation links between South Asia and the Middle East.

The North Korean Nuclear Test and South Asia

As expected, North Korea's nuclear test put renewed focus on the dangers of nuclear proliferation, and policymakers in India assumed it would lead to more stringent criticism of its nuclear agreement with the United States. Indian experts expected the North Korean test to impact especially on any nuclear test-related provisions of the nuclear agreement with the United States. Consequently, New Delhi swiftly condemned the test and indirectly highlighted Islamabad's contribution to Pyongyang's nuclear test.

Some Indian officials even stated that Pyongyang's illegal acquisition of nuclear technology would actually spur reluctant supplier countries (such as Australia) to legitimately sell nuclear fuel to India, especially since it would be used for civilian purposes.

On the other hand, Islamabad refuted any suggestion that the activities of the A.Q. Khan network had contributed to Pyongyang's test, stating that North Korea's nuclear program is based on plutonium while Pakistan relies on uranium. In this manner, both India and Pakistan tried to ensure that proliferation in South Asia was not equated with proliferation in Northeast Asia. To a certain extent, the Bush administration obliged the subcontinental nuclear powers, as senior officials dismissed any parallels between North Korea's path to nuclear weapons to those of India and Pakistan. However, while Pakistan denied any links to the test, it did not help Islamabad's case when Japanese sources stated that days before Pyongyang's test, several Pakistani nuclear technicians arrived in North Korea through China. This augmented the suspicions that Pakistani agencies may have had some role in the test, perhaps through data sharing before or after the explosion.

The A.Q. Khan Network and Proliferation Dynamics

The A.Q. Khan network, which provided nuclear assistance to North Korea and Iran, has represented the most serious proliferation problem in recent years. Since Khan's public confession in February 2004, the Musharraf regime has consistently asserted that this network was the work of a rogue scientist and that the Pakistani government and its military leaders were not involved in these activities. However, it is not clear to what extent this assertion is accurate. Analysts and officials in Pakistan as well as in the United States have expressed skepticism over Khan's confession as well as the implicit professed innocence of the Pakistani political and military establishment. A highly publicized report released in April 2007 by the London-based International Institute for Strategic Studies, also stated that individuals and entities involved in the network could still be dormant and can conceivably be reactivated in the future.

So far, Islamabad has refused to allow foreign interrogators to question Khan even though the U.S. government has regularly expressed dissatisfaction over information released by Pakistan. > Furthermore, most individuals connected to the network are still at large, including important figures such as B.S.A. Tahir, while others, such as Henk Slebos, have been given light sentences. Moreover, the Khan claimed in a signed statement that successive army chiefs in the 1990s (Generals Mirza Aslam Beg and Jehangir Karamat) had authorized the sales of nuclear technology. While this could be taken as Khan's attempts to remove the burden of guilt, it is true that the military was closely associated with the nuclear and missile programs. In fact, in 1990, Gen. Beg warned U.S. government officials that Pakistan would be forced to provide nuclear technology to Tehran if Washington did not offer support to Pakistan.

Other circumstantial evidence, such as visits by the Pakistani military leadership to North Korea throughout the nineties, suggests that there was a barter deal between Pyongyang and Islamabad (uranium enrichment technology in exchange for missiles). Additionally, in August 2005, Gen. Musharraf conceded that Khan had transferred centrifuge machines to North Korea through which uranium hexafluoride (which was also transferred) can be enriched for eventual processing into civilian reactors fuel or for military purposes. Shipping out such large centrifuge machines without the military's knowledge would have been impossible. Therefore, it would have been highly unlikely that these activities were carried out without the military's acquiescence. On a side note, it is possible that Washington's attitude was colored by the need to retain Islamabad's support in the anti-Taliban/Al Qaeda campaign in Afghanistan.

Additionally, for a country to acquire a nuclear delivery system (such as the No Dong missiles transferred to Pakistan), the decision-making process incorporates several factors, as well as the opinions of numerous government agencies to ensure compatibility among the various systems. It is therefore not very plausible that a nuclear-missile barter deal with such serious and risky international consequences could have been approved without cooperation from senior levels of the political-military establishment in Pakistan. The issue of the Pakistani military-scientific establishment's involvement (or endorsement) in the Khan's network activities is crucial due to its implications for contemporary proliferation routes and processes. If these elements within and outside Pakistan (including non-Pakistani nationals) and their methods and routes remain undiscovered, it has two broad consequences for proliferation in South Asia.

First, it allows Islamabad to potentially procure missile and nuclear technology in the future, in an attempt to catch up with India. In this regard, a Pakistani national, Mohammed Aslam, working at the Tabani Corporation's Moscow office, was named by the Russian government in 2006 as having attempted to acquire dual-use technology and other materials for Pakistan's nuclear and missile development programs. This example demonstrates that elements of the network are still active, though it is unclear if they are directly connected to Pakistani nuclear and missile development programs. Given Islamabad's need to construct a secure deterrent against India (especially long-range missiles that can reach southern and eastern India), it is possible that the above case is an instance of continuing efforts to exploit non-state networks to procure prohibited equipment. As one analyst noted, due to Pakistan's apparent inability to acquire nuclear weapons components legally, it is encouraged to look toward illegal sources. Furthermore, according to some experts, apart from Pakistan, other countries can easily utilize the same supply networks. The Iranian government has made use of these networks for its nuclear and missile programs. As the previously mentioned IISS report states, Tehran controls a clandestine nuclear materials network comparable to the one run by Khan, and in the past has procured technology from some of the same suppliers used by Khan. In context of nuclear proliferation networks, a further concern is that if North Korea dismantles its nuclear weapons program, it will create a potential source of unwanted nuclear materials in the process. Such discarded, but nevertheless lethal technology, could be bought by illegal nuclear supply entities that may or may not have had any connection to the Khan network.

Second, the continued existence of the kind of middlemen that the network generated increases the possibility of nuclear technology leakage out of Pakistan in the event of a coup or widespread instability from radical groups. Since 9/11, there have been periodic fears of internal upheavals in Pakistan, especially from groups linked to the Taliban. Recent reports have also stated that two nuclear scientists from the Pakistan Atomic Energy Commission (PAEC) were kidnapped by the Taliban in late 2006, and as of March 2007 remained in captivity in the Waziristan area. > Soon after that kidnapping, there was an aborted attempt to capture six more PAEC officials in the North West Frontier Province of Pakistan in January 2007. While it is not clear if the officials and scientists were targeted specifically because of their links to Pakistan's nuclear program, these incidents demonstrate the potential danger of non-state actors' participation in the illegal market in nuclear technology. In order to demonstrate to the international community that it is a responsible nuclear power, Islamabad has decided to set up a "Strategic Export Control Division" in its foreign ministry that will ostensibly prevent prohibited WMD-related technology from being exported. However, this does not necessarily address the problem of possible involvement of government entities and officials that have remained under the radar even after the network was uncovered. In general, the proliferation-related fear for U.S. policymakers is twofold-first, that nuclear technology could be transferred to a terrorist organization; and second, that the Musharraf regime could be overthrown, resulting in uncertainty for the counter-terrorism as well as nonproliferation campaigns.

The case of Pakistan demonstrates the difficulty that arises when nonproliferation goals collide with other strategic imperatives such as counter-terrorism. While the Khan network problem is one of the reasons why Washington has refused to offer a nuclear cooperation agreement to Pakistan, the perceived tilt toward India (through the Indo-U.S. nuclear agreement) can also be a reason why Washington has not pressured Islamabad any further on the A.Q. Khan issue. Nevertheless, in January 2007, in a proactive step, the U.S. Congress under the Democratic leadership passed the Nuclear Black Market Counter Terrorism Act, which authorizes the administration to implement "punitive actions" against states condoning or cooperating with entities actively engaged in nuclear proliferation.

2

Nuclear Weapons and Strategy

Such deliberate use takes the threat of use to its next logical conclusion. Such use is itself illegal for the various reasons examined in the cases given below, but in addition and more importantly such use is illegal if it is likely to bring about limited or general nuclear exchanges leading to a gross breach of all the principles of the laws of war.

DETONATION OF SINGLE WEAPON IN WATER

Use of a single, one kiloton nuclear warhead accurately targeted upon a surface ship even as large as an aircraft carrier would completely destroy it, with the probably loss of all hands. This would be in breach of the laws of war to the extent that disproportionate force would have been used. The same military objective could be achieved with the use of several successful torpedo or conventional missile attacks. If the weapon was detonated at very low altitude very substantial amounts of soluble radioactive isotopes would be generated and dispersed creating a large local environmental impact to the aquatic food-chains and a radioactive fallout plume lethal several miles downwind. Injection of radioactive material into the upper atmosphere would be unlikely. These effects would bring a further charge of unlawfulness to the extent that an. area would be poisoned.

Use of Single Weapon on Land

Assuming that a small detonation was made in a remote pass before enemy troops could reach the area and that prevailing winds did not blow fallout over the territory of neighbouring countries the only breach of the law is that of poisoning of the environment. In reality it is very difficult to envisage all such eventualities being fulfilled and such use would be most likely to breach the neutrality of any neighbouring countries, to kill civilians, and to be indiscriminate use.

Use of Single Weapon as Demonstration

Such use would be a very explicit example of terroristic diplomacy and a very clear threat of further use on a possibly inhabited area or upon a military target.

Tendency of Weaponry and Strategies Towards Use

Here the Tribunal considered factors such as the disposition of various nuclear states to use nuclear weapons, cumulative tendencies to use nuclear weapons, crisis stability, specific technologies and strategies leading towards use and the likely influence of possible defensive components (for example, the SDI) in conjunction with the highly offensive nuclear weapons. A large body of evidence was presented and several specialist witnesses were cross-examined.

Strong evidence was presented to the Tribunal that nuclear strategies currently in force, particularly western strategies, had detailed contingency plans for the first-use of nuclear weapons in response to conventional attack — known as 'extended' deterrence. Nuclear weapons were not seen as purely existing to make a devastating response to any nuclear attack. Soviet declared strategy differed in that the Soviets had made a unilateral pledge not to use nuclear weapons first, against non-nuclear states or neutrals. Despite this declared strategy, evidence was presented that the Soviet Union might in certain circumstances, such as in anticipation of an imminent nuclear attack by NATO, launch nuclear weapons first. Nevertheless the strategic trends were that NATO was more ready to threaten or actually to initiate nuclear weapons use than the Soviet Union. This was a clear asymmetry between the positions of the two superpowers.

Relating to the weapons themselves, the trend in weaponry is towards larger numbers of smaller and more accurate warheads.

The accuracy of present-day warheads is far above that needed to target cities, which gives rise to the fear that these weapons are targeted upon other nuclear weapons in their silos and that they might be used in a nuclear 'first strike'. Neither side has sufficient weapons of sufficient accuracy to achieve such a disarming first strike over the other, also both sides possess submarine launched weapons whose positions were not sufficiently well-known to be hit. Nevertheless this trend in weaponry and in anti-submarine warfare was to increase the numbers of weapons systems potentially vulnerable to first-strike. The US was 5 to 10 years ahead of the Soviet Union in this technology.

New conventional weapons also 'fudge' the firebreak between nuclear and non-nuclear use for two reasons: (a) new dual-capable weapons systems are planned using cruise and Pershing type missiles to strike Warsaw Pact airfields and fixed targets, these launches would be indistinguishable from nuclear launches; (b) certain weapons such as the fuel-air explosion have explosive powers larger than the smallest nuclear weapons, others are intended to be just as destructive as neutron warheads to tank concentrations (MLRS Phase 3 warhead), others such as the cluster bomb can devastate large areas with withering blasts of shrapnel and deposit plastic minelets for area denial purposes. Witnesses (Boyle, Meyrowitz) referred to the Rand Study to support a proposition that more accurate and smaller weaponry could be an attempt to legitimize nuclear weaponry by reducing collateral damage. Evidence was presented that although individual warheads are smaller, intermixing of military and civilian targets would lead to inevitable and unlawful killing of civilians. Also increased forward basing of land-based weapons in highly populated areas such as Europe could only exacerbate the problem.

Both sides have deployed weapons which could be targeted upon the other's command and control networks and reaching them in 5 to 10 minutes from launch. These deployments were judged by the Tribunal to be diminishing stability in a crisis by reason of the very short flight times and the vulnerability of command and control networks. This trend represented, in the view of the Tribunal an increase in risk taking which was deemed to be both unnecessary and reckless endangerment.

The influence of possible future defensive measures was considered. The US SDI is defensive only insofar as its intention is to destroy incoming warheads. Both the US and the USSR possess large numbers of highly offensive weapons including long-range nuclear warheads. Such offensive capability in conjunction with a new defensive ability, would enhance both the defensive and the offensive capability of any power deploying an SDI system. If one side deploys SDI the result is simply a greater degree of threat to the side not possessing it, because as far as it is successful a certain proportion of the nuclear warheads of one's opponent are made useless. SDI could be interpreted as enhancing a possible first strike option because any response after first strike could be stopped by the shield. It can also be interpreted as removing the deterrent ability of the smaller nuclear powers. In both these respects it is de-stabilizing. SDI as presently envisaged cannot defend Europe, because tactical weapons do not go up into space, or defend against low-flying weapons of longer range. Anti-tactical Ballistic Missile (ATBM) systems are being considered for the point defence of US airfields in Europe. As far as SDI is successful and the belief that any retaliatory strike may be sufficiently blunted is enhanced, the likelihood of further unlawful and unethical risk-taking is increased.

Evidence was given to the effect that the nuclear state could only exist by means of excessive state security and was thus by its nature counter-democratic leading to a gradual erosion of human rights (Kaldor).

The existence of nuclear weapons had led to a militarization of international relations since the Second World War. Successive nuclear threats were known to have been made by the US in Korea, but the effectiveness of these threats as a means of nuclear coercion or blackmail was severely questioned. It seemed that the only successful case of nuclear blackmail was by a small nuclear state (Israel) against the US.

The Tribunal found that the trends in weaponry and strategy made the unlawful use of nuclear weapons more likely, both the threat of use and the actual detonation of weapons. Many of the newer, smaller types of weapons particularly the US cruise missile, made verification of future treaties more difficult (cruise is outside existing arms control treaties such as Salt-2).

This also applied to a lesser extent to mobile weapons such as the Soviet SS-20. Modern developments made the likelihood of escalation to all-out nuclear war from serious conventional conflicts almost inevitable and constituted an unlawful and unethical degree of risk taking. The US SDI initiative was seen as a further destabilizing development, particularly as an existing arms control treaty, the ABM treaty, was likely to be threatened.

One positive trend which emerged from the technology was that with the extremely high sensitivity of satellite monitoring operating at many different frequencies and new technologies for higher frequency seismic analysis-the transparency revolution-the possibility of any side cheating on any arms control agreements was more remote. This could not be used as a valid reason for not ratifying the Comprehensive Test Ban Treaty (CTBT) or a implementing a freeze on deployment, testing and development.

WEAPONS DEVELOPMENT AND THE NATIONAL DEFENCE ECONOMY

It is common knowledge that modern warfare is not only the competition of weapons on the battlefield but is also, at the same time, an all-out competition of the total strength of the opposing side's politics, economics, military, and science and technology. During the development of weaponry, the four aspects of politics, economics, military and science and technology are completely brought into play. In today's climate of rapid development of national defence science and technology and the daily emergence of new weapons, the material base of the actual national defence economy should be not only strong but also exceptional.

- With the upgrade in the tactical and technical performances of weapons, manufacturing costs would correspondingly be also more expensive. Since the end of WWII, science and technology development has flourished. There has been a multitude of achievements in science and technology that have continuously increased weapon precision, its powers to cause casualties, and its military effectiveness. The explosive power of a small atomic bomb has the same effectiveness as 100 bombers from WWII. The fire power of today's tank is tenfold greater than that of WWII. A mission to destroy 60 percent of the equipment of a tank division would today require only 1 percent of the aircraft used 40 years ago. During the Falklands War between England and Argentina, the EXOCET missile, which cost only $200,000, fired by the Argentinean Air Force was able to sink a British SHEPHARD missile destroyer that costs $200 million. The ratio of the two costs effectiveness is 1:1,000. The precision of precision-guided bombs and artillery shells is 2 to 3 times better than that of non-guided bombs and artillery shells. However, the upgrading of weapons performance has also brought with it the consequence of more expensive manufacturing costs. The cost of scientific research and technical components compared to the cost of a system with microcomputer technology, new materials, and new techniques imported in great quantities would appear to be prominently greater. Each of the U.S.'s HELLFIRE antitank missile costs about $28,100 to buy, but the scientific research to produce it costs $310 million. Each of the LEOPARD-II tanks of the Federal Republic of Germany costs $3.58 million to buy, yet the scientific research cost was $360 million. The research cost of Japan's MODEL 61 tanks cost •500 million to research and develop in the 1950s, its MODEL 74 tanks cost •2.5 billion to develop in the 1960s, and the MODEL 88 tanks that currently are under research and development have a budgeted cost that could reach •25 billion. The research and development expenditures of three generations of tanks seem to have increased geometrically. According to statistics, the costs of fighters and tanks increase about tenfold every 20 years and the costs of aircraft carriers increase by tenfold every 30 years. Weapons development has come to rely more and more on the national defence economy, causing great burdens for many countries.

- The increase in weapon power has also created battlefield situations where the consumption of battlefield material and economic losses are immense. It requires a huge quantity of material reserves. The 4th Middle East War lasted only 18 days and both sides, Egypt and Israel, suffered economic losses of over $5 billion. The loss of aircraft by both sides was comparable to the combined loss in aircraft in a year by all of the participant countries during WWII. In the first 3 days after the war started, the total number of tactical missiles launched by both sides was equivalent to the combined total of all the reserves of the countries in NATO. The loss of tanks was equal to one-third the number of those in the possession of NATO countries at that time. Both sides strategic reserves and materials were exhausted a week into the war. We can infer the amount of economic loss that could be created by modern warfare from this. In the Falklands War, the English spent a total of $2.16 billion, about $1.2 million every hour. This kind of consumption, to fight one mid-size modern war, is difficult for even an economically great power to support.

In addition to the above, research and production of weapons, ammunition, technical facilities and engineering equipment all consume large amounts of metal and various kinds of nonferrous metals. They also need the support of the chemical industry and energy resources, as well as military industrial products. According to the statistics from affiliated departments at the United Nations, 15 to 16 percent of the world's copper output and 10 percent of it tin, nickel, lead, and zinc outputs are used for weapons production and toward the building of other national defence installations. The consumption of energy resources is even greater. During WWI, the consumption of fuel by each soldier for each day averaged about 6 kg. During WWII, it was increased to 20 kg for each person each day. In the several local area wars fought in recent years, the fuel consumption of each man each day increased to 90 kg. The consumption level is shocking! This not only raises problems for logistics support, it also increases the economic and energy resources burden.

- The rapid increase and shorter intervals in the updating and replacement of weaponry have sharply increased military expenditures and expenses. The advancements of science and technology have caused new weapons to emerge in an endless stream and greatly accelerated replacement and updating of weaponry. Before and after WWI, the time period for a weapons system to go from research and design, through trial tests and production to its deployment within the service required about 20 to 30 years. At present, this procedure requires only 10 to 15 years or an even shorter period. According to the analysis of a Soviet economist, Maj. Gen. Guluofu, a new weapons system for the Soviet military from research to its deployment in the services requires 10-15 years. Since the 1960s, Soviet missiles have already been updated three generations. The majority of its aircraft, submarines, and surface ships underwent updating long ago. Its anti-air defence missiles, radar, command equipment, communications equipment, and other equipment have also been through several generations of updating. The research of new weapons and the updating of existing weapons have greatly increased the military expenditures and expenses of every country. According to an analysis by western observers, "The world economy is already shouldering a burden of massive destructive weapons, poverty, and debt. Militarization will further sap its strength." Since the 1960s, the global expenditure for weapons has been about $14 trillion. In 1985 it was about $800 billion, in 1986 about $900 billion. Every second of every year about $1.7 million are spent. Immense military expenditures have become serious economic problems for each of the world's countries.

- The research and production of modern weapons have made even greater demands on the national defence economy and national defence industries. Since WWII, especially during the 1960s and 1970s, the unceasing discovery of new technology has led to a great revolution in weapons and military-use equipment.

In 1945, the atomic bomb appeared. The research of computers for weapons use came in 1946. In 1952, the first transistorized computer was developed. In 1953, the world's first hydrogen bomb was exploded. In 1955, the first nuclear-powered submarine was launched. In August 1957, the first intercontinental ballistic missile was fired, and in October of that same year, the first manmade satellite was orbited. In 1960, mankind recovered its first satellite. In 1961, the world's first manned satellite did an orbit around the earth and returned to the surface.

In 1967, the first integrated circuit was successfully developed. In 1969, man had his first landing on the moon. In 1977, the neutron bomb was researched and developed. In April 1981, the world's first spacecraft flew. The research and production of all these new weapons and equipment and a large portion of the new technology that entered into the sphere of the national defence economy not only greatly changed the production and industrial structure of the national defence economy, it also added a series of new production and industrial sectors. These changes helped to restructure the traditional national defence industries, moving them in the direction of technological improvement, and development of a technological reserve. The diffusion of a large quantity of high technology made it possible to turn a consuming national defence economy into a propagating field of national defence economy.

Weapons development is reliant on the development of the national economy. It also encourages the growth of national defence science and technology. Military high-technology also gave impetus to the development of the economy. Looking at this from two-dimensional space, this big "O" cycle could possibly expand further. Analyzing it from a three-dimensional space, this kind of spiraling trend is perfectly suited to the objective laws of material development.

WEAPONS AND EQUIPMENT DEVELOPMENT STRATEGY RESEARCH

The weapons development strategy is dictated by the realpolitik of politics, economics, national defence and science and technology. These situations suggest comprehensive ideas for the development of weapons. Weapons development hinges between the needs of combat and military construction, and what is possible economically and in science and technology. At the same time it is also determined by a country's political system, its national defence strategic policies, and its fundamental appraisal of the international condition. Thus, different countries have different weapons development strategies.

China is a socialist country and a part of the Third World. This is the political basis from which China formulates its national defence development strategy. China espouses a foreign policy of independence and self-determination. It is against all expansionism and aggression.

It supports all struggles and movements for justice. China, together with the rest of the Third World, is a major force for the preservation of world peace. This demands that China have the necessary military strength and an appropriate weapons development program to defend itself against outside aggression. It also demands that it have the ability to completely protect its territory and rights, to protect its country's unity, legitimate rights, interests and self-respect, to prevent the breakout of world wars and to protect world peace.

China is a country that is still economically, scientifically, and technologically undeveloped. This in itself imposes a limit on the amount of money it can possibly commit to weapons development and makes it even more impossible for it to be involved in an arms race. Thus, the development of China's weaponry must be based on the needs of national defence and military construction and economic strength, the level of potential in construction and its economic strength, the level of potential in the development of its science and technology, and the independent, self-determining and self-reliant road it takes toward developing weaponry. In the near future, our actions must be firmly directed toward transforming our present weaponry, so that our military weapons will be improved by the end of the century and they will have the ability to meet the demands of a localized conflict. We must also face the future by developing weapons systems for our country, striving to reach world advanced standards in weapons in the next century and carrying out the modernization of our weapons. In order to realize the objectives of the above-mentioned weapons development strategy, our military must develop suitable strategic nuclear weapons and tactical nuclear weapons, strengthen its research for precision-guided weapons and electronic and technological equipment, and work even more toward modifying various conventional weapons.

Strategic nuclear weapons are not only a combat tool of immense destructive power; they also serve as powerful deterrents and an anti-deterrent force. After our country had successfully exploded its first atomic bomb on October 16, 1964, it went on to successfully explode its first hydrogen bomb in June 1967. With every step China takes in the development of its strategic nuclear weapons, the strength of world peace is also increased by those steps. China's development of its limited nuclear capability is completely for the purpose of defence, for breaking up the nuclear monopoly and nuclear threats of the United States and the Soviet Union, and for preserving long-lasting world peace. To win time for the world to stabilize within this nightmarish nuclear situation and to provide our socialist modernization greater security in the international environment, to completely destroy the nuclear blackmail of the U.S. and the Soviet Union, to strive for the thorough destruction of nuclear weapons, to proceed toward preventing a world from exploding into war, and to increase the strength for world peace over war so that China and Third World countries can play a greater role in international affairs, China must continue to develop proper strategic weapons and move toward upgrading their precision, lessening their weight, and increasing their mobile combat capability.

Field tactical nuclear weapons are an effective antipersonnel weapon. The extent of their destructive area is above 300 km. This weapon not only has the superior tactical technical capabilities of long range, fast firing rate, high accuracy, and great destructive power, but it could also be used as a surprise weapon in major field operations to strive for and grasp the field initiative. In its tactical use, in an offensive situation it could directly break up the effective fire power of the enemy and destroy the defence points of the enemy from a distance, or it could attack the depth defences of the enemy and cut off the enemy's retreat. In a defensive situation it could attack the enemy rear echelon troops, stop the continuous assault of the enemy, and defend against the enemy making a direct deep push. Coordinated and complementary field tactical nuclear missiles used with various other conventional weapons systems could give the military greater military benefits and battlefield power. In a situation where, temporarily, no global wars are being fought, localized wars will be the major forms of combat for a period of time. In localized wars, the possible use of field tactical nuclear weapons by the enemy cannot be dismissed. Thus, China appropriately and within reason must develop field tactical nuclear weapons in order to further break down the various kind of nuclear threats of the hegemonists and restrain the use of field tactical nuclear weapons by the enemy.

After the implementation of the strategical changes in the guiding ideologies of military construction, the serious research of various weapons systems for localized wars will become the major tasks of our country's weapons system development for a period of time. The effective use in recent years of conventional precision-guided weapons in several localized combat theaters of operations has been followed with general interest by various countries around the world. Our national socialist characteristics have also determined that the major combat form of our military will hereafter still be that of defending our national territory. In a defensive war, the major missions assumed by our military will be defending against the enemy's surprise air attacks and stopping a mass invasion by the enemy's tanks. In our military's conventional arms buildup, the development of different precision-guided weapons for anti-air and antitank defence will be of special importance.

The level of modernization of our weapons directly corresponds to how sophisticated our electronic technology is and this will have a direct impact on victory or defeat in modern warfare. After our forces are equipped with a large quantity of electronic equipment and computers, not only will the electronic command, control, communications and information systems (C3I) within our combat and control become highly automated, and simple platforms and partial electronic equipments of warfare like reconnaissance and antireconnaissance, jamming and antijamming, destructive and antidestruction devices be completely transformed for "electronic wars;" they will also allow electronic technology to spread and permeate into all of the other weapons systems until it becomes the mainstay of our modern weaponry. The energetic development of our country's military use of electronic technology is of utmost importance to upgrading the modernization level of our military weapons and closing the weapons gap with advanced countries.

For a long time, our military had summarized a complete set of combat methods and experience on how to gain victory with inferior equipment over a superiorly equipped enemy. Facing a strong opponent, our military would be inferior in terms of weapons. Our country's economic strength is still very weak, our science and technology is still not very developed and compared to a strong enemy, the gap in our weapons will be difficult to overcome immediately. After our country implemented the strategic change of "transferring the work emphasis towards economic construction," there has been little possibility that military expenditures will be increased greatly and also little possibility that more money will be forthcoming for the research of sophisticated weapons. Thus, we must begin exploring new ways to develop weapons that possesses Chinese characteristics.

On the one hand, we can track the development of global high technology, build a good technological reservoir, and actively research new weapons systems in order to lay a foundation to close the gap with the advanced standards in foreign countries. On the other hand, we can use what we currently have and what high-technology results we have already achieved to change the low-tech conventional weapons system in our military, and upgrade the tactical technological capability of our present weapons so that with these slightly improved low-tech weapons systems we can still win a victory over our enemy's hi-tech weapons.

A weapons development strategy is an important component of our national defence development strategy. In the historical situation where our guiding ideology for military buildup is undergoing grave strategic changes, the somber formulation of a military weapons development strategy, the development of military weapons in a planned, focused, and measured way, and the acceleration of the pace of development of our military weapons will all have practical and long term impacts on encouraging our military's modernization and standardization.

WEAPONS AND EQUIPMENT DEVELOPMENT AND MILITARY SCIENTIFIC THEORY

"Technology determines the tactics." The appearance of large quantities of technical equipment inevitably brings about great transformations in military theory and tactics; this in turn leads to great changes in strategic thinking, patterns of combat, combat style, and military structures:

- Weapons development enhances man's strategic consciousness, deepens his strategic reflections, and increases the emphasis on strategic projections. In today's world, strategic research is extremely dynamic. With the development of strategic rockets and various spacecrafts, as well as the gradual development of energy beam weapons, kinetic energy weapons, and other space weapons systems, war has extended from the surface, air, and sea toward outer space. The areas of man's activities have already extended beyond the earth and moved into space. This has opened up man's field of vision and expanded his modes of thinking. In the wideness of space, the earth is no longer "boundless and limitless," but has become one of the "global villages" in the universe. In the eyes of the strategist, the earth has become small and man's strategic reflection is becoming more profound and his strategic consciousness has been greatly enhanced. Man's heart embraces the whole of the universe. The development of strategic research is even more important than at any time in history and has become an especially important issue for all countries globally. What is coming will be conflicts in space. One of the conflicts will be the military struggle for "control of the high ground in space." The other will be exploitation and use of space, the struggle for the resources of space. For this reason, every country in the world is busily formulating and developing strategic plans. In March 1983, the United States became the first to formulate a "Star Wars

Plan." This caused global commotion in strategy research. The Soviet Union responded with "defensive measures" to the "Star Wars Plan." Western Europe came up with the "Eureka Plan." Each of the COMECON countries announced a "Plan for the integrated advancement of science and technology by the year 2000." Japan had its "Policy outline for science and technology;" China had a "Policy for a new technological revolution;" India came out with "Policy statements for new technology;" South Korea had its "Conceptions for long range national growth;" and Yugoslavia had its "National science and technology development strategy." To rank within the world's family of nations, to live and survive in the "global village" in this universe, each nation must come up with ideas for a "grand strategy." "To stand shoulder to shoulder with the giants" one must intensely fix one's eye on the growth of national defence construction and weapons in the next century.

- Modern weapons are not only direct combat strengths between opposing combat opponents, they are also strategic deterrents and tools for international political struggles. The appearance of offensive strategic weapons like missiles, atomic bombs, nuclear-powered submarines, and long-range bombers has caused great changes in military strategy. The research, production, and large stockpiles of strategic weapons are already more than needed to seek out and kill an enemy. It has turned into a tool for political and diplomatic struggle. The large-scale arms race have caused the United States to stockpile over 9,400 nuclear warheads with a total nuclear weight equivalent of over 4 billion tons. The Soviet Union's stockpile of over 8,000 nuclear warheads has a total nuclear weight equivalent of over 5 billion tons. The quantity of nuclear warheads possessed by these two nuclear powers comprises above 97 percent of the global total. Both have the capacity to destroy the other several times over. Living under these conditions, the military strategy of both sides has gone through many changes; strategic ideologies have been revised about every 10 years. However, pressure from the threat that "destroying the enemy doesn't necessarily mean one's own survival" has kept them from crossing the "nuclear threshold" and taking the next step of pressing the button to launch those nuclear missiles. England, France, and China have independently and on their own developed into national nuclear powers. The limited power of these countries is not enough to compete with the capabilities of the United States and the Soviet Union, but they do play a role in the even development of political, economical, and military affairs within the world. This power is entirely a symbol of a country's independence and its existence within the world of politics, economics, military affairs, and science and technology.

In addition to nuclear weapons, the emergence of strategic weapons has definitely caused reforms within the military, changing past combat theories that we must go through war and campaigns to achieve strategic objectives to the possibility that strategic weapons could directly attack the opponent's strategic targets and achieve the strategic objectives. The development of various space weapons has not only intensified military struggles in space, it has also increased ways in which strategic objectives could be directly achieved.

- Today's weapons systems are very mobile. They also have long range, high accuracy, and great power, causing the time and spatial aspects as well as the intensity of war to change greatly. The development of these weapons and the great number of these weapons being deployed within the services have caused the arenas of war to be extended into deep sea and space, the length of war to shorten, and the suddenness, destructiveness, savageness, and mutation to increase unprecedentedly. In the "blitzkrieg" of the German armoured troops during WWII, they could advance only about 30 km daily. Today, under normal circumstances, the Soviets could do 50 km and under nuclear conditions it could reach above 100 km. When the Soviet Union invaded Afghanistan, its push towards Kabul, a distance of 900 km took only 6 days. The time it takes for an intercontinental ballistic missile to travel its whole distance is only slightly more than 30 minutes and there is no more than 20 minutes of early warning for its defence.

During the Falklands War, England's SHEFFIELD class missile destroyer did not even have the opportunity to react before it was hit by Argentina's EXOCET missile. With this short span of time, it is very difficult to react. This has made even greater demands on command and control. The largeness of the battlefield and the number of troops involved have given rise to immense increases in technical weaponry and specialized technology and have caused even greater problems in the coordination of operations and commands. According to reports, there were only 20 different military specialties during Word War I. It grew to 160 during World War II, and at present, the number of military technologies and specializations exceed 2,000. During combat, the army, navy, air force, and the other different service branches are all involved at the same time. The types of weapons used are never less than a dozen and usually are in the hundreds. This alone would demand that the commander prepare detailed plans and coordinate his commands well. There must be no mistakes in differentiating missions, allotting time, and coordinating activities. Any small error could lead to major mistakes and even greater disasters.

First strike has always been the combat phase that militarists attach greatest importance to. The success or failure of the first strike impacts the whole battle. In modern combat, because of the short time needed for combat, the phases of combat are no longer clearly delineated. The long range surprise attack or the counterattack during the preliminary period of the combat has become the main combat model for first strike. Thus, every nation has given special attention to studying the first strike phase of a war. The United States emphasizes that "every preparation must be made to win with the first strike." The Soviet Union also believes that "surprise attacks are the most effective combat opening moves to implement in future wars.... Victory can basically be determined in the first phase of a war." This will demand that commanders make complete preparations for first strikes. Intelligence, reconnaissance, personal observations with automatic and rapid analysis, processing and judgment, decisionmaking, formulating careful plans, and even reactions must be quick and accurate because only then could the "first strike win" objective be achieved.

- The extensive use of modern weapons has caused great changes in military structures. Before WWI, the military was basically composed of land forces that included the infantry, artillery, calvary, and navy. Before WWII, there was a great deal of aircraft and tanks in the military, thus the air force, armoured troops and motorized troops came into existence. The air force itself was divided into bomber, fighter, and attack aircraft forces. There were surface vessels, submarines, naval aviation forces and marines in the navy. After WWII, strategic rocket forces, army airborne forces and other service branches were formed. With the development of space technology and the successful development of various spaceflight vehicles as well as the development of various space weapons, the militarization of space will possibly strengthen the military deployment of a new independent military service branch "Space Forces." In 1982, the United States established the Air Force Spaceflight Command (a command comparable to the Strategic Air Force and Tactical Air Force Commands combined), and in 1983, the United States established the Naval Spaceflight Command. In 1985, the two commands and affiliated army commands were combined to form the U.S. Spaceflight Command. Not long after the United States had established the Air Force Spaceflight Command (1982), the Soviet Union appointed Lt. Gen. Sadaluofu as the "Aeronavigation Forces Commander." Some reports have said that "it is possible that the Soviet Union had already established a military spaceflight command like the U.S. Air Force Spaceflight Command and that the aeronavigation force was nothing but a subforce of that command." Various evidence has shown that the growth of the militarization of space has brought about the birth of the "Space Forces." With the advancements made in microelectronics, computers, and artificial intelligence technology, multipurpose robots could soon be used more and more in military applications and in those work areas where the labour is heavy and environmentally dangerous; thus a "robot force" would have to be deployed. The influence of weapons development on military administrative systems and deployment and on the overall structure can be easily seen. At present, the strategic course for overall military development is: a reduction in the overall personnel strength, a rise in the proportion of technical military personnel in the overall structure, a decrease in the proportion of personnel directly involved in combat, and a different scale for the increase in the proportion of logistic personnel (including technical support personnel).

The impact of modern weapons on military theory has been profound and extensive. The various sophisticated tools, means and methods of modern policy decision studies, projection studies, and futures studies have scientifically given impetus to and provided directions for military theories and strategic growth. It has allowed the military to grow scientifically so that it can completely anticipate conflicts and play a better leadership role.

LAWFUL USE OF NUCLEAR WEAPONS

In evidence before the Tribunal, Professor Meyrowitz stated that, of all those scholars who have expressly considered the topic, the substantial majority have concluded that the use of nuclear weapons would contravene international law. The minority opinion, predominantly American, is that the use of nuclear weapons would be lawful so long as their use complies with the standards of discrimination and proportionality. To be meaningful, this last assertion requires an answer to the question of whether the real (and not theoretical) use of nuclear weapons could be discriminating and proportionate. The Tribunal did not consider that the likely reality supports the assertion, and reached this conclusion based upon the evidence of the capabilities of existing nuclear weapons, the unlikelihood of a limited use of nuclear weapons and the medical and environmental consequences of their actual use.

Professor Boyle stated, "one might be able to conceive some totally insignificant situation in which a bomb could be blown off and perhaps not violate international law". Professor Griffith offered a few examples such as the use of a small 'clean' tactical weapon against an enemy ship in mid-ocean or against a small force in mid-desert.

The Tribunal considered these examples to be unlikely. In reality any major nuclear exchange would be an unprecedented human and environmental catastrophe proving a serious threat to the survival of all life on the planet. Even the use of a few tactical nuclear warheads would result in substantial incidental loss of civilian life and civilians would be subjected to unnecessary suffering far outweighing any immediate political or military objectives.

There are the strongest religious and moral objections to the destruction of a society through the use of nuclear weapons. Indeed, it is difficult to identify any real value system that justifies their use. As for the rights of neutral states, missiles, which are not included within any of the treaties regulating air traffic, but which will inevitably fly over neutral territory are in breach of Article II of the fifth Hague Convention. The use of nuclear weapons would inflict considerable damage on neutral nations, most obviously upon Austria and Switzerland. It is the most extraordinary proposition that two warring states, engaged in a private conflict, may legitimately destroy their neutral neighbours.

Upon the evidence, the use of nuclear weapons cannot distinguish between combatants and non-combatants, that it could not represent a proportionate use of force, that it cannot be selective or discriminating, and that it violates the rights of neutral nations. In short, the use of nuclear weapons is unlawful. It is clear therefore that the use of nuclear weapons involves, inter alia, infringements the Charter of the United Nations, the Hague Conventions of 1899 and 1907 on the Law of War, the Geneva Conventions of 1949 and the Geneva Protocols of 1977. It is also clear that mere *possession* (certainly in terms of testing nuclear weapons) has already involved quite unlawful actions against civilian populations and exposed certain populations to unacceptable risks and actual damage.

FLEXIBILITY OF NUCLEAR POWER PLANTS

It is often claimed that nuclear stations are inflexible in their output, implying that other, typically fossil stations would be used to meet peak demand. Whilst it may have been true for certain reactors, this is not longer true of at least some modern designs. Nuclear plants are routinely used in load following mode on a large scale in France.

Economics

The economics of nuclear power plants are primarily influenced by the high initial investment necessary to construct a plant. In 2009, estimates for the cost of a new plant in the U.S. ranged from $6 to $10 billion. It is therefore usually more economical to run them as long as possible, or construct additional reactor blocks in existing facilities. In 2008, new nuclear power plant construction costs were rising faster than the costs of other types of power plants.. A prestigious panel assembled for a 2003 MIT study of the industry found the following: In deregulated markets, nuclear power is not now cost competitive with coal and natural gas. However, plausible reductions by industry in capital cost, operation and maintenance costs, and construction time could reduce the gap. Carbon emission credits, if enacted by government, can give nuclear power a cost advantage. —The Future of Nuclear Power Comparative economics with other power sources are also discussed in the Main article above and in nuclear power debate.

Future of the Industry

As of 2007, Watts Bar 1, which came on-line in February 7, 1996, was the last U.S. commercial nuclear reactor to go on-line. This is often quoted as evidence of a successful worldwide campaign for nuclear power phase-out. However, even in the U.S. and throughout Europe, investment in research and in the nuclear fuel cycle has continued, and some nuclear industry experts predict electricity shortages, fossil fuel price increases, global warming and heavy metal emissions from fossil fuel use, new technology such as passively safe plants, and national energy security will renew the demand for nuclear power plants. According to the World Nuclear Association, globally during the 1980s one new nuclear reactor started up every 17 days on average, and by the year 2015 this rate could increase to one every 5 days.

Many countries remain active in developing nuclear power, including China, India, Japan and Pakistan. all actively developing both fast and thermal technology, South Korea and the United States, developing thermal technology only, and South Africa and China, developing versions of the Pebble Bed Modular Reactor (PBMR). Several EU member states actively pursue nuclear programs, while some other member states continue to have a ban for the nuclear energy use. Japan has an active nuclear construction program with new units brought on-line in 2005. In the U.S., three consortia responded in 2004 to the U.S. Department of Energy's solicitation under the Nuclear Power 2010 Program and were awarded matching funds—the Energy Policy Act of 2005 authorized loan guarantees for up to six new reactors, and authorized the Department of Energy to build a reactor based on the Generation IV Very-High-Temperature Reactor concept to produce both electricity and hydrogen. As of the early 21st century, nuclear power is of particular interest to both China and India to serve their rapidly growing economies—both are developing fast breeder reactors.. In the energy policy of the United Kingdom it is recognized that there is a likely future energy supply shortfall, which may have to be filled by either new nuclear plant construction or maintaining existing plants beyond their programmed lifetime. There is a possible impediment to production of nuclear power plants as only a few companies worldwide have the capacity to forge single-piece reactor pressure vessels, which are necessary in most reactor designs.

Utilities across the world are submitting orders years in advance of any actual need for these vessels. Other manufacturers are examining various options, including making the component themselves, or finding ways to make a similar item using alternate methods. Other solutions include using designs that do not require single-piece forged pressure vessels such as Canada's Advanced CANDU Reactors or Sodium-cooled Fast Reactors.

The World Nuclear Industry Status Report 2009 states that "even if Finland and France each builds a reactor or two, China goes for an additional 20 plants and Japan, Korea or Eastern Europe add a few units, the overall worldwide trend will most likely be downwards over the next two decades". With long lead times of 10 years or more, it will be difficult to maintain or increase the number of operating nuclear power plants over the next 20 years. The one exception to this outcome would be if operating lifetimes could be substantially increased beyond 40 years *on average*. This seems unlikely since the present average age of the operating nuclear power plant fleet in the world is 25 years.

However, China plans to build more than 100 plants, while in the US the licenses of almost half its reactors have already been extended to 60 years, and plans to build more than 30 new ones are under consideration. Further, the U.S. NRC and the U.S. Department of Energy have initiated research into Light water reactor sustainability which is hoped will lead to allowing extensions of reactor licenses beyond 60 years, in increments of 20 years, provided that safety can be maintained, as the loss in non-CO_2-emitting generation capacity by retiring reactors "may serve to challenge U.S. energy security, potentially resulting in increased greenhouse gas emissions, and contributing to an imbalance between electric supply and demand." In 2008, the International Atomic Energy Agency (IAEA) predicted that nuclear power capacity could double by 2030, though that would not be enough to increase nuclear's share of electricity generation.

NUCLEAR REACTOR TECHNOLOGY

Just as many conventional thermal power stations generate electricity by harnessing the thermal energy released from burning fossil fuels, nuclear power plants convert the energy released from the nucleus of an atom, typically via nuclear fission. When a relatively large fissile atomic nucleus (usually uranium-235 or plutonium-239) absorbs a neutron, a fission of the atom often results. Fission splits the atom into two or more smaller nuclei with kinetic energy (known as fission products) and also releases gamma radiation and free neutrons. A portion of these neutrons may later be absorbed by other fissile atoms and create more fissions, which release more neutrons, and so on.

This nuclear chain reaction can be controlled by using neutron poisons and neutron moderators to change the portion of neutrons that will go on to cause more fissions. Nuclear reactors generally have automatic and manual systems to shut the fission reaction down if unsafe conditions are detected. A cooling system removes heat from the reactor core and transports it to another area of the plant, where the thermal energy can be harnessed to produce electricity or to do other useful work. Typically the hot coolant will be used as a heat source for a boiler, and the pressurized steam from that boiler will power one or more steam turbine driven electrical generators.

There are many different reactor designs, utilizing different fuels and coolants and incorporating different control schemes. Some of these designs have been engineered to meet a specific need. Reactors for nuclear submarines and large naval ships, for example, commonly use highly enriched uranium as a fuel. This fuel choice increases the reactor's power density and extends the usable life of the nuclear fuel load, but is more expensive and a greater risk to nuclear proliferation than some of the other nuclear fuels. A number of new designs for nuclear power generation, collectively known as the Generation IV reactors, are the subject of active research and may be used for practical power generation in the future. Many of these new designs specifically attempt to make fission reactors cleaner, safer and/or less of a risk to the proliferation of nuclear weapons. Passively safe plants (such as the ESBWR) are available to be built and other designs that are believed to be nearly fool-proof are being pursued. Fusion reactors, which may be viable in the future, diminish or eliminate many of the risks associated with nuclear fission.

Life Cycle

A nuclear reactor is only part of the life-cycle for nuclear power. The process starts with mining. Uranium mines are underground, open-pit, or in-situ leach mines. In any case, the uranium ore is extracted, usually converted into a stable and compact form such as yellowcake, and then transported to a processing facility. Here, the yellowcake is converted to uranium hexafluoride, which is then enriched using various techniques. At this point, the enriched uranium, containing more than the natural 0.7% U-235, is used to make rods of the proper composition and geometry for the particular reactor that the fuel is destined for. The fuel rods will spend about 3 operational cycles (typically 6 years total now) inside the reactor, generally until about 3% of their uranium has been fissioned, then they will be moved to a spent fuel pool where the short lived isotopes generated by fission can decay away. After about 5 years in a cooling pond, the spent fuel is radioactively and thermally cool enough to handle, and it can be moved to dry storage casks or reprocessed.

CONVENTIONAL FUEL RESOURCES

Uranium is a fairly common element in the Earth's crust. Uranium is approximately as common as tin or germanium in Earth's crust, and is about 35 times more common than silver. Uranium is a constituent of most rocks, dirt, and of the oceans. The fact that uranium is so spread out is a problem because mining uranium is only economically feasible where there is a large concentration. Still, the world's present measured resources of uranium, economically recoverable at a price of 130 USD/kg, are enough to last for "at least a century" at current consumption rates. This represents a higher level of assured resources than is normal for most minerals. On the basis of analogies with other metallic minerals, a doubling of price from present levels could be expected to create about a tenfold increase in measured resources, over time. However, the cost of nuclear power lies for the most part in the construction of the power station. Therefore the fuel's contribution to the overall cost of the electricity produced is relatively small, so even a large fuel price escalation will have relatively little effect on final price. For instance, typically a doubling of the uranium market price would increase the fuel cost for a light water reactor by 26% and the electricity cost about 7%, whereas doubling the price of natural gas would typically add 70% to the price of electricity from that source. At high enough prices, eventually extraction from sources such as granite and seawater become economically feasible.

Current light water reactors make relatively inefficient use of nuclear fuel, fissioning only the very rare uranium-235 isotope.

Nuclear reprocessing can make this waste reusable and more efficient reactor designs allow better use of the available resources.

Breeding

As opposed to current light water reactors which use uranium-235 (0.7% of all natural uranium), fast breeder reactors use uranium-238 (99.3% of all natural uranium). It has been estimated that there is up to five billion years' worth of uranium-238 for use in these power plants. Breeder technology has been used in several reactors, but the high cost of reprocessing fuel safely requires uranium prices of more than 200 USD/kg before becoming justified economically. As of December 2005, the only breeder reactor producing power is BN-600 in Beloyarsk, Russia. The electricity output of BN-600 is 600 MW — Russia has planned to build another unit, BN-800, at Beloyarsk nuclear power plant. Also, Japan's Monju reactor is planned for restart (having been shut down since 1995), and both China and India intend to build breeder reactors.

Another alternative would be to use uranium-233 bred from thorium as fission fuel in the thorium fuel cycle. Thorium is about 3.5 times as common as uranium in the Earth's crust, and has different geographic characteristics. This would extend the total practical fissionable resource base by 450%. Unlike the breeding of U-238 into plutonium, fast breeder reactors are not necessary—it can be performed satisfactorily in more conventional plants. India has looked into this technology, as it has abundant thorium reserves but little uranium.

Fusion

Fusion power advocates commonly propose the use of deuterium, or tritium, both isotopes of hydrogen, as fuel and in many current designs also lithium and boron. Assuming a fusion energy output equal to the current global output and that this does not increase in the future, then the known current lithium reserves would last 3000 years, lithium from sea water would last 60 million years, and a more complicated fusion process using only deuterium from sea water would have fuel for 150 billion years. Although this process has yet to be realized, many experts and civilians alike believe fusion to be a promising future energy source due to the short lived radioactivity of the produced waste, its low carbon emissions, and its prospective power output.

Water

Like all forms of power generation using steam turbines, nuclear power plants use large amounts of water for cooling. At Sellafield, which is no longer producing electricity, a maximum of 18,184.4 m^3 a day (over 4 million gallons) and 6,637,306 m^3 a year (figures from the Environment Agency) of fresh water from Wast Water is still abstracted to use on site for various processes. As with most power plants, two-thirds of the energy produced by a nuclear power plant goes into waste heat, and that heat is carried away from the plant in the water (which remains uncontaminated by radioactivity). The emitted water either is sent into cooling towers where it goes up and is emitted as water droplets (literally a cloud) or is discharged into large bodies of water — cooling ponds, lakes, rivers, or oceans. Droughts can pose a severe problem by causing the source of cooling water to run out. The Palo Verde Nuclear Generating Station near Phoenix, AZ is the only nuclear generating facility in the world that is not located adjacent to a large body of water. Instead, it uses treated sewage from several nearby municipalities to meet its cooling water needs, recycling 20 billion US gallons (76,000,000 m^3) of wastewater each year.

Like conventional power plants, nuclear power plants generate large quantities of waste heat which is expelled in the condenser, following the turbine. Colocation of plants that can take advantage of this thermal energy has been suggested by Oak Ridge National Laboratory (ORNL) as a way to take advantage of process synergy for added energy efficiency. One example would be to use the power plant steam to produce hydrogen from water. (Separation of water into hydrogen and oxygen can use less energy if the water begins at a high temperature.)

Solid Waste

The safe storage and disposal of nuclear waste is a significant challenge and yet unresolved problem. The most important waste stream from nuclear power plants is spent fuel. A large nuclear reactor produces 3 cubic metres (25–30 tonnes) of spent fuel each year. It is primarily composed of unconverted uranium as well as significant quantities of transuranic actinides (plutonium and curium, mostly). In addition, about 3% of it is made of fission products. The actinides (uranium, plutonium, and curium) are responsible for the bulk of the long term radioactivity, whereas the fission products are responsible for the bulk of the short term radioactivity.

High-level Radioactive Waste

Spent fuel is highly radioactive and needs to be handled with great care and forethought. However, spent nuclear fuel becomes less radioactive over the course of thousands of years of time. After about 5 percent of the rod has reacted the rod is no longer able to be used. Today, scientists are experimenting on how to recycle these rods to reduce waste. In the meantime, after 40 years, the radiation flux is 99.9% lower than it was the moment the spent fuel was removed, although still dangerously radioactive.

Spent fuel rods are stored in shielded basins of water (spent fuel pools), usually located on-site. The water provides both cooling for the still-decaying fission products, and shielding from the continuing radioactivity. After a few decades some on-site storage involves moving the now cooler, less radioactive fuel to a dry-storage facility or dry cask storage, where the fuel is stored in steel and concrete containers until its radioactivity decreases naturally ("decays") to levels safe enough for other processing.

This interim stage spans years or decades or millennia, depending on the type of fuel. Most U.S. waste is currently stored in temporary storage sites requiring oversight, while suitable permanent disposal methods are discussed. As of 2007, the United States had accumulated more than 50,000 metric tons of spent nuclear fuel from nuclear reactors. Underground storage at Yucca Mountain nuclear waste repository in U.S. has been proposed as permanent storage. After 10,000 years of radioactive decay, according to United States Environmental Protection Agency standards, the spent nuclear fuel will no longer pose a threat to public health and safety. The amount of waste can be reduced in several ways, particularly reprocessing. Even so, the remaining waste will be substantially radioactive for at least 300 years even if the actinides are removed, and for up to thousands of years if the actinides are left in. Even with separation of all actinides, and using fast breeder reactors to destroy by transmutation some of the longer-lived non-actinides as well, the waste must be segregated from the environment for one to a few hundred years, and therefore this is properly categorized as a long-term problem. Subcritical reactors or fusion reactors could also reduce the time the waste has to be stored. It has been argued that the best solution for the nuclear waste is above ground temporary storage since technology is rapidly changing. There is hope that current waste may well become a valuable resource in the future.

Low-level Radioactive Waste

The nuclear industry also produces a huge volume of low-level radioactive waste in the form of contaminated items like clothing, hand tools, water purifier resins, and (upon decommissioning) the materials of which the reactor itself is built. In the United States, the Nuclear Regulatory Commission has repeatedly attempted to allow low-level materials to be handled as normal waste: landfilled, recycled into consumer items, et cetera. Most low-level waste releases very low levels of radioactivity and is only considered radioactive waste because of its history.

NUCLEAR STRATEGY

Nuclear warfare strategy is a way for either fighting or avoiding a nuclear war. The policy of trying to ward off a potential attack by a nuclear weapon from another country by threatening nuclear retaliation is known as the strategy of nuclear deterrence. The goal in deterrence is to always maintain a second strike status (the ability of a country to respond to a nuclear attack with one of its own) and potentially to strive for first strike status (the ability to completely destroy an enemy's nuclear forces before they could retaliate). During the Cold War, policy and military theorists in nuclear-enabled countries worked out models of what sorts of policies could prevent one from ever being attacked by a nuclear weapon.

Different forms of nuclear weapons delivery allow for different types of nuclear strategy, primarily by making it difficult to defend against them and difficult to launch a pre-emptive strike against them. Sometimes this has meant keeping the weapon locations hidden, such as putting it on submarines or train cars whose locations are very hard for an enemy to track, and other times this means burying them in hardened bunkers. Other responses have included attempts to make it seem likely that the country could survive a nuclear attack, by using missile defence (to destroy the missiles before they land) or by means of civil defence (using early warning systems to evacuate citizens to a safe area before an attack). Note that weapons which are designed to threaten large populations or to generally deter attacks are known as strategic weapons. Weapons which are designed to actually be used on a battlefield in military situations are known as tactical weapons. There are critics of the very idea of nuclear strategy for waging nuclear war who have suggested that a nuclear war between two nuclear powers would result in mutual annihilation. From this point of view, the significance of nuclear weapons is purely to deter war because any nuclear war would immediately escalate out of mutual distrust and fear, resulting in mutually assured destruction. This threat of national, if not global, destruction has been a strong motivation for anti-nuclear weapons activism.

Critics from the peace movement and within the military establishment have questioned the usefulness of such weapons in the current military climate. The use of (or threat of use of) such weapons would generally be contrary to the rules of international law applicable in armed conflict, according to an advisory opinion issued by the International Court of Justice in 1996.

Perhaps the most controversial idea in nuclear strategy is that nuclear proliferation would be desirable. This view argues that, unlike conventional weapons, nuclear weapons successfully deter all-out war between states, and they are said to have done this during the Cold War between the U.S. and the Soviet Union. Political scientist Kenneth Waltz is the most prominent advocate of this argument. It has been claimed that the threat of potentially suicidal terrorists possessing nuclear weapons (a form of nuclear terrorism) complicates the decision process. Mutually assured destruction may not be effective against an enemy who expects to die in a confrontation, as they may feel they will be rewarded in a religious afterlife as martyrs and would not therefore be deterred by a sense of self-preservation. Further, if the initial act is from rogue groups of individuals instead of a nation, there is no fixed nation or fixed military targets to retaliate against. It has been argued, especially after the September 11, 2001 attacks, that this complication is the sign of the next age of nuclear strategy, distinct from the relative stability of the Cold War.

NUCLEAR IMPLICATIONS OF THE 'TWO FRONT' FORMULATION

A 'Two Front' conflict is a 'worst case' scenario that has exercised military minds at least since 1963 when Pakistan sought to curry favour with China by ceding the trans-Karakoram Shaksgam area. That a joint threat was perceived by India ever since is evident from late Field Marshal Manekshaw's insistence in April 1971 that any military confrontation in East Pakistan be postponed to winter so that Pakistan could not bring to bear the 'China factor'. A combination of India's diplomacy since the late eighties and military preparedness demonstrated in the Wangdung incident has ensured that the 'worst case' scenario does not arise. While this will continue to be the endeavour, the military for the sake of deterrence and as a professional obligation requires thinking through the implications of a 'two front' conflict.

Here two scenarios are taken up: one, a collusive attack on India by China and Pakistan, and, two, opening up of India's second front by the other power in case India is engaged in a conflict on the other front. As to the first albeit unlikely one, India may need allies who can threaten meaningfully to widen the conflict. With respect to avoiding the second, precedence of 1971 War exists in orchestrating strategy so as to restrict the war to only one front. The third scenario, of Indian contemplation of proactive offensive action on both fronts, is likely only in case it wishes to pre-empt the first when inevitable and imminent. Such thinking has been done earlier. Writing in wake of the 1971 victory on security in the coming decade, K. Subrahmanyam stated:

India will have to develop and keep at readiness adequate forces to deter China and Pakistan from launching an attack either jointly or individually and in case deterrence fails to repel aggression effectively...faced with the possibility of two adversaries, our aim must be to hold one and reach a quick military decision with the other. It is obvious that the latter can only be Pakistan. Consequently, our force requirements must be planned to achieve this aim ('Our National Security', *Economic and Scientific Research Foundation*, 1972).

Similar reflection was done also by Jasjit Singh a couple of decades on, though he did not envisage in the improved conditions on the China front then prevailing a 'two front' situation. Given the economic constraints of the mid-nineties he opined at a Seminar at the USI on 'Impact of decreased defence spending on the armed forces' (USI, 1996) that against Pakistan there was a need to keep conventional 'deterrence' capabilities honed, while against China a 'dissuasive' posture would suffice. To him developing a conventional deterrent capability in the North was likely to strain our economy considerably. However, he required that "there is no reduction in the dissuasive capability for the foreseeable future till further substantial and formalised improvement in relations."

The current debate was initiated by K. Subrahmanyam acknowledging in his *Indian Express* column that, "Professionally, Indian armed forces officers have a duty to anticipate such adventures by our potential adversaries in future and plan to forestall them. It would be justified to think about such a contingency..." He is however, of the opinion that, "the international situation has radically changed with the end of the Cold War" and that "most strategic opinion today discounts the possibility of a war among major powers with nuclear weapons." Therefore he avers that "the choice of the term 'two-front war' appears to be inappropriate." He instead prefers that, "In such circumstances what should be planned for is exercise of deterrence and dissuasion in each case using the most modern technology available."

The crucial question remains as to the response in case deterrence fails. The military's options could be called for in short order. Doctrinal preparedness enables relevance by preceding such an eventuality. Strategies of response would require being mindful of prevalent doctrine. In case Indian Army had continued with an attritionist mindset, it would not be able to cope with the political demands on it in such circumstance. Therefore its shift over the past decade has been warranted. This is arguably the appropriate doctrine to underpin conflict strategy, even if a war of manoeuvre in a short, limited war, is not, in the event, the preferred political choice. Not enabling the option would be a lapse on part of the Service.

That this movement has made an impression across the border is evident from Pakistan's Army Chief stating, "Proponents of conventional application of military forces, in a nuclear overhang, are chartering an adventurous and dangerous path, the consequences of which could be both unintended and uncontrollable." This implies that the conflict option would have to be deliberately thought through, along with alternatives to conflict being discussed in interdisciplinary forums alongside as suggested by Subrahmanyam, particularly since the nuclear angle, perhaps alluded to by Kayani, requires being factored in. What is its profile in a 'Two Front' War?

India professes No First Use as a principal plank of its nuclear doctrine, one diluted to an extent by the tenet of consideration of the nuclear option in case also of a major CBW attack. China also subscribes to the NFU, though believed to be qualified by it reserving the right to use nuclear weapons first on its own territory. In case territories it claims are taken by it as its 'own' then these would not be covered by the NFU. The Indian perspective of the Chinese NFU has it that it does not apply to Indian areas claimed by China. Pakistan, on the other hand, not having declared its nuclear doctrine, is believed to be preserving the option of 'first use'.

For the single front phase in this scenario, with respect to an India-Pakistan initial phase, deterrence stability has been assessed as existing up to a point. The arguable expectation is that Pakistan's high nuclear threshold permits limited Indian conventional attacks. In case of an initial phase of an India-China confrontation, war expansion would be against grand strategies of both states that privileges economic growth. But in case China, nursing superpower ambitions and out to 'teach India a lesson', is met with a face-altering bloody nose by India, it could find in its NFU caveat an opening for nuclear resort. In the reverse scenario, in case of Chinese 'hordes' poised to sweep into the plains along the rivers Brahmaputra or Teesta, a repeat of Nehru's speech leading to evacuation in Tezpur is unlikely. Instead India in self-defence may rescind its self-imposed NFU as a first step, thereby giving itself the option of nuclear first use.

In the collusive case, the two adversaries would attack under the perception of relative advantage. Nuclear use would not likely figure in their initial calculus. India, under pressure, could contemplate rescinding the NFU with the intent of nuclear signalling. This may be the minimum necessary in case the adversaries apply nuclear pressures by also brandishing the nuclear card. This would have operational dividend in making any enemy advances cautious and thereby slower. Declaring nuclear thresholds may deter the enemy threatening these, depriving them of war gains of significance. Balancing nuclear capabilities of allies could deter enemy nuclear use. However, the danger is in tempting a joint first strike, leaving India only a much degraded second strike capability. However, any semblance of even victory subsequent to nuclear use may be a worse outcome than losing the war. Therefore, restricting any nuclear resort to the lowest possible level makes sense. This has implications for the Indian deterrent based on the promise of infliction of 'unacceptable damage', needlessly disadvantageous in a two front situation.

In the second scenario of war expansion from two to three powers, in case of an initial India-China conflict, NFU, howsoever qualified, of both can be expected to hold since in the middle term future only limited border wars can be envisaged. Neither state would wish to let the dangerously escalatory nuclear card enter into the equation. In case of Pakistan joining in hyena-like, it would rely on its conventional capability since the nuclear card would be dependent on the senior partner's intent. India, if pressured, may resort to nuclear signalling at best, since it cannot reasonably prefer the alternative of limited nuclear war that may result.

The nuclear 'backdrop' carries dangers even in a single front. This is exponentially more so in the 'two front' situation, particularly since a move to rescind the NFU tenet of doctrine may be necessary.

Even as the military can be expected to delve into the issue, avoiding the predicament through diplomatic manoeuvre, deepening interdependence, managing extra-regional partnerships and evolving appropriate regional security forums are the more pertinent implications for grand strategy.

NUCLEAR STRATEGIES AND THE ROLE OF NUCLEAR DETERRENCE TODAY

Nuclear strategy is still relevant in the landscape of contemporary security issues, and today's approach to nuclear strategy is mainly focused on the concept of deterrence. That said, the prominent role of deterrence is not an exclusive one: the first strategies, as the bombings of Hiroshima and Nagasaki show, treated atomic bombs as merely more powerful versions of their conventional equivalents. However, soon the nuclear device became 'the absolute weapon' (as Brodie calls it in his 1946 book of the same title), and the strategies contemplating its use on the battlefield were replaced by deterrence. Today, the two approaches coexist. Since the end of the Cold War, the actual utilisation of tactical or theatre nuclear weapons have been reintroduced on the security agenda (Levi, 2004: 93), but nuclear deterrence has not abandoned its prominent role: in fact, strategic deterrence and regional deterrence remain the fundamental elements in the Nuclear Posture Review Report of the US, published in 2010. Moreover, the prospects of utilising low-yield tactical nuclear weapons have so far remained just a possibility, while nuclear deterrence is a well-established reality.

In the light of the current spending plans of the two Cold-War era superpowers, it would be naïve to consider the relevance of nuclear strategy concluded with the end of the Cold War. Both Russia and the US, in fact, are planning to develop in the next years more sophisticated delivery systems for their long-range strategic nuclear forces, as well as spending on keeping operational the old hardware (Kearns, 2011: 4). Despite the signing of the

"New Strategic Arms Reduction Treaty" (New START), both sides are currently working to modernise their arsenals, with the US alone planning to invest over $ 100 billion in its nuclear stockpiles (Ibid. 11): new, more effective delivery systems, as for example a new generation of strategic bombers, are currently under design, and the limitations imposed by the New START merely show that a new arms race is possible and feared by both states.

However, there are elements of discontinuity. The growing importance of actors like the PRC, together with the imbalance in the nuclear Powers' arsenals, explains why Mutual Assured Destruction (MAD) has lost its validity (Lieber and Press, 2006: 10). This system was based on the bipolar order of the Cold War, and its inapplicability today is one of the main reasons that has led to the current reinterpretation of deterrence by strategists, in both its nuclear and conventional form. In fact, the current situation of unipolarity does not permit a strategic balance: even if the eventuality of a first strike still may involve catastrophic consequences (the fear of which allegedly prevented war to break out during the Cold War), the "healthy fear of devastation" which made deterrence so easy then (according to Jervis, 1979-1980: 618) is no longer applicable to a scheme so profoundly changed.

Another key factor in shaping today's policies is the emergence of international terrorism. With the declaration of war on terror in 2001 (although the process started well before), the threats posed by non-state actors have replaced interstate conflict as the primary source of insecurity for the US. The National Security Strategy of the United States of America, published in 2002, explicitly recognised that traditional deterrence, as it was conceived during the Cold War, was useless when facing an adversary of this kind (US Department of State, 2002: 15). Anyway, rather than discharging the whole concept, the new strategy adopted by the US just proposed its adaptation to the new security scenario.

An interesting point in this context is the fact that flexible response plans are not part of the strategy actually adopted by the US, and, although they are seriously taken into consideration by the Nuclear Posture Review of 2010, the empirical approach of US chain of command is so far inconsistent with the prospects of the document. As already mentioned, the role of nuclear weapons in actual war-fighting has been limited to just two cases in history, and it is very unlikely that this tendency will change in the foreseeable future. The major obstacle to any nuclear utilisation theory is the consolidation of the nuclear taboo: the use of nuclear arms in the battlefield would probably confine any actor that used them to the status of a pariah state. This attitude by the international community is reinforced by the presence of international regulations which severely affect the legitimacy of a nuclear first-strike use (Tannenwald, 1999: 436). The time elapsed since the only event of actual use of nuclear weapons in war is another factor that strengthens the consolidating of this taboo. Having said that, the only use that remains for nuclear weapons is deterrence, since the consolidation of the nuclear taboo does not hinder the credibility of a state's threat of nuclear retaliation in response to a severe attack to its national security, especially if this attack threatens the state's survival.

The greatest innovation in the field of nuclear strategy is probably the concept of expanded deterrence – that is, deterrence aimed at governments that support terrorist organizations: this is one of the two possible responses which have been conceived to counter the risk of a terrorist use of WMDs, the other being preventive war (Gallucci, 2006: 52). The other nuclear powers of NATO have in a sense modelled their innovations in contemporary strategy over those of the United States: France has clearly affirmed in 2006 that states sponsors of terrorism could be attacked by a French nuclear warhead in retaliation of a terrorist attack (Yost, 2006: 702), and the British government did a similar declaration the same year, revealing a joint strategic line (Boese, 2007).

Specular to this concept, but representing an element of continuity with the Cold War-era strategies, is that of three-party extended deterrence. This is the official strategic policy adopted by many non-nuclear states under the NPT regime: they do not develop their own devices, choosing instead to rely on the arsenal of a nuclear power, sheltering under what is called a "nuclear umbrella". This strategy is designed to prevent nuclear attacks conducted mainly by state actors, but can as well be applied to conventional attacks (Quackenbush, 2006: 563). Its application to conventional threats is crucial with regard to its validity in the contemporary world: for example, one of the states which currently most relies on this strategy – Taiwan – is faced with an adversary – the PRC – whose hostile intentions, although fully proven, are unlikely to include a nuclear attack (Dunn, 2007: 28). However, the risk of a nuclear crisis between the PRC and the US (of which Taiwan is the protégé) cannot be underestimated, even if the likelihood of this happening is mainly linked to the possibility of miscalculations on both sides (Ibid.).

Given its importance within the US strategic doctrine, it is not surprising to find out that nuclear deterrence also continues to be an important part of NATO strategy today: in fact, according to the Deterrence and Defence Posture Review issued by the Alliance in 2012, "nuclear weapons are a core component of NATO's overall capabilities for deterrence and defence" (NATO, 2012). This document clearly delineates the common position of the Atlantic allies towards the role of nuclear weapons in today's security scenario and characterises it as a conservative one, mainly focused on the threat posed by state actors and oriented to solve it through the classic scheme of deterrence.

The actual validity of the concept of nuclear deterrence in the post-Cold War world will be now valued through the examination of two broad categories into which can be split the whole range of possible threats to the survival of a country, that is deterrence of nuclear and of non-nuclear attack.

NUCLEAR DETERRENCE OF NUCLEAR ATTACK

The eventuality of a nuclear attack has always represented one of the most dangerous threats to the safety of a country, inasmuch the precision and lethality of nuclear devices permit an adversary to cripple in an extremely short period of time the command, control and communication (C3) structure of the attacked state, in what is called a "decapitation strike" (Walton, 2010: 215). The only effective deterrent for such an attack remains the threat of another nuclear strike, in what is called a "second-strike capability". Anyway, today's nuclear threats are extremely different from the ones that lead to the establishment of the classic balance of terror during the Cold War. In a 2008 report, the US Secretary of Defense indicates as the current most urgent causes for concern terrorism and nuclear proliferation (US Secretary of Defense, 2008: 9). The two phenomena are closely linked, since the two most likely scenarios of terrorist acquisition of nuclear weapons – acquisition of HEU (highly enriched uranium) with or without the assistance of a government and theft or transfer of a completed weapon – require the existence of a nuclear arsenal in a sympathising or unreliable country (Gallucci, 2006: 53). As previously said, the main strategy developed to deal with the threat of a nuclear attack conducted by a non-state actor is expanded deterrence; anyhow, this measure must be implemented by steps to prevent horizontal nuclear proliferation, that is, the growth in the number of actors armed with nuclear weapons.

In fact, the enlargement of the nuclear club has increased the likelihood of a nuclear strike taking place: since a single weapon is sufficient to conduct such an attack, it can be deduced that, while vertical proliferation (the growth in the number of warheads within a country) does not make the eventuality of such an attack more likely, horizontal proliferation does. Nuclear deterrence has traditionally been associated with the neorealist view that a world with more nuclear actors, and ideally a world composed only by nuclear actors, is the prerequisite to a lasting peace founded on the fear of nuclear war (Berkowitz, 1985: 115). However, this model does not consider the current relevance of non-state actors and so-called rogue states and their asymmetrical relationship with the traditional players.

One of the most serious challenges to nuclear deterrence in the Second Nuclear Age is, in fact, represented by the issue of its applicability to actors with a different behaviour than the Cold War-era US and USSR (Walton, 2010: 214). These new actors may not conform to a model of rational behaviour, the latter being a fundamental prerequisite for deterrence to work. Hence, the major contemporary challenge for nuclear deterrence is to find ways to adapt itself to actors that may be non-rational: this means forcing them to assume a rational behaviour. The reduction of the "nuclear threshold" referred to in the US Nuclear Posture Review can be read in the light of these facts not as an introduction of flexible response strategies in nuclear policy, but as an action consistent with the need for improved deterrence schemes. Being credibility far more influential than capability as a variable that decides the effectiveness of a nuclear deterrent (Lowther, 2009: 32), the aggressive policy of nuclear pre-emption which is discussed in the above said document and in the US National Military Strategy to combat Weapons of Mass Destruction (US Chairman of the Joint Chiefs of Staff, 2006: 18) can be seen as a way to make the prospect of nuclear attack more real in the minds of the potential enemies of the US. Since the nuclear taboo does not apply to terrorist organisations or rogue states ruled by irrational leaders, the only way to counter them is acting as if its validity was lost also for the traditional actors (in this case, the US).

The matter is different with regard to the relationships within the circle of the established nuclear powers. In this case, nuclear deterrence is based on the schemes of the Cold War, as the policies of Russia and the US show. In fact, the current expenditure for nuclear weapons, despite significant cuts, is still extremely high, as previously mentioned. China has a considerably inferior arsenal compared to that of the two former superpowers, sufficient only to assure a policy of "minimal deterrence" (Lieber and Press, 2006: 8). The concept of minimal nuclear deterrence could be the most suitable to today's security issues regarding the relations among declared nuclear armed states, and there are sectors of the public opinion lobbying for an even greater reduction in the nuclear stockpiles of the US: among the others, this position is supported by the Federation of the American Scientists (Kristensen et al., 2009: 21). Anyway, at the moment the official strategy of the US is oriented differently, and the same can be said for Russia. While at the beginning of the First Nuclear Age the US relied on nuclear weapons to counterbalance Soviet conventional forces, today the situation has reversed, and Russia keeps an apparently anachronistic large storage of nuclear weapons to cope with the drastic reductions which took place after the Cold War in its non-nuclear offensive capabilities. NATO has stated in its Deterrence and Defence Posture Review that the current amount of its strategic nuclear weapons is dependent on the reciprocal level of these weapons on the Russian soil, so it is very unlikely that there will be drastic reductions, similar to those that occurred at the end of the Cold War, by the US and its allies in the foreseeable future.

NUCLEAR DETERRENCE OF NON-NUCLEAR ATTACK

The role of nuclear deterrence in averting the threat of a conventional attack is currently proving to be alive especially with regard to non-traditional nuclear actors, that is, non-declared nuclear powers, states outside the NPT and states that have violated the terms of the NPT. Countries in this category have not been attacked militarily in recent times, and there is some evidence that their nuclear capabilities could have played a major role in defending them. It is the case of North Korea, a part of Bush's "axis of evil": her policy towards the development of WMD programs was far more aggressive than that of Iraq (on her current and past programs: NTI, 2012), but she has not suffered any attack by the US nor by any of their local allies. It can be argued that it was her very progress in the development of WMDs, and especially of nuclear weapons, that permitted her to avoid an external aggression. Given the sensitivity of the American public opinion toward the number of casualties during recent conflicts, it is easy to understand that a retaliatory strike conducted by an actor facing foreign invasion is considered as an unacceptable condition by the US. On the other side, the threat of a nuclear attack should be questioned the survival of the state apparatus must be considered seriously: in fact, the price to pay to break the nuclear taboo is high, but certainly lower than that of regime capitulation: so, these actors gain in credibility what they lack in capability.

Nuclear deterrence has a role also in averting conventional attacks in a regional context. The conflict between India and Pakistan exemplifies this point: in fact, despite the existence of sources of tension between the two countries, these actors have not engaged in major open hostilities since their development of a nuclear arsenal. The fear of nuclear escalation may be the explanation for the restraint of these governments in an area like

Kashmir, where since the acquisition of nuclear weapons both sides have only supported a low-intensity conflict (Joeck, 1997: 36).

In any case, nuclear deterrence of non-nuclear attack seems inconsistent with regard to the traditional nuclear actors. In fact, these have continued to experience major conventional conflicts (it is, for example, the case of Russia with Georgia). It is possible that the threat of a nuclear retaliation lacks credibility when only the aggressor is armed with nuclear weapons – as the behaviour of many nuclear powers in time of war may lead to think – but this would be hardly true in the case of a WMD attack. In this respect, the biggest innovations are those developed by the US within its strategy to combat global terrorism. The same policy of expanded deterrence which has been discussed above is applied also to non-nuclear threats, in particular with regard to the scenario of a terrorist use of WMDs (Huntley, 2006: 49-50). In the National Military Strategy to Combat Weapons of Mass Destruction, Washington has confirmed its willingness to pursue a policy aimed at

"dissuading, deterring and defeating those who seek to harm the US directly [...] especially extremist enemies with weapons of mass destruction" (US Chairman of the Joint Chiefs of Staff, 2006: 9).

Nuclear deterrence is the most likely way to counter terrorism to be used in the future, since pre-emptive war lacks popular support and has been recognised to be an excessively expensive strategy. As Trager and Zagorcheva argue, nuclear deterrence may prove to be an effective method to counter the threat posed by non-state actors, as long as terrorists' political aims will be influenceable by states (2005/2006: 88).

Conclusion

Nuclear deterrence is still relevant in dealing with contemporary security issues. Although different strategies concerning the use of nuclear weapons have been proposed in recent times, their application would be extremely controversial, and for this reason is very unlikely. Nuclear deterrence is still an important part of the official strategy of the US to fight traditional threats, and has been adapted to meet also today's new security concerns. The other nuclear armed states, the traditional as well as the non-traditional ones, have shown their willingness to maintain the nuclear taboo, pursuing in most cases a minimal deterrence policy.

The threat of a nuclear strike can deter both nuclear and non-nuclear attacks, the contemporary security scenario requires an evolution of deterrence rather than a discharge of the concept as a whole. In fact, nuclear weapons are still among the most powerful and intimidating weapons with which states can arm themselves, and the stability of a system based on deterrence still remains attractive, although since the end of the Cold War maintaining this system has become far more complicated.

However, nuclear deterrence alone cannot be the answer to every security issue in the contemporary world, and its application needs to be strengthened by other strategies. The main role it held during the First Nuclear Age is lost, but its relevance, although resized, is not.

THE DEVELOPMENT OF NUCLEAR WEAPONS WILL CONTINUE

The dropping of atomic bombs on Hiroshima and Nagasaki in August 1945 by U.S. troops proclaimed the advent of a nuclear era. With their unprecedented tremendous power, it shocked people's hearts, became a significant bargaining chip of military strength, and cast a nuclear shadow over warfare. Between the 1960s and 1970s, the role of nuclear weapons was inappropriately exaggerated. The prolonged situation of the Cold War and particularly the emergence of high-tech weapons and high-tech warfare have made people understand more clearly the limitations of nuclear weapons. However, we must note that the existence of a large number of nuclear weapons and the continuous development of nuclear technology are facts that brook no argument. We cannot simplistically think that the emergence of high-tech weaponry has replaced the position and role of nuclear weapons, neither can we believe that because of their extremely gigantic destructive power, nuclear weapons have totally negated their own prospects for use.

For several decades after World War II, various military powers vied with one another in the research and development of nuclear weapons. At present, countries possessing nuclear weapons include the United States, Russia, Britain, France, and China, and the total number of nuclear warheads currently throughout the world exceeds 20,000. Of this total, 95 percent are in the hands of the United States and Russia, who have the power to destroy the world many times. A series of treaties and agreements on nuclear disarmament has been concluded in recent years.

However, even after they have been completely implemented, in the year 2003, the United States will still possess 3,500 strategic nuclear warheads, with a total equivalent weight of approximately 900 million tons, and 999 carrier vehicles; Russia will still possess 3,000 strategic nuclear warheads, with a total equivalent weight of more than 700 million tons, and 975 carrier vehicles. If we compare the above two sets of figures with the amount of bombs dropped by the U.S. troops during their 3-year war of aggression in Korea and the 8-year war in Vietnam, which totaled 680,000 tons and 1.5 million tons, respectively, it is not difficult to imagine that the force of the "remnant" nuclear weapons is still extremely formidable.

Since the Cold War ended, the danger of a world war has been growing smaller and smaller, but local military conflicts have never ceased. In light of the issues cropping up in various local wars, especially in the Gulf War, and to meet the requirements of the new pattern of military strife, some military powers stepped up their research and production of new-type nuclear weapons with very small TNT equivalents.

Such small-sized nuclear weapons have a degree of destructive power, yet the possibility of using them will not be negated because their equivalent weights are not too big and the destruction they cause is not too disastrous.

As disclosed in the autumn 1992 issue of Strategic Review, some people proposed that three kinds of nuclear weapons with small TNT equivalents should be developed:

- One is a small-size, ground-penetrating nuclear weapon with an equivalent of 10 tons. It explodes at 10 to 15 meters beneath ground surface, and its pressure will reach 25 meters deep, with a capability to destroy heavily fortified command posts and all underground defence works except bunkers. The shock waves produced by the nuclear explosion cause only slight damage to the building facilities within about 100 meters, and the danger of radiation is also controlled within a relatively small range. This kind of nuclear weapon can also effectively wreck enemy airports and other important military facilities. During Desert Storm, the multinational troops repeatedly bombed Iraqi airports, but that did not produce a satisfactory result because the craters blasted by the bombs were rapidly filled in. However, a ground-penetrating nuclear warhead is capable of creating a strong radioactive crater with a radius of 15 meters and a dimension of 3,000 cubic meters, which is very hard to repair. Hence, it can disable the functions of an airport.
- The second is a small-size, anti missile nuclear weapon with an equivalent of 100 tons. If an antimissile missile is equipped with a nuclear warhead with a small equivalent, it will not only accurately intercept the attacking missile in the sky, but also disable the nuclear, biological, and chemical warheads of the attacking missile.
- The third proposed nuclear weapon is a small-size, ground-to-ground or air-to-ground nuclear weapon with an equivalent of 1,000 tons. According to the article, "the appropriate scale of U.S. nuclear weapons could prevent the recurrence of the tragic retreat in Dunkirk. When the U.S. emergency troops arriving at the war zone were unable to hold back the enemy's attack, a display of a small-sized nuclear weapons with an equivalent of 1,000 tons would probably have made the enemy submit obediently."

Certainly, the future development of nuclear weaponry is far beyond the issue of size; indeed, the focus is on other aspects, including the individualized antipersonnel and destructive effect, the method of lead-in explosion, the technology of adjustable equivalent (with plug-in component), and the enhanced ability to penetrate defence lines and survivability, all of which are well along in development. All this has added to the flexibility of nuclear use in actual operations.

As a matter of fact, both the United States and Russia clearly understand that the existence and continued development of nuclear weapons is an objective reality in the present world. Because so many of nuclear weapons still exist and their functions are further improving, then there is a material foundation for using them. In this regard, nuclear weaponry is still the sword of Damocles hanging over the people of the world.

A Nuclear Environment in Future Battlefields

Today, the world is in a historical period of drastic changes, the pattern of multipolar forces is taking shape, the international situation is moving toward relaxation, and peace and development have become the theme of the present world. Therefore, we can anticipate that a new world war will not break out and nuclear warfare is avoidable. However, the world today is not trouble free, hegemony and power politics still have not withdrawn from the historical arena, the international situation is still very complicated, and the flames of war arising from local conflicts have never died out. Owing to multifarious factors, the nuclear shadow still cannot be cast away from future battlefields. Warfare is violent action. More than 100 years ago, the capitalist strategist Clausewitz pointed out, "The use of violence knows no bounds. Therefore, a belligerent will oblige its opponent to use force as it will itself, thus producing a kind of interaction.

As viewed from this conception, such interaction will inevitably lead to extreme." Warfare is the continuation of politics, and a kind of bloody politics at that. Nuclear warfare and high-tech warfare are both instruments subordinate to the purposes and requirements of wars. When countries possessing nuclear weapons and high-tech conventional weapons are involved in a war in which the conflict is intensifying, the possible use of nuclear weapons cannot be ruled out. Nuclear weapons, therefore, are still a trump card in the hands of nuclear nations.

Thomas F. Ramos, science adviser to the senior officer responsible for nuclear weapons in the U.S. Department of Defence said: "No reasonable evidence indicates that conventional weapons will be reliable shelters to cope with enemies possessing and intending to use nuclear weapons." His remarks express the consensus of some military strategists studying the Gulf War. As estimated by some Western specialits/analysts, there are at least 12 countries which claim to have ballistic missiles and at least 25 countries that have probably developed or are developing nuclear, biological, and chemical weapons. Using this estimation, some Western publications maintain that "the world has ushered in an age of nuclear proliferation." In 1974, India carried out its first nuclear blast, which kicked off the nuclear emulation in South Asia. In 1988, India successfully developed the PRITHVI medium-range ground-to-ground missile with a range of 2,000 meters, and the capability of carrying nuclear warheads. On March 24, 1993, South African President De Klerk addressed a special session of the National Assembly, saying that South Africa worked out a limited nuclear deterrent program in 1974 and had produced six atomic bombs by the end of 1989, and that all the said nuclear weapons had been dismantled and destroyed in early 1990. It was also revealed by the South African media that if the expansion of nuclear powers shown an intimidating color, South Africa will install warheads into its missiles and will probably develop and deploy neutron weapons. Israel is one of the countries that had nuclear weapons in its possession relatively earlier. Moreover, it was prepared to use them during the fourth Middle-East war.

Other data also stated that countries like Argentina and Brazil will also be able to manufacture nuclear weapons. With the rapid development of science and technology, the technology of making nuclear weapons has almost become an open secret. The disintegration of the former Soviet Union not only resulted in a brain drain of a vast number of scientists engaged in nuclear weapon development, but also threw the supervision of nuclear materials into chaos, considerably enlarging the scope of nuclear proliferation. A terrorist organization or a maniac could, some day, claim possession of an atomic bomb and use it as a tool of intimidation and blackmail, and no one would think that this was a tale from the Arabian Nights. What merits our attention is that in a high-tech conventional war, a nuclear environment may still emerge even if nuclear weapons are not used. The more society advances, the greater the demands for energy will be. In order to satisfy the demands for energy, nuclear power stations were built. According to the data released by the International Atomic Energy Agency in March 1994, at the end of 1993 there were 430 nuclear power plants with a total installed capacity of approximately 345 million kw operating in various places throughout the world; these accounted for more than 17 percent of the world's gross power generation. It had been predicted that by 2001, there will be 558 nuclear power generating units with a total installed capacity of approximately 460 million kw all worldwide, which will account for 24 percent of the world's gross power generation. The peaceful utilization of nuclear energy is a piece of joyous news to mankind.

Meanwhile, the extensive use of nuclear energy also constitutes a latent threat to peace and the existence of human beings. The accident at the Chernobyl Nuclear Power Plant that occurred in April 1986 inflicted air pollution on 16 Russian oblasts and victimized 250,000 people. In Ukraine, 370,000 people suffered injuries in varying degrees as land covering 40,000 square meters was polluted, and more than 2,000 residential areas were evacuated. In future high-tech warfare, if an enemy intentionally or unintentionally attacks nuclear power plants or other facilities using nuclear energy with high-tech conventional weapons, the secondary nuclear radiation produced and the nuclear environment brought about would likewise do harm. In June 1981, Israel dispatched four aircraft to launch a sudden attack on an Iraqi nuclear reactor southeast of the capital Baghdad, dropping 16 tons of bombs in two minutes and hitting all the targets. Fortunately, the reactor was not yet operational; otherwise the attack would have resulted in very serious consequences.

Nuclear Deterrence Will Be Used in Local Wars

The local wars that broke out after World War II were mostly carried out under the conditions of nuclear deterrence if the Western powers were involved in them. During the Korean War, U.S. Commander-in-Chief MacArthur once threatened a sudden attack of atomic bombs on China's northeast and coastal strategic targets. After Eisenhower came to power, he again ordered the Pentagon to formulate a nuclear program aimed at China. During its war of aggression in Vietnam, the United States also made nuclear threats and was prepared to resolve the issue with nuclear weapons. After the armed conflicts on Zhenbao Island between China and the Soviet Union in 1969, Brezhnev considered initiating a nuclear attack on China in an attempt to ruin China's nuclear facilities. In the Malvinas Islands War, Britain carried tactical nuclear weapons on its huge fleet and was prepared to use them if its conventional operations failed. In particular, the multinational coalition troops headed by the United States used extremely advanced high-tech weapons in the Gulf War, and although they held the trump card, they still deployed 800 to 850 tactical nuclear weapons on three sides of Iraq.

What is more, U.S. troops considered using radio flash bombs but, because of political considerations, they were not approved by U.S. President Bush. In response to Saddam's repeated threats to use chemical weapons, the British Government warned again and again that its troops would retaliate by using tactical nuclear weapons should Iraq resort to using chemical weapons. Bush also hinted that he would give field commanders freedom when necessary. These countries threatened to use nuclear weapons in conventional wars because they believed that with nuclear weapons in hand, psychologically they would be able to hold a dominant position, which would enhance troop morale and frighten the enemy on the one hand, and restrict the enemy's use of some conventional means on the other, thus changing the direction of the war. These past events should not be forgotten.

At present, nuclear deterrence is still a strategic pillar of military power. U.S. President Clinton thinks that the United States must build up military muscle that suits the new age, and this military muscle must have the capacity of nuclear deterrence. Nuclear deterrent force is an effective form of security. The 1993 defence report submitted by the U.S. Defence Department to Congress proposed that an all directional global defence system of strategic nuclear deterrence to prevent limited nuclear attacks should be set up, under which the former nuclear deterrent strategy chiefly aimed at the Soviet Union should be readjusted to an all-direction and multilevel nuclear deterrent strategy aimed at both the former Soviet Union and other regions.

On September 25, 1995, President Clinton ordered the Energy Department to maintain the three major nuclear weapon laboratories to ensure that U.S. nuclear deterrent capacity remains effective. Russia set up a defence ministry in March 1992, then founded its nuclear strategic forces and made the development of strategic nuclear weapons a top priority in the future development of eight technical weapons.

President Yeltsin said that a strategic nuclear force was the foundation of Russia's military strength. In November 1993, giving sanction to the new Russian military theory, he officially abandoned the Kremlin's 11-year-old commitment that in a conflict it would not be the first to use nuclear weapons. In its 1992 defence report, France claimed that it merely wanted to have the "most rudimentary" nuclear deterrent for as a way to cope with various kinds of unexpected events and check possible encroachments on its interests by potential enemies.

In the meantime, France announced that it is continuing to focus on the development of a submarine-launched strategic nuclear missile system to ensure the reliability of its nuclear deterrent strategy. At his first news conference after assuming office as president on June 13, 1995, Chirac declared that France would resume its nuclear tests in the South Pacific. The French Defence Minister maintained that President Chirac had made a "very serious decision." British Prime Minister Major said, "As far as Britain is concerned, laying down the nuclear shield in whatever manner is an indiscreet move. Britain holds on to its views that as long as the CIS countries are still in possession of nuclear weapons, Britain should retain its own. The number of British nuclear weapons will not be determined by that of other countries, but by whether or not they are sufficient to make potential enemies feel incapable of sustaining their losses."

Deterrence and actual combat are complementary and closely interrelated. Generally speaking, the military strategy of all countries has a dual character of deterrence and actual combat. Before a war breaks out, a country will, by way of military deterrence, try to make the opposite side refrain from launching an attack rashly, so as to provide a powerful backing for its own political, economic, and diplomatic activities. Once military deterrence does not work, it will strive to win a victory through actual combat, so as to remove obstacles to its political, economic, and diplomatic activities.

Militarily, the immense effect of nuclear weaponry is that it can serve as a deterrent force and, at the same time, as a means of actual combat. Some countries, even those of the Third World, also consider possession of limited nuclear strength to be a significant way to contend against the deterrence of big powers or to deter one another in order to make up for the deficiency of their conventional forces. Military history after World War II has principally centred on the two superpowers that applied nuclear deterrence to each other and contended with each other for nuclear hegemony. After one of the superpowers disintegrated, a "crowd of heroes" rose up. As a result, conflicts that were in the past covered up by the Cold War surfaced with each passing day, and the collision and coalition of various political forces intensified simultaneously. Some regional powers were not weakened by the superpowers' relaxed control over them. On the contrary, they will, perhaps, go their own way even more wilfully on the issues of possessing and using nuclear weapons. Both the United States and Russia believe that future nuclear threats will primarily stem from small nuclear nations in certain regions. Hence, the world situation of nuclear deterrence will be transformed from the previous global nuclear deterrence and confrontation between the United States and the Soviet Union to multiple and regional nuclear deterrence and confrontation. In future high-tech local wars, the struggle between nuclear deterrence and counter nuclear deterrence will be even more complex.

We are materialists, so when we study an issue, we must proceed from the objective reality rather than from a subjective wish and, through investigation and study of objective reality, we derive our principles, policies, and measures. The study of issues concerning warfare can be conducted in the same way. Comrade Mao Zedong said a long time ago:

> Investigation and study are very important. When we see someone hold something in his hand, we should look into the matter. What is he holding in his hand? It is a knife. What is the use of a knife? It can kill a person. Whom will he kill with the knife? He will kill the people. After probing into these matters, we should further the investigation: The Chinese people also have hands, and they can hold knives too. They can forge one if they have none....

We love peace. China's development and possession of a small number of nuclear weapons is entirely for self-defence. Since the very first day when China had nuclear weapons in 1964, it solemnly proclaimed that it would never be the first to use nuclear weapons at any time and under any circumstances. China also made the commitment that it would never use or threaten to use nuclear weapons toward nuclear-free countries or regions. At the same time, we clearly understand that only by relying on the arduous work of the people all over the world can the objective of genuinely eliminating nuclear wars and genuinely obtaining world peace be realized: "It is a universal truth since ancient times that proficiency in warfare is not tantamount to bellicosity." The stronger our national defence muscle and the more sufficient our preparations for high-tech warfare under the condition of nuclear deterrence, the smaller the possibility of the outbreak of nuclear war.

We wish that the day will come when the nuclear shadow will disappear from the blue sky and the people the world over will live under the sunshine of genuine peace. To hail the early arrival of this day, we should work with greater stamina and diligence.

3

Nuclear Proliferation

The global nuclear order is changing. Concerns about climate change, the volatility of oil prices, and the security of energy supplies have contributed to a widespread and still-growing interest in the future use of nuclear power. Thirty states operate one or more nuclear power plants today, and according to the International Atomic Energy Agency (IAEA), some 50 others have requested technical assistance from the agency to explore the possibility of developing their own nuclear energy programs. It is certainly not possible to predict precisely how fast and how extensively the expansion of nuclear power will occur. But it does seem probable that in the future there will be more nuclear technology spread across more states than ever before. It will be a different world than the one that has existed in the past.

This surge of interest in nuclear energy – labelled by some proponents as "the renaissance in nuclear power" – is, moreover, occurring simultaneously with mounting concern about the health of the nuclear nonproliferation regime, the regulatory framework that constrains and governs the world's civil and military-related nuclear affairs. The Nuclear Non-Proliferation Treaty (NPT) and related institutions have been taxed by new worries, such as the growth in global terrorism, and have been painfully tested by protracted crises involving nuclear weapons proliferation in North Korea and potentially in Iran. (Indeed, some observers suspect that growing interest in nuclear power in some countries, especially in the Middle East, is not unrelated to Iran's uranium enrichment program and Tehran's movement closer to a nuclear weapons capability.) Confidence in the NPT regime seems to be eroding even as interest in nuclear power is expanding.

This realization raises crucial questions for the future of global security. Will the growth of nuclear power lead to increased risks of nuclear weapons proliferation and nuclear terrorism? Will the nonproliferation regime be adequate to ensure safety and security in a world more widely and heavily invested in nuclear power? The authors in this two-volume (Fall 2009 and Winter 2010) special issue of *Dædalus* have one simple and clear answer to these questions: It depends.

On what will it depend? Unfortunately, the answer to that question is not so simple and clear, for the technical, economic, and political factors that will determine whether future generations will have more nuclear power without more nuclear proliferation are both exceedingly complex and interrelated. How rapidly and in which countries will new nuclear power plants be built? Will the future expansion of nuclear energy take place primarily in existing nuclear power states or will there be many new entrants to the field? Which countries will possess the facilities for enriching uranium or reprocessing plutonium, technical capabilities that could be used to produce either nuclear fuel for reactors or the materials for nuclear bombs? How can physical protection of nuclear materials from terrorist organizations best be ensured? How can new entrants into nuclear power generation best maintain safety to prevent accidents? The answers to these questions will be critical determinants of the technological dimension of our nuclear future.

The major political factors influencing the future of nuclear weapons are no less complex and no less important. Will Iran acquire nuclear weapons; will North Korea develop more weapons or disarm in the coming decade; how will neighboring states respond? Will the United States and Russia take significant steps toward nuclear disarmament, and if so, will the other nuclear-weapons states follow suit or stand on the sidelines?

The nuclear future will be strongly influenced, too, by the success or failure of efforts to strengthen the international organizations and the set of agreements that comprise the system developed over time to manage global nuclear affairs. Will new international or regional mechanisms be developed to control the front-end (the production of nuclear reactor fuel) and the back-end (the management of spent fuel containing plutonium) of the nuclear fuel cycle? What political agreements and disagreements are likely to emerge between the nuclear-weapons states (NWS) and the non-nuclear-weapons states (NNWS) at the 2010 NPT Review Conference and beyond? What role will crucial actors among the NNWS – Japan, Iran, Brazil, and Egypt, for example – play in determining the global nuclear future? And most broadly, will the nonproliferation regime be supported and strengthened or will it be questioned and weakened? As IAEA Director General Mohamed ElBaradei has emphasized, "The nonproliferation regime is, in many ways, at a critical juncture," and there is a need for a new "overarching multilateral nuclear framework." But there is no guarantee that such a framework will emerge, and there is wide doubt that the arrangements of the past will be adequate to manage our nuclear future effectively.

The authors in both this and the subsequent volume address these and other vexing issues that will affect the spread of nuclear power and the spread of nuclear weapons. As is necessary to understand such a complex set of real-world issues, the authors represent diverse academic disciplines (including physical sciences, engineering, and social sciences) and many professions (including lawyers, nuclear regulators, nuclear industry executives, and experienced diplomats and political leaders). As is appropriate to address a global issue, the authors come from many different countries, from both NWS and NNWS. And as is appropriate for an objective intellectual enterprise, the authors represent both strong advocates for and skeptics of the global expansion of nuclear power, as well as both supporters and opponents of complete nuclear weapons disarmament.

In this introductory essay, we aim first to demonstrate why the question of which states will develop nuclear power in the future matters for global security. To do so, we briefly discuss the connections between nuclear power, nuclear proliferation, and terrorism risks; we present data contrasting existing nuclear-power states with potential new entrants with respect to factors influencing those risks. Second, we introduce major themes addressed by the authors in both volumes, and explain why the expansion of nuclear power, the future of nuclear weapons disarmament, and the future of the NPT and related parts of the nuclear control regime are so intertwined. Finally, we conclude with some observations about what is new and what is not new about current global nuclear challenges. The American Academy of Arts and Sciences has published three important special issues of *Dædalus* on nuclear weapons issues in the past – in 1960, 1975, and 1991 – and reflecting on the differences between the concerns and solutions discussed in those three issues and the nuclear challenges we face today is both inspiring and sobering.

Although many experts talk about the "expansion" or "renaissance" of nuclear power around the globe, it is important to differentiate between two related phenomena: a potential *growth* in the production of nuclear energy in states that currently have nuclear power facilities and the potential spread of nuclear power plants and related facilities to states that are new entrants to the "nuclear energy club." The existing nuclear-power states and the aspiring states that have requested IAEA assistance in exploring nuclear programs, by regions of the world. With respect to climate change, it would, in theory, make relatively little difference which nations increase their use of nuclear energy (and other non-carbon-producing energy technologies); what matters is the overall global reduction in carbon emissions. With respect to the safety and security dimensions of the nuclear future, however, it will matter greatly which states acquire what kinds of nuclear technology. Thus, there are three broad reasons to be concerned about an unconstrained spread of nuclear power to new nations that have not previously managed the technology.

First, for nuclear energy programs to be developed and managed safely and securely, it is important that states have domestic "good governance" characteristics that will encourage proper nuclear operations and management. These characteristics include low degrees of corruption (to avoid officials selling materials and technology for their own personal gain as occurred with the A.Q. Khan smuggling network in Pakistan), high degrees of political stability (defined by the World Bank as "likelihood that the government will be destabilized or overthrown by unconstitutional or violent means, including politically-motivated violence and terrorism"), high governmental effectiveness scores (a World Bank aggregate measure of "the quality of the civil service and the degree of its independence from political pressures [and] the quality of policy formulation and implementation"), and a strong degree of regulatory competence. Fortunately, we have a great deal of information measuring these domestic good governance factors across the globe. Unfortunately, the data highlight the grave security challenges that would be created if there were rampant proliferation of nuclear energy production facilities to each and every state that has expressed interest to the IAEA in acquiring nuclear power. The World Bank publishes annual aggregate data, derived from multiple sources, on each of these good governance characteristics, and the average scores of the potential new nuclear-energy states on each of these dimensions is significantly lower than the scores of states already possessing nuclear energy.

Second, all NNWS under the NPT must accept IAEA safeguards inspections on their nuclear power facilities in order to reduce the danger that governments might cheat on their commitments not to use the technology to acquire nuclear weapons; therefore, it is illuminating to examine the historical record of NNWS violating their NPT commitments. Here there is one very important finding about how domestic political characteristics influence the behaviour of NPT members: each known or strongly suspected case of a government starting a secret nuclear weapons program, while it was a member of the NPT and thus violating its Article II NPT commitment, was undertaken by a non-democratic government. (The confirmed or suspected historical cases of NPT member states starting nuclear weapons programs in violation of their Treaty commitments include North and South Korea, Libya, Iraq, Yugoslavia, Taiwan, Iran, and Syria, all of which were non-democratic at the time in question.) It is therefore worrisome that, the group of potential new states seeking nuclear power capabilities is on average significantly less democratic than the list of existing states with nuclear energy capabilities.

Third, states that face significant terrorist threats from within face particular challenges in ensuring that there is no successful terrorist attack on a nuclear facility or no terrorist theft of fissile material to make a nuclear weapon or dirty bomb. The United States Counterterrorism Center comparing the five-year totals of terrorism incidents in the existing states that have nuclear power facilities and the iaea list of aspiring states. India and Pakistan, both of which have nuclear weapons and nuclear power facilities and which face severe terrorist threats from homegrown and outsider terrorist organizations, clearly lead the pack. The states that are exploring developing nuclear power would take up six of the slots on a "terrorist top ten risk list" if each of them develops civilian nuclear power in the future.

These figures clearly represent worst-case estimates about the security implications of the spread of nuclear power, for as a number of authors in these volumes note, many of the aspiring states will not be able to progress with nuclear power development programs any time soon due to financial or other constraints. Indeed, most of the growth in nuclear power over the coming decade is likely to come from new plants in states that already operate nuclear power plants. But the figures do dramatically highlight the intertwined political, technical, and economic challenges we face if the world is to see both the expansion and spread of the use of nuclear power on a global scale. It seems almost certain that some new entrants to nuclear power will emerge in the coming decades and that the organizational and political challenges to ensure the safe and secure spread of nuclear technology into the developing world will be substantial and potentially grave. The proposals in these two volumes – for international control of the fuel cycle, for sharing best practices for physical security, and for enhancing the international nuclear safety regime – are designed to mitigate the inherent security risks that the nuclear renaissance will bring.

The essays collected in these two volumes of *Dædalus* focus on three broad, interlocking subjects: nuclear power, nuclear disarmament, and nuclear proliferation. The new nuclear order that will emerge years hence will be the result of the interplay of state motives for pursuing nuclear power and constraints on that pursuit. Contributors to the volumes consider in detail the changing technical, economic, and environmental factors that are making nuclear power seem more attractive around the globe. But they also address factors inhibiting the growth of nuclear power: enormous capital costs, the need for public subsidies, limited industrial capacity to build power plants, inadequate electricity grids, the possible emergence of alternative energy technologies, concern about the cost and risks associated with nuclear wastes, public fear of nuclear technology, as well as concern about the security risks created by the possible spread of weapons-usable nuclear technologies. When the constraints are taken into account, it may well be that the spread of nuclear power will be neither as fast nor as extensive as many anticipate. Nevertheless, some expansion and spread seems inevitable, and accordingly these volumes consider the standards for safety and physical protection that must be met to reduce the risks that could emerge along with the spread of civilian nuclear power capacity.

Concerns about proliferation (whether to states or terrorists) arise at the intersection of nuclear power and nuclear weapons. Indeed, the connection between power and weapons is somewhat inevitable because key technologies in the nuclear sector – notably, uranium enrichment and plutonium reprocessing capabilities – are relevant to both. In the nonproliferation context, this is the dual-use dilemma: many technologies associated with the creation of a nuclear power program can be used to make weapons if a state chooses to do so. When a state seems motivated to acquire nuclear weapons, a nuclear power program in that state can appear to be simply a route leading to the bomb or a public annex to a secret bomb program. The crisis over Iran's nuclear activities is a case in point. Depending on what capabilities spread to which states, especially regarding uranium enrichment and plutonium reprocessing, a world of widely spread nuclear technologies could be a world in which more states, like Iran, would have the latent capability to manufacture nuclear weapons. This could easily be a world filled with much more worry about the risk of nuclear proliferation – and worse, a world where more states possess nuclear weapons. A fundamental goal for American and global security is to minimize the proliferation risks associated with the expansion of nuclear power. If this development is poorly managed or efforts to contain risks are unsuccessful, the nuclear future will be dangerous.

What can be done to limit future proliferation risks? The contributors to these volumes explore two fundamental answers to that question. First, some authors discuss policies that could create a world in which the incentives to acquire nuclear weapons are minimized. If nuclear weapons remain the currency of the realm, if they are the ticket to the high table of international politics, if they are believed to confer enormous diplomatic and security benefits, if the existing NWS insist on the necessity to retain their nuclear weapons for the indefinite future, then it will be very difficult over the long run to make the case that for all other states nuclear weapons are unnecessary and undesirable. On the other hand, the context for future nuclear decision-making will be very different if that context is a world where nuclear weapons are being devalued and marginalized and where the NWS are reducing their arsenals and perhaps even heading meaningfully in the direction of eliminating nuclear weapons altogether. This is why the nuclear disarmament debate comes into play in considering the future global nuclear order.

The disarmament-nonproliferation connection is formally codified in the famous Article VI of the NPT, which calls for the NWS (and all other states) to make good faith efforts to achieve nuclear disarmament. Under the general rubric of arms control, work over several decades has gone toward efforts to regulate, constrain, reduce, and eliminate nuclear weapons – efforts that have helped contain the dangers of nuclear rivalry. Nevertheless – and despite their obligations under Article VI and their repeated rhetorical commitments to nuclear disarmament – the NWS have not, in the opinion of many observers, moved genuinely and significantly in the direction of nuclear disarmament. Indeed, there have been multiple statements by some government officials in NWS that suggest that they are firmly committed to keeping nuclear weapons indefinitely, and the failure of the U.S. Senate to ratify the Comprehensive Test Ban Treaty (CTBT) and help bring that Treaty into force opens up the prospect of testing new nuclear weapons in the future. The result has been growing dissatisfaction among many key NNWS about the failure of the NWS to live up to their NPT obligations, recurrent acrimonious collisions over Article VI at NPT review conferences, mounting frustration with and disaffection from the NPT regime, and a consequent protracted inability to address other key NPT issues in a constructive fashion. From the perspective of many NNWS, Article VI was one of the core bargains of the NPT and the weapons states are simply not living up to their end of the bargain.

The current debate over nuclear disarmament is crucial to the evolution of the global nuclear order for two reasons. One way or the other, the debate will influence future incentives to acquire nuclear weapons, and it will have significant implications in terms of preserving, effectively managing, and strengthening the NPT regime. It is therefore very important that nuclear disarmament has now made it onto the public and policy agenda in a prominent way, having been galvanized by the efforts of four distinguished American statesmen and reinforced by President Obama's remarkable embrace of the nuclear disarmament objective in his speech in Prague in April 2009. It is generally understood that nuclear disarmament is a long-term goal, not an immediate policy objective. Yet much can be done in the interim to constrain nuclear forces and reduce their role in international politics; such steps can help to address the concerns that have commonly arisen in the nonproliferation context. The origins, rationale, meaning, and prospects of nuclear disarmament are therefore addressed in these volumes of *Dædalus.*

Future proliferation risks can also be limited in a second fundamental way: by preserving and improving the nonproliferation regime, that system of rules and institutions that is meant to allow the use of civilian nuclear power while providing reassurance against the use of nuclear technology for weapons purposes. As the protracted nuclear crises of recent decades – Iraq, Iran, North Korea – have shown, the system is not perfect or foolproof even today. But looking to the future, will the nonproliferation regime be adequate in a world where there is more nuclear knowledge and technology spread across more states? The essays collected in the second volume confront that question. Some of the essays explore various ways in which the nonproliferation regime could be improved: transparency could be enhanced, safeguards bolstered, the IAEA further empowered to monitor nuclear programs and explore suspicious activities. NPT rules can be more uniformly and universally enforced, with exceptions like the U.S.-India nuclear deal not permitted. The nuclear fuel cycle can be organized in a way that minimizes the spread of sensitive dual-use technology; various schemes for assuring fuel supplies could reduce the need and incentive for individual states to acquire enrichment capabilities, for example. Any fuel-cycle arrangement or agreed norm that limits the spread of enrichment and reprocessing technology will greatly circumscribe the proliferation risks associated with expanded nuclear power. It would also be desirable to find more effective methods of enforcement when instances of noncompliance are discovered. These ideas and more are examined in volume two.

But the NPT is a nearly global regime – all but four states are members (Israel, India, and Pakistan never joined, and North Korea withdrew in 2003) – and none of the ideas for improving the regime will be feasible if they do not inspire wide assent among NPT members. The regime therefore must be considered from a diverse set of national perspectives in order to gauge what steps might be possible and what constraints will need to be addressed in order to adapt the nonproliferation regime to the emerging global nuclear order. It is far from certain that key NNWS will share the diagnoses and support the remedies preferred by the Western nonproliferation community. The essays in these *Dædalus* volumes address these contrasting perspectives, and the decision to include authors from multiple NWS and NNWS was designed to ensure that the analysis does not suffer from American-centric or NWS biases.

The growth and spread of nuclear power raises a set of concerns about the risk of nuclear proliferation and nuclear terrorism; working on the problem of nuclear proliferation raises the issue of nuclear disarmament. These topics do not completely overlap, but it is not possible to think comprehensively about the future of the global nuclear order without considering them together and without appreciating the extent to which they are interrelated.

This two-volume special issue of *Dædalus* represents the fourth time that the American Academy has dedicated its journal to issues concerning arms control and nuclear weapons. Special issues were published on "Arms Control" in 1960, on "Arms, Defence, and Arms Control" in 1975, and on "Arms Control: Thirty Years On" in 1991. It is valuable to look back on the articles in these volumes, and the strategic issues upon which they focused, in order to appreciate the significant successes that have occurred in the past, as well as to understand the enduring nature of many of the problems we face and the novelty of some emerging challenges.

The 1960 volume, a product of a special summer study at the American Academy, is widely recognized as a seminal contribution to the development of arms control as a tool to reduce the danger of nuclear war and to manage Soviet-U.S. relations. Indeed, it has been called "the Bible" of arms control, and "the Cambridge school" has been credited with identifying and promoting three key insights that helped maintain nuclear peace during the height of Cold War tensions. First, the authors strongly argued for the creation of a high threshold between conventional military forces and nuclear forces, in stark contrast to the earlier plans developed during the Eisenhower administration to use nuclear weapons earlier in any conflict with the Soviet Union or the People's Republic of China – the so-called Massive Retaliation doctrine. Second, while the *Dædalus*authors cannot be credited with being the first to identify the maintenance of "secure second-strike forces" as a prerequisite for nuclear deterrence stability (credit for that insight belongs to Albert Wolhstetter and Warren Amster), the *Dædalus* authors were the first to argue that the pursuit of secure second-strike forces was a *mutual* interest between the USSR and the United States, and thus that arms control negotiations could usefully seek constraints on offensive and defensive forces with this form of strategic stability as an objective. Third, the *Dædalus* authors identified the prevention of the spread of nuclear weapons to new nations as a key national security interest and arms control objective. Again, this was an innovative argument coming at the end of the Eisenhower administration, which had widely distributed nuclear power technology under the Atoms for Peace program and was considering providing nuclear weapons to U.S. NATO allies in Europe.

The 1960 *Dædalus* authors went on to become a veritable "Who's Who" of arms control during the Cold War, both in terms of scholarship and government service: Herman Khan, Edward Teller, Henry Kissinger, Paul Doty, Thomas Schelling, and Hubert Humphrey. All were relatively young men at the time, but they were to play even more important roles in developing U.S. grand strategy and arms control in subsequent years. With the benefit of hindsight, however, it is as interesting to note the major future security issues that were *not* addressed in the 1960 volume as it is to recognize those that were. Concerns about nuclear proliferation focused primarily on states within U.S. and Soviet alliance systems – in NATO and the Warsaw Pact, and to a lesser degree, China. The idea that many states in what was then deemed the "third world" might be capable of producing nuclear weapons was generally beyond the horizon of vision for the authors. Similarly, future fears about the danger of nuclear terrorism were simply not on the intellectual agenda of the early 1960s: indeed, it is noteworthy that in his *Dædalus* essay Herman Khan feared what he called "nuclear diffusion" primarily because it would provide nuclear weapons to "criminal organizations" and give the Soviets a new opportunity "to act as agent-provocateurs." Finally, it bears mentioning that the 1960 "Bible" of arms control was written entirely by American authors. In the Cold War atmosphere of 1960, Americans might speculate on Soviet or Chinese views about nuclear weapons, but it was not possible for experts or policy-makers from either Communist state to contribute directly to the emerging literature.

Much had changed by the time the special issue on "Arms, Defence, and Arms Control" appeared in 1975. As suggested by the title, arms control had become a significant part of U.S. foreign policy, and many of the essays were now devoted to analyzing how best to balance potential arms control agreements with the Soviet Union with perceived U.S. national security requirements for secure and effective nuclear weapons delivery systems. In contrast with the 1960 authors, many of whom used early game theory methods and assumed "rational actors" inside both the United States and the Soviet Union, the 1975 *Dædalus* authors developed new ideas about how domestic politics, organizational interests, and bureaucratic politics influenced defence programs and arms negotiations. The NPT had been negotiated and had come into force in 1970, and that development, coupled with India's 1974 test of a "peaceful nuclear explosive," led to much more attention on proliferation dangers in the developing world. This *Dædalus* issue therefore had a much less bilateral Soviet-U.S. focus, with essays addressing the spread of nuclear weapons and other advanced military systems from the superpowers to third-world states around the globe. Nevertheless, the discussion was still taking place exclusively among Americans, and not one expert from an allied nation, much less a Cold War rival or a neutral third-world state, contributed to the 1975 *Dædalus* volume.

The contributions to the 1991 volume, "Arms Control: Thirty Years On," were written amid great geopolitical change, as the Cold War ended and the Soviet Union was breaking into separate independent states. It is not entirely surprising therefore that many of the essays – indeed, even the volume's title – have a historical emphasis: looking in the rear-view mirror at the role of arms control in the Cold War, albeit with attempts to use that history to predict possible future trends. The 1991 volume did have more international authors, with a leading Russian nuclear strategist, Andrei Kokoshin (who was soon to become a senior Ministry of Defence official), contributing an essay, along with articles by leading European arms control specialists Lawrence Freedman and Johan Jørgen Holst. Many of the specific arms control topics addressed in the volume, such as the conventional weapons balance in Europe and the spread of chemical weapons, are simply no longer as significant a concern today as they were in the waning years of the Cold War and the start of a new, uncertain era in international politics. Other issues addressed by the *Dædalus*contributors, however, notably the failure of leading powers to negotiate a CTBT and concerns about the fragility of the NPT and its future ability to constrain states from acquiring nuclear weapons, remain as salient today as they were in 1991.

This special double issue on "The Global Nuclear Future" thus stands in a proud line of *Dædalus* volumes seeking to bring new ideas into the global public policy debate about how to reduce the risks of nuclear proliferation and nuclear weapons use. We do so, however, in the context of a new global topic: how to manage the potential growth and spread of nuclear power. And this special double issue includes far more voices from NNWS, among U.S. allies and others in the developing world, because their governments' decisions will be as important in determining the global nuclear future as are decisions made in Washington.

We hope that the analyses presented in these *Dædalus* volumes will inform and influence policy debates in both NWS and NNWS in the future. Today, the nature of the global nuclear future remains highly uncertain. What is clear is that the decisions we make in the coming years regarding arms control and disarmament, the spread of nuclear power technology, and the reform of international regimes will strongly determine whether a hopeful or frightening nuclear future emerges just over the horizon.

4

Nuclear Command and Control in India and Pakistan

THE POKHRAN AND CHAGAI TESTS

The nuclear tests conducted by India and Pakistan in May 1998 - Pakistan's tests being a predictable, direct response to those of its neighbour's - sent shock waves across the globe. The tests were quickly followed by both countries declaring themselves as nuclear-weapon states. The justifications put forth by them for their actions were anchored on the well-known virtues of the bomb as propagated by the the 'N-5' countries before them. The prime factor which motivated the tests in India were the domestic political ambitions of the Bharatiya Janata Party (BJP) government and pressure from the scientific community engaged in the nuclear weapons programme. The continued neglect by the nuclear-weapon states of Article VI of the Non-Proliferation Treaty (NPT) provided added justification.

THE PAKISTAN-INDIA NUCLEAR EQUATION: SOME GENUINE CONCERNS

The continuing adversarial relationship between the two countries has already resulted in three wars, and a limited war in Kargil in April-May 1999, barely a year after the nuclear tests. Some people in responsible positions, both in India and Pakistan, advocated the use of the nuclear weapons during the war in Kargil. In view of this, and also the existing, rather primitive command and control facilities, genuine concerns have been expressed by many observers regarding the safe and proper management of nuclear weapons by both India and Pakistan. Dr. Shaun Gregory dismisses this view rather summarily by stating *"this analysis oversimplifies the situation, pays insufficient attention to balancing factors, and smuggles a number of unfounded assumptions."* He goes on, *"the point at issue is whether a stable nuclear relationship can be constructed in South Asia. Much of the answer to this question rests on whether robust command and control arrangements can be put in place to meet the requirements of stable deterrence."*

Stable Deterrence

'Stable deterrence' is but a mirage! This concept pre-supposes a mind- and technology-freeze by potential adversaries. It also assumes a halt to proliferation after a certain number of weapons and delivery systems have been reached. Unfortunately the quest for superior technology, combined with the desire to have an edge over the adversary, creates, if anything, a perpetually asymmetrical situation, leading to anything but stability.

Command and Control

As of now, there is simply no robust command, control, communications and intelligence systems (C3I) in place in either state. Given the economic and technological constraints, this is not likely to materialise for some time to come. All this makes the entire security environment in South Asia extremely dangerous and highly unstable.

The credit given by Dr. Gregory to both India and Pakistan for their 'reflection on the understanding' of the experience of the N-5 countries, is expressed as follows: *"...this reflection encompasses a rich understanding of nuclear deterrence, nuclear doctrine, strategy, posture, command and control arrangements and the role of arms control and confidence building measure..."*

This sounds reassuring, but in the view of many who have studied and worked in this field, it is, unfortunately, neither convincing nor backed up by the situation on the ground in both countries. To illustrate this point, it might be useful to briefly recount some recent incidents concerning 'command and control' and crisis management in India.

- The Purulia Incident (December 1995), where weapons were air-dropped by a civilian aircraft in the eastern part of India without any detection and/or interception of the said aircraft
- The shooting down of the Pakistan Navy's 'Atlantique' aircraft by the Indian Air Force in peacetime (August 1999)
- The hi-jacking of the Indian Airlines aircraft (December 1999) and the consequent lack of timely and efficient management of the situation
- The recent earthquake in Gujarat and the near total collapse of administrative machinery and rescue efforts
- The poor safety record in the nuclear power and mining industry

Given this kind of track-record, it is difficult to accept the reassurances regarding 'safety' and 'command and control' which have been provided from time to time by government agencies, their nuclear scientists, and also independent analysts. This is not to say that there is absolutely nothing in place by way of command and control systems, but the technologies to ensure safety and to prevent accidental deployment of nuclear weapons are still at an embryonic stage.

Dr. Gregory's suggestion that *"the imposition of high level control can be addressed by relatively low-tech procedural means such as the two-person rule (reinforced by command authority separation) and the expedient of keeping warheads and delivery systems separated until required"* merits further examination. What Dr. Gregory is suggesting is virtually the 'de-alerting' of weapons.

From my own standpoint, this is indeed an excellent idea, and a wonderful first step towards total nuclear disarmament. However, as far as 'command and control' is concerned, the two-person formula is fraught with danger unless there are matching technological interlocks in place.

This holds true especially in the context of South Asia and also raises the question as to who will oversee this 'de-alerting' of nuclear weapons. The operationalising of nuclear weapons from a de-alerted state, given India's stated doctrine of 'no-first use', is unworkable because of the inordinate time delays this will impose on a second-strike response. This suggestion is therefore unlikely to be accepted or implemented, a sad fact which once again highlights the inadequacies of the 'command and control systems' currently available.

THE BILATERAL NUCLEAR RELATIONSHIP

Whilst sketching the historical development of nuclear capabilities of India and Pakistan, Dr. Gregory goes on to say that *"consequently both parties have already managed a functional bilateral nuclear relationship for more than a decade, and have steered this relationship through three important crises... Brasstacks in 1986/87... Zarb-e-Momin in 1990... and Kargil in 1999."*

The point to note about Brasstacks and Zarb-e-Momin is that these were major exercises conducted, by India and Pakistan respectively, after prior notification to each other. The question of adroit management of the nuclear environment was therefore not the real issue. Some analysts have given the 'crisis' label to these events. Whilst, no doubt, these exercises were closely followed by professionals on both sides, there was really no war hysteria prevalent at the time. Last but not least, delivery systems for the nuclear weapons were simply non-existent except for the air-dropping of nuclear bombs, procedures for which had not been perfected.

As for Kargil, we only managed to avert a catastrophe by the closest of margins, with some individuals in responsible positions in both countries advocating the use of nuclear weapons. This narrow escape was not due to any special nuclear relationship or understanding, but to heavy international pressure, especially that exerted by the United States. Such pressure worked in this case because the war was limited to Kargil and no international boundaries had been crossed.

War-Fighting Traits of India and Pakistan

Sundry points brought out by Dr. Gregory in this regard include the following:

- Intra-war escalation control
- Propensity to bilateral political and military dialogue to contain conflict
- Aversion to systematically attacking civilian targets
- Mutual assured destruction - of Islamabad, Lahore and Karachi in Pakistan, and of Delhi and Mumbai in India - as a powerful deterrent against nuclear risk-taking
- The continuing presence of Muslim populations in India in excess of those in Pakistan, as a restraining factor against attack on civilian targets
- The overarching dependence by Pakistan on the influence of the international community, especially the USA, in respect of its nuclear policy

As far as intra-war escalation control - the ability of political and military dialogue to contain conflict - is concerned, no such mechanism actually existed during any of the conflicts that have taken place. Such dialogue usually either preceded or followed a conflict - be it 1948, 1965, or 1971. The only exception was when India asked Pakistan to surrender during the 1971 war in the erstwhile East Pakistan, which led to the creation of Bangladesh.

The effectiveness of 'mutually assured destruction' of major cities as a factor against nuclear risk taking would be a dangerous assumption.

Should the two nations go to war with conventional weapons, and should one of Pakistan's major cities be directly threatened, it is quite on the cards that they may be tempted to carry out a first strike with nuclear weapons against Delhi or Bombay, or both. The deterrence factor is therefore most unlikely to work in this case. In such a case even international intervention is unlikely to avoid such a development.

Civil Military Interface

In India as of now, the military has not been fully integrated into the nuclear weapons control chain. In Pakistan on the other hand, the nuclear button is solely in the hands of the army. Neither of these situations are conducive to effective command and control.

Dyadic Coupling

The 'dyadic coupling' mentioned by Dr. Gregory for integrating the national nuclear command and control systems of both India and Pakistan is certainly a novel idea - but one that is perhaps still ahead of its time. Unless the two countries are able to resolve outstanding bilateral problems, including that of Jammu and Kashmir, any meaningful 'coupling' is totally unrealistic. This observation is based on the experience of numerous 'Track II' initiatives which have failed primarily because of the inability to integrate the 'techno-fix' with the political aspects which underpin India-Pakistan relations.

Fundamentalism and Terrorism

South Asia is also witnessing a trend of rising fundamentalism. India, Pakistan and Afghanistan each have their own brands of extremists. It will indeed be a frightening day should such groups gain access to nuclear weapons - a possibility which cannot be totally ruled out. Such groups do not work on the basis of conventional political logic or other norms of behaviour, and can therefore be totally unpredictable. A recent example was the open advocacy of 'jihad' or holy war as a legitimate means of defending a particular 'Vision of the Nation State', a view proffered by a former Chief of Army Staff and currently head of a well known Policy Research Institute in Pakistan.

NUCLEAR COMMAND AND CONTROL

Nuclear weapons are the most destructive and unrelenting instruments ever created by mankind. The whole world can be destroyed by less than 200 nuclear weapons within the space of a few days. Given the potentially disastrous complexities involved in nuclear force employment and contrasting control methods, building up a formidable command and control system has always remained a daunting and costly task for nuclear weapon states. Nuclear command and control systems are developed by states to ensure that nuclear weapons are used only when authorised by legitimate decision-makers, and that the possibility of accidental or unauthorised firing of nuclear weapons can be entirely ruled out. Thermonuclear weapons are so powerful that they can wipe out whole cities, killing tens of millions of people.

The unimaginable death and destruction that could result from the unauthorised use of a nuclear weapon has led the US, Russia and other nuclear powers to spend hefty amounts of money every year to develop a 'fail-safe' command and control system. A robust command and control system is also seen as an essential ingredient in the equation of deterrence between the two sides. US nuclear weapons laboratories — Lawrence Livermore, Sandia and Los Alamos — worked during the Cold War to make nuclear materials as safe as possible, using almost unlimited budgets. A strong command and control system for nuclear weapons involves hundreds of people working at different levels from top to bottom but the authority to take key decisions remains concentrated in the hands of a few individuals. At the heart of the complexity of this system lies a paradox. Governments try to ensure that weapons should always be ready for use when asked for by the authorised leader and a similar assurance that they will never be used unless commissioned by such authority. These apparently contradictory objectives become extremely important in the case of nuclear weapons because of the political and diplomatic utility they have acquired in addition to their enormous destructive power.

Some nuclear weapon states have developed a set of interlocked administrative and technological systems including combination locks aka Permissive Action Links (PALs), which can block unauthorised use of a nuclear weapon. Pakistan's nuclear security establishment also claims to have indigenously made coded locks that completely rule out the possibility of unauthorised use of nuclear weapons even if they fall into the hands of terrorists. However, there is no authentic information available about the nature of those combination locks. The standard 'two-man rule' is also believed to be in practice in Pakistan's command and control structure. This rule ensures that at every stage, from manufacturing to storage, at least two people capable of stopping unauthorised use remain present. Other procedural aspects include 'special safety design features' that reduce the risk of a warhead detonating if it catches fire or is otherwise damaged.

The strategic command organisations in all nuclear weapon states have evolved with the passage of time. During the Cold War, the US had a very loosely defined command and control structure and even nuclear weapons were dispersed in a number of European countries under the control of NATO forces. However, a number of crises, particularly the Cuban missile crisis of 1962, caused President Kennedy to take quick steps towards attaining higher standards of robustness in the command and control structure. President Kennedy, after consultations with leading experts at the Pentagon and the department of energy, ordered a review of the US's nuclear command and control, which led to the creation of a nuclear 'football'. The atomic football (also known as the president's emergency satchel, the black box, the button) is a briefcase that contains the information needed to enable the US president to authorise a nuclear attack while he is away from command centres such as the White House 'situation room'. The nuclear football works as 'a mobile hub' in the strategic defence system of the US and follows the president wherever he goes.

According to a Washington Post article, a military aide always accompanies the president, carrying the football in a black leather jacket. Bill Gulley, the former director of the White House military office, revealed in his famous book, Breaking Cover, that the contents of the football include: (a) the "black book" containing nuclear weapons' launch options, (b) a booklet outlining classified site locations, (c) a folder giving a description of the procedures for the 'emergency broadcast system', and (d) a three-by-five inch card with authentication codes. During their presidencies, Jimmy Carter and Ronald Reagan preferred to keep the launch codes in their pockets. According to some accounts, the football was immediately separated from President Reagan after the 1981 assassination attempt against him. Like the US, in most nuclear weapon states, only the highest political authorities are in a position to authorise the use of nuclear weapons. The possession of a nuclear weapon by military units does not give them the ability to use it.

In Pakistan, due to some serious imbalance between civil and military relations, the military enjoys absolute authority over the control and use of nuclear weapons. Unfortunately, the civilian prime ministers in our country do not even dare to ask the military authorities about the exact location of the nuclear arsenal — what to talk of any control over their use.

The unpredictability of integrated administrative procedures and technologies can sometimes result in major failures in command and control systems. One of the major threats associated with the event of a nuclear war is 'decapitation'. This involves a successful attack on a country's command and control system, which results in rendering its nuclear arsenal unusable. There are a number of steps that have been taken by nuclear weapon states to mitigate the possible loss of command. These include early warning of an impending attack by ground based radars, comprehensive planning to secure command centres, alternative command posts and establishment of multiple communication links between the decision makers and nuclear armed units that can survive an attack. However, these measures are extraordinarily costly and complex. Another alternative to avoid decapitation is to delegate the authority to use nuclear weapons to other officials but that increases the likelihood of unauthorised nuclear use.

COMMAND AND CONTROL OF NUCLEAR

Command and control of nuclear arsenals is a complex subject and involves many issues. There are different models, as we have seen in other countries, which are built on their doctrines, goals and type of adversary capabilities. There is a lot we can take from there and a lot we need not take from there. I would like to focus on what I consider to be a few central principles on which command and control of nuclear weapons should be established in India. It is not sufficient to say, let us take a little bit of this and a little bit of that and let us put it together in some form. Or even allow single Service ambitions or turf to be promoted unless it serves the larger purpose. The stakes are very high. This is not a business where failure at any level or in any form can be condoned or compensated by some other steps or organisations. It will be disastrous for this country if our system of command and control does not function the way it must function. How do we want it to function? To get the answer, we need to decide first what is the task we expect the system to perform.

Doctrine and Strategy

The core element is that the nuclear doctrine that we adopt will decide the nuclear strategy. Nuclear strategy in turn will decide the nature and substance of the command and control system which is going to execute the strategy in accordance with that doctrine. There is a linkage here-between the doctrine, strategy, and structure. If we are clear that our doctrine is going to be deterrence only, rather than fighting a nuclear war, the arsenal will have to be designed for that purpose and the command and control will have to correspond to that goal. Considering that nuclear threats to India are likely to emerge essentially from the immediate neighbourhood across the country's territorial boundaries, the very short time of flight due to the proximity factor will need to be catered for in the strategy.1 It is also clear that there is no conceivable political purpose which would require India to initiate a nuclear threat first, leave alone use of nuclear weapons first.2 The central elements and objectives of our doctrine should be:

(a) First, to deter nuclear threat and possible use by another state against us. This rules out deterrence of war as such (which would require inclusion of conventional forces into the spectrum of threats to be deterred) and an acceptance of the reality that nuclear weapons cannot deter each and every type of threat to national security (which may include transnational terrorism, for example). Deterrence of nuclear weapons could be achieved by adopting an offensive ordefensive strategy. In 1999, the National Security Advisory Board of the National Security Council (NSC) had proposed the defensive strategy and recommended a doctrine and strategy based on the principle that India would not be the first to use nuclear weapons. 3 The Indian political leadership had also affirmed, both before and after the nuclear tests, that India would not be the first to use nuclear weapons.

(b) Second, if deterrence fails (and an aggressor launches a nuclear strike against India or its forces), our nuclear forces should be able to immediately retaliate with adequate power to inflict an "unacceptable" level of punishment and destruction on the aggressor. Taken together, these two principles imply that India will not be the first to use nuclear weapons and, therefore, will also not be the first to threaten another country with nuclear weapons. With a defensive strategy of deterrence there would be no requirement of continuing control of nuclear forces during a nuclear exchange as was the case in the North Atlantic Treaty Organisation (NATO) strategy of flexible response.

(c) Third, the proposed strategy of "no-first-use" would require a single massive retaliatory punitive strike more in tune with what was the French strategy during the Cold War.4 A no-first-use strategy also means that our nuclear arsenal does not have to be maintained at hair-trigger alert of operationally deployed and instantly ready weapon systems like the two superpowers maintained during the Cold War. The command and control of nuclear forces, therefore, will have to be created and operated on that basis.

(d) Fourth, the nuclear strategy and posture must ensure a very high level of credibility and effectiveness that there will surely be a massive retaliatory punitive strike which would inflict unacceptable punishment. In the context of giving up the first strike option, this requires a very high degree of survivability of the nuclear arsenal, including its command and control system. This means that the command and control must be able to survive and continue functioning with high efficiency to achieve the political goals even after absorbing a first (attempted decapitation) strike. A high level of survivability has to be built on a combination of measures including:

(i) High degree of mobility of assets, particularly the delivery means and warheads, separately as well as complete weapon systems. The greater the mobility of the arsenal, the greater would be its survivability. For example, a nuclear-powered submarine launched nuclear missile force would provide the greatest survivability and, hence, would require the smallest size of arsenal.5

(ii) Extensive dispersal, including frequent moves and relocation of these assets along with an ability to operate from a myriad locations.

(iii) Extensive deception measures, including decoys and dummies. We are partly fortunate that overall Chinese surveillance capability (of course, Pakistan's is even less) to track in real-time or near real-time the position of the Indian nuclear arsenal in any form is not very strong. The Chinese capabilities will keep building in the coming years, but we must capitalise on the technological weaknesses of our neighbours to be able to execute a real decapitating strike. We need to build an arsenal of highly mobile delivery systems and high capability to match the delivery systems with nuclear warheads in a short period of time. The logic for the national planning parameter is that we need the capability to be able to launch a nuclear retaliatory strike within a very short time, say, 30 minutes, if the forces are already on a degree of alert, following a certain amount of tension or precautionary measures. If not, then within a maximum of one to two hours. The technical reasons of fusing/putting it together, putting on the warhead, aligning it, the process of loading it, should not exceed that, and the weapon systems must be launched within that time-frame. If it gets launched in two hours, it should be considered acceptable. But I think it is very important that we reduce this to a minimum credible period.

(iv) The fourth important element for command and control is the question: will India acquire battlefield nuclear weapons, or nuclear weapons for use in the battlefield scenario-in the conventional normal sense that we have understood use of weapons in the past? My answer is a categorical, absolute "NO" to tactical nuclear weapons. There are many reasons for this. Firstly, there is no tactical use of nuclear weapons of any size or yield which will not result in an impact that is not strategic. If that is so, then the linkage and its escalation into a full-fledged strategic exchange can be considered as almost inevitable and automatic (unless the adversary does not possess nuclear weapons). Even if it is argued that escalation may not take place or gets controlled, then you land up with a situation on the other side that the local exchange of nuclear weapons between the two armies gets delinked from the larger strategic equation. This implies fighting a war with nuclear weapons. I don't have to spell out the implications of that. It may well be the preferred option of some people and foreign governments at that stage, to try and stop such exchange at that point which most certainly implies not only a substantial loss of life, but also implicitly that India would lose that war.

Some Principles

The second set of issues here revolves around the question: what should be principles on which we should build our command and control system? There are accepted norms of command and control systems for military formations. Military power itself is an instrument for achieving political objectives and, hence, constitutes a political instrument of the state. Similarly, a nuclear weapon essentially exists as a political tool which must also, in the extreme case, be employed as a military weapon, although with little military utility as such. To maximise the political utility of nuclear weapons, therefore, the following must be kept in mind:

(a) First, firm political control over the nuclear arsenal. I will revert to that later.

(b) Second, a highly efficient and responsive military command and control system. With that I mean that decision-making must remain at the highest political level with the advice of the military and other experts, but essentially the operational command and control system as such must remain with the military forces for a series of reasons.

(c) The third principle is that there must be minimum disruption of well-tested existing organisations and procedures. Our goal should be to see where they need to take on additional responsibilities, with minimum modification. It would be a gross mistake of truly monumental dimensions to attempt an organisational revolution to manage a multiple set of things- fundamentally new type of weapons, new set of command and control systems and a new set of procedures to handle these. Any major experimenting or violation of basic principles of controlling military systems will lead to serious and irreversible problems for many years, perhaps decades, to come. Therefore, we must build on existing systems and procedures wherever they exist, and do so in an incremental form, review these constantly as we go along, and then at a future stage, if we still need to introduce significant changes, we should do so in an incremental, planned manner. A conservative approach will be well worth the effort. We are entering a stage where not enough thought has been given to the details of the circumstances and the way in which nuclear weapons are to be used. The military in particular has been kept out of most of the decision-making and examination of the implications in this process. The case of chemical weapons is symptomatic. Therefore, it is essential that we move into the nuclear weapons command and control through an incremental, evolutionary process built on existing capabilities, procedures and past experiences.

(d) The fourth principle is that costs must be minimised, otherwise we are likely to land up with an expensive system which may or may not work. Experimenting or rushing into something here is the last thing we should be thinking of. If that is so, do we have any models that exist at least partially, in which the military at least has handled similar tasks in the past? I would like to draw attention to the command and control of "Chiefs of Staff Committee

(COSC) Targets" which have been effectively managed for more than four decades, in peace and war. The three Services, under the sanction and direction of their chiefs, have evolved the framework and procedures which authorise their staff to work out the targetting policy for a set of targets considered of central and strategic value, as the strategic targets to be released under the combined authority of the three chiefs of staff. Targetting and planning for this purpose has been maintained by the Indian Air Force (IAF) in all its details. The planned air effort takes into account the commitment for the COSC targets. The concept, in principle at least, is no different from targetting with nuclear weapons. Targetting with nuclear weapons needs additional factors to be considered, but lesser involvement of all three Services will be necessary if the delivery systems belong to one Service only. But the basic requirements and parameters of management are not very different, either in terms of organisational needs or management techniques. Secondly, the IAF has been undertaking, like air forces in other countries, strategic reconnaissance missions over the decades. The way command and control has been managed and the lessons derived from decades of highly successful operations would be extremely relevant to the issues related to command and control of strategic strike with the nuclear arsenal

(e) The fifth principle is that the bulk of the work related to effective management of the nuclear arsenal has to be done during peace-time. This involves scenario building and assessing the other country's postures, likely trends, changes that may take place, signalling of intent, etc. For example, what are the implications when the Chinese say during a crisis situation that "Los Angeles could burn?" Or if Pakistanis threaten grave destruction? How seriously should such pronouncements be taken? Do they constitute a firm form of escalation moving towards use of nuclear weapons or not?

(f) Last, but not the least, is the issue of assessment of what it will take to deter the other side under different sets of circumstances. This will remain a matter of judgement, but one derived from extensive and deep study of the cultural, socio-political and strategic factors affecting the likely response of a country to the threat and use of nuclear weapons. I am sure many more aspects and principles can be added to what the command and control system should be expected to do, and what it can do in the framework of a time horizon.

Having considered this and a few other factors, it is obvious that at the political level, command and control of nuclear weapons, in the ultimate analysis, must be exercised by the prime minister of India. Given our political constitutional system, it cannot be anybody else. This can change only if the constitutional basis of our governance changes. A concurrent issue is that there is a need for a consultative group or a decision-making group to assist the prime minister at that level of political leadership. This has two aspects. One relates to the chain of command to cater for a contingency if the prime minister is not available or is incapacitated. The Constitution lays down the succession process very clearly. But the process may be inadequate since it did not visualise the need to plan a response with nuclear weapons. So we have to evolve a suitable system of national command authority. Whatever system is evolved, the prime minister of India will have the prerogative to make changes to it. What is required is that each prime minister, at any one time, should have a well-defined system of national command authority for command and control of nuclear weapons. Which one it is, is not the point. It may also not be possible to formally declare the system, nor is it necessary, as long the operating formations that have to execute the orders are clear about the chain of command. In fact, there are strong reasons for not publicising the chain of command for obvious reasons besides the potential for domestic political difficulties of the type experienced often when a deputy prime minister was appointed. So let the prime minister decide who will be his successor. The prime minister, who selects his Cabinet ministers, will always have the prerogative to make even frequent changes to the chain of command; but he will have to ensure that the new person(s) concerned are briefed thoroughly and they understand the role fully.

At the same time, a decision-making-cum-planning body at the political-strategic level is needed which will then authorise the planning of targetting policy and the force development and deployment policies. If the NSC functions, then the Cabinet Committee would be the obvious organisation. Even in that case, there is a need to immediately resurrect the Defence Committee of the Cabinet (DCC) with the three chiefs in attendance, on a permanent basis, not just on invitation, which should start taking the planning process forward. Their attendance implies that they would not participate in the deliberations of the Cabinet, but will be available to answer queries and provide explanations where needed.

It may be recalled that when the higher defence organisation was reorganised in 1947, it was based on the experiences of the UK and the USA (the latter being a nuclear weapon power) during World War II. In fact, Lord Ismay, who planned the post-War higher defence organisation for the UK and the USA was also the person who planned the organisation for independent India. This was based on corporate decision-making at each level with a Defence Committee of the Cabinet at the apex, with a Defence Minister's Committee, the Chiefs of Staff Committee, Joint Planning Committee, a Joint Intelligence Board and another dozen committees of the government to take decisions concerning various aspects of defence below that within the governmental framework, located in the Cabinet Secretariat. Interestingly, the Joint Planning Committee was to be in permanent session with a permanent staff "in particular to prepare plans for the joint employment of the three armed forces." Unfortunately, the permanent staff was never set up. In 1986, the government established a joint Defence Planning Staff of the Chiefs of Staff Committee. However, its relationship with the Joint Planning Committee was never clear. The result was that the operations branch of the individual Services kept operating nearly autonomously. This, in turn, created numerous incidents that have tended to increase the gap of mutual understanding of roles and missions, especially between the army and the air force. Over the decades, the effort of the army and the navy then has been to try and bring as much of the air power as possible under their own control. But classic cases of failure of joint planning naturally arose out of the failure to establish the requisite structures for this purpose which in turn also adversely affected the development of a culture of jointness that is so much talked about but rarely practised these days.

There is a need to address the question of where the inputs to the DCC or the Cabinet Committee on National Security would come from. These inputs will be a mixture of the military elements and political-diplomatic implications of decisions. Thus, an increasing amount of military component gets introduced into the command and control system as we move down the ladder of national command and control of the nuclear arsenal. The logical locus of such component of the management system is the Ministry of Defence. Other ministries and departments like the Finance Ministry have an important role to play in the force planning though their role in force employment would perforce be limited. In my view, the Defence Minister's Committee (DMC) should be resurrected (with some modifications) at an early date with the clearly defined role of decision-making about strategic planning and force structure planning, including that for nuclear weapons. The DMC would naturally be chaired by the defence minister, and have as its members, the minister for state for defence, the three defence Services chiefs, the defence secretary, the foreign secretary, secretary Department of Atomic Energy, the home secretary, scientific adviser (SA) to the defence minister, the chairman Joint Intelligence Committee (JIC) and the finance secretary. The DMC should be logically served by a professional strategic planning staff under the defence minister (in the Ministry of Defence) which should be able to situate the nuclear strategy and policy within a broader strategic planning for defence.

Below the ministerial level, the requirement shifts to more military-specific planning and direction-the nuts and bolts, so to say. This is really what should be treated as a task of what may be termed as the Nuclear Planning Group which would work out the detailed targetting policy. This is the sort of function that the IAF has been undertaking for decades in respect of COSC targets. The Nuclear Planning Group should preferably be headed by the defence minister himself with the three chiefs of staff, SA to the defence minister, and the defence secretary as members. The Defence Planning Staff is really now in a position to perform the role of an integrated staff and provide staff support for the Nuclear Planning Group that will go into detailed planning in respect of targetting policy, dispersal policy, deception policy, survivability policy, communication policy, etc.

INDIA AND PAKISTAN: ON THE NUCLEAR THRESHOLD

This briefing book contains material from the National Security Archive's project on U.S. policy toward South Asia, which is documenting nuclear developments in India and Pakistan from the 1950s to the present. The archive is collecting U.S. government records that illustrate American policies and perspectives. Information is being collected from the National Archives and the presidential libraries, and through Freedom of Information Act (FOIA) and Mandatory Review requests, used to obtain the declassification of now-secret materials. A selective and focused collection of documents will be made available to researchers.

The project is creating a comprehensive history of nuclear developments in South Asia, including weapons programs in India and Pakistan, as well as international efforts to curtail proliferation in the region. Information about factors that influenced nuclear issues, such as the unresolved enmity between India and Pakistan, and India's perception of China as a security threat, will also be incorporated. The U.S. has generally opposed nuclear proliferation in South Asia, while seeking to preserve good relations with both India and Pakistan. At times, however, its commitment has been questioned, because it has seemed to subordinate nonproliferation policy to other concerns. During the Soviet occupation of Afghanistan, for instance, the U.S. provided massive levels of economic and military aid to its ally, Pakistan. The assistance was widely criticized, because Pakistan was demonstrably importing nuclear-related material, from China and other nations. Few doubted that it was engaged in an active nuclear weapons development program.

China's role as a leading provider of sensitive technology to Pakistan has repeatedly strained U.S.-China relations, and has complicated efforts to expand U.S.-China trade. The Archive's South Asia project is using the FOIA to seek the declassification of documents discussing this issue, and other contemporary and controversial topics. Materials collected for this project will, of course, reflect a U.S. perspective. As noted, nonproliferation policy is influenced by other concerns, including competition among the major powers. The Archive's efforts are directed toward enhancing understanding of U.S. decisions and the issues that influenced policy formulation. The analyst for the South Asia nuclear project is Joyce Battle, who prepared this briefing book. She is also the analyst for the Archive's documentation projects on the Persian Gulf and U.S. policy toward Iraq. Materials collected for the latter project were published in a document set, Iraqgate: Saddam Hussein, U.S. Policy and the Prelude to the Persian Gulf War, 1980-1994.

BRIEFING BOOK DOCUMENTS

The documents in the briefing book date from 1961 to 1983. In 1961, India had an advanced civilian nuclear program, while Pakistan's was in its early stages. In 1983, nine years had elapsed since India's explosion of a nuclear device, and Pakistan's nuclear weapons program was well under way. During the early 1960s, India under Prime Minister Jawaharlal Nehru strongly advocated global disarmament, but was apprehensive about China's nuclear weapons program. India's concern increased following its October 1962 territorial war with China. The stakes were raised by China's first nuclear weapons test in October 1964. Many observers thought it increasingly likely that India would respond to China's actions by seeking its own weapons capability. War with Pakistan in 1965 further alarmed India: it was angered by China's outspoken support for Pakistan during the conflict, and disappointed by what it viewed as insufficient Western attention to its security needs. The U.S. considered various options that might dissuade India from developing nuclear weapons, including scientific cooperation aimed at enhancing India's national prestige. It also joined in cooperative arrangements with both India and Pakistan to monitor nuclear and missile developments in China and the Soviet Union. India, for its part, launched a campaign seeking security guarantees to shield it from Chinese nuclear attack, arguing that such assurances might make a nuclear weapons program of its own unnecessary. Various options were proposed: U.S. guarantees, joint U.S.-Soviet guarantees, guarantees from all the nuclear states, British guarantees, or guarantees in conjunction with the nuclear nonproliferation treaty, then being negotiated. U.S. policy makers seriously considered these proposals, although some doubted that they would deter India from developing a bomb.

The Embassy in New Delhi viewed India's overtures sympathetically, while the Defence Department opposed any commitment to India that would alienate Pakistan, a U.S. military ally. In 1967, both President Lyndon Johnson and Defence Secretary Robert McNamara supported the concept of guarantees during meetings with a visiting Indian representative. Later that year, U.S. and Soviet officials were still discussing security guarantees, hoping to induce India to sign the nuclear nonproliferation treaty. No agreement was ever reached, however, in part because India itself concluded that such commitments would not guarantee its security in the event of actual nuclear conflict. In May 1974, India tested a nuclear device, although it called the event a "peaceful nuclear explosion."

Its terminology did not forestall censure, both within the international community and from domestic critics. The test had serious consequences: India lost much of the foreign technical assistance that had till then sustained its civilian nuclear program. A Pakistani reaction to India's test of a nuclear explosive was predicted, and confirmed within a few years. By the mid-1970s, intelligence reports indicated that Pakistan had an active nuclear weapons program, and in 1983 the State Department noted that it had "unambiguous evidence" of this fact. Documents in this briefing book illuminate aspects of the internal debate among U.S. officials, as they attempted to formulate effective policies toward nuclear proliferation in South Asia while protecting sometimes conflicting interests and objectives.

INDIA'S PROPAGANDA AGAINST PAKISTAN AND CHINA

Although Indian officials and media have always implicated Pakistan and China on various issues, now with the help of American media, they have started a new phase of propaganda against these two countries in respect of Gilgit-Baltistan. In this respect, Indian writer B. Raman has already been maligning both Beijing and Islamabad, while Selig Harrison, former correspondent of the "Washington Post" in New Delhi has left no stone unturned in this regard.

On August 27, 2010, the "New York Times" carried an article by Selig Harrison who wrote, "While the world focuses on the flood-ravaged Indus River valley, a quiet geopolitical crisis is unfolding in the Himalayan borderlands of northern Pakistan, where Islamabad is handing over de facto control of the strategic Gilgit-Baltistan region in the northwest corner of disputed Kashmir to China. The entire Pakistan-occupied western portion of Kashmir stretching from Gilgit in the north to Azad (Free) Kashmir in the south is closed to the world…but reports from a variety of foreign intelligence sources reveal, "two important new developments in Gilgit-Baltistan: a simmering rebellion against Pakistani rule and the influx of an estimated 7,000 to 11,000 soldiers of the People's Liberation Army."

The report caused considerable sensation in India. The Government of India, while expressing its concern, ordered a verification of it by its agencies. A strong denial of the report came from the Pakistani Embassy in Beijing. "A senior Pakistani official on August 31 denied recent reports that Chinese troops are stationed in the area of Pakistan-controlled Kashmir to build a high-speed rail and road there. Masood Khan, ambassador of Pakistan to China told the Global Times, "The story is not true," and "It is totally fabricated."

Selig Harrison, in his article referred to the Gilgit-Baltistan region as "Pakistan-controlled Kashmir". On the other hand, Chinese Government officials and journalists describe Jammu and

Kashmir as "Indian-controlled Kashmir." On the September 1, 2010, the Government-controlled Xinhua news agency disseminated the report: "China rejected reports of the presence of over 11,000 Chinese troops in northern Pakistan, saying that such "groundless reports" were made with "ulterior motives." Chinese Foreign Ministry spokesperson Jiang Yu remarked, "We believe the attempts of some people to fabricate stories to provoke China-Pakistan are doomed to fail." The comment came in response to recent reports of some American and Indian press that China had deployed more than 10,000 troops in the Gilgit-Baltistan region of Pakistan. The next day, during the regular briefing of Bejing-based journalists including some from India, Jiang Yu reportedly used the expression "northern Pakistan" while referring to Gilgit-Baltistan in context of the article of Selig Harrison.

As Pakistan's close neighbour and all-weather friend, China has been helping Pakistan for its severe natural disaster. The Chinese Government has offered several instalments of humanitarian relief supplies worth more than RMB 100 million. An international relief team sent by the Chinese Government has arrived in the hardest-hit southern part of Pakistan and set up a mobile hospital which is in operation now. Beijing has provided sincere and timely assistance to Pakistan without any strings attached. According to reliable sources, China recently refused to grant a visa to Lieutenant General Jaswal, head of Indian Army's Northern Command, and the Indian side said that the refusal was about the Kashmir issue. China's visa policy towards the residents of Indian-held Kashmir is consistent and remains unchanged. Unlike the western countries, Beijing more strongly holds that the Kashmir issue should be properly handled through dialogue and consultation between India and Pakistan.

The fact of the matter is that the Chinese reference to northern Pakistan could have been the result of the use of a similar expression by Selig Harrison who has referred to Gilgit-Baltistan as "Himalayan borderlands of northern Pakistan." Nevertheless, it is evident that the Chinese, while sticking to the decisions to issue stapled visas to residents of Jummu and Kashmir and to assist Pakistan in the development of its infrastructure in Gilgit-Baltistan have irked the Indian eyes—whose high officials and journalists have misperceived the close ties of Beijing with Islamabad.

As regards Beijing's contention that their troops were present in the Gilgit-Baltistan region only for humanitarian relief work, the Chinese have made two humanitarian interventions in the area this year. The first was in January last. On January 4, a landslide created a huge artificial lake in the Hunza area, which subsequently burst submerging a large number of villages in the Gojal Tehsil. About 22 KMs of the Karakoram Highway were submerged under water totally disrupting road communications with Xinjiang in China and with the rest of Gilgit-Baltistan. The Pakistan Army was able to go to the assistance of the affected villages only in the downstream area. It was not able to reach the affected villages in the upstream area for want of helicopters. The Pakistan Government appealed to the Chinese for assistance. Workers of the Chinese Red Cross and engineers of the People's Liberation Army entered the Hunza area for relief.

In that connection, The Xinhua reported: "On January 19, at the request of the Pakistani government, the Chinese side made special arrangements to open the Kunjirap border and facilitate the purchase of relief goods from China and its clearance. The second humanitarian intervention at the request of Islamabad was made after the recent floods.

It is mentionable that during the visit of President Zardari, under Memorandum of Understanding (MoU) officials of the two Governments signed—that China will build the 165-km long Jaglot-Skardu road and the 135-km long Thakot-Sazin road. Under another MoU to be jointly executed by Chinese company Datang and Norwegian company EBT—500 MW electricity would be produced through wind power.

China and Pakistan plan on building a rail link, which would pass through Gilgit-Baltistan near the Karakoram Highway. This has sparked a debate in India. In this regard, Indian Minister of State for Defence M M Pallam Raju said, "It is definitely a matter of concern." Besides, the two leaders of Pakistan and China discussed a host of issues relating to strategic partnership. The most prominent area of this bolstering of ties—especially for the world is the Sino-Pak civilian nuclear deal which is now beginning to see complete formalisation and initiation. It is unfortunate that the US and India have expressed their concerns about this deal, where the main goal is to address the acute power crisis in Pakistan. While rejecting particularly US objections, China has once again clarified that it will supply two nuclear reactors to Pakistan under the old nuclear deal.

It is also regrettable that, until now, we have been denied the same right to civil nuclear technology that India was granted by the US in 2008. It provides the precedent, and in fact, has opened the door for any similar sort of nuclear deal in the future. Indeed, after setting precedent by themselves, both India and the US have no legal and moral grounds to challenge the legality of the Pak-China nuclear deal. In fact, Pakistan's province, Balochistan where China has invested billion of dollars to develop Gwadar seaport that could link Central Asian trade with rest of the world, irritates both Washington and New Delhi. It has even shifted the central gravity of the Great Game to Pakistan.

Returning to our earlier discussion, Selig Harrison's information about the presence of Chinese troops in Pakistan has not independently be confirmed as it is part of a new propaganda game against China and Pakistan. —Opinion-Maker

OBAMA & AMERICA'S CONTINUING AFGHAN MUDDLE

The latest, released earlier this week, is Obama's Wars by Bob Woodward, one of the two journalists who exposed the Watergate scandal. The earlier one published in May is The Promise by Jonathan Alter, which reviewed the first year of the Obama Presidency. The descriptions in these books – based on briefings by White House officials and interviews including with the President himself – of how decisions on Afghanistan were made last year reveal intense policy rifts and personality clashes within the Administration over the course to follow in what is now America's longest war. They offer instructive insights into the tensions that continue to afflict the US approach. Both books confirm the deep divisions within the US government over how to handle Afghanistan. The most protracted Presidential consideration of a national security decision since the 1962 Cuban missile crisis – which led up to President Barack Obama's announcement of a military surge last December.

Woodward's book focuses on the Afghan war and the internal 'wars' over it by recounting what happened in the strategy discussions. Both books depict Obama as having doubts about investing more deeply in the Afghan conflict and who felt that his military advisers were trying to manoeuvre him into a decision of escalation that he was uneasy with, recognising as he did its risks and the political and economic costs of prosecuting an open-ended war. From the coverage and extracts of Obama's Wars, it seems the US President was deeply conflicted about expanding the war as was his national security team. Obama is left in Woodward's book with the realisation that the policy review process did not yield a clear solution.

Accounts in both books show Vice President Joe Biden advocating a narrow counterterrorism mission in Afghanistan with a lighter footprint and greater reliance on drones and Special Forces and opposing the large-scale counterinsurgency campaign proposed by the military and the Pentagon. "Obama and his senior staff", writes Alter, "believed (Admiral) Mullen and (General) Petraeus were using McChrystal to jam the President, box him, manipulate him, game him" into a policy of extending the war by an unlimited commitment lasting ten years or more.

Woodward's book depicts an exasperated Obama asking his commanders for an exit plan. What he gets instead is military advisers "steering him towards one option and thwarting his search for an exit plan." In response he writes a six-page "terms sheet" that spells out the conditions for the surge so as to prevent any mission creep. Reports of the book cite Obama telling Defence Secretary Robert Gates and Secretary of State Hilary Clinton in an October 2009 meeting: "I'm not doing 10 years – I am not doing long-term nation building – I am not spending a trillion dollars (in Afghanistan)." In confronting the choice between the Biden plan and the one presented by Generals McChrystal and Petraeus, President Obama opts for a middle path, combining elements of both. He gives the military substantially what they wanted but imposes resource and time limits. Most importantly, he announces a date, July 2011, when a withdrawal of American forces would begin from Afghanistan. This surge-and-exit approach was designed to give something to both supporters and opponents of the war. As he tells a senator in Woodward's book: "I can't let this be a war without end and I can't lose the whole Democratic Party."

These anecdotal details about the crafting of Obama's Afghan strategy raise a number of questions. Have the fierce policy differences been reconciled behind an approach that has strategic clarity? Did the "hybrid" plan promote a consensus or leave differences to persist? Has this compromise injected insoluble tensions in US strategy? Does July 2011 reflect a political position rather than a firm deadline in a coherent strategy? Does the date signal a desire to exit but without having a credible exit plan? Answers to these questions go to the very heart of where the US-led mission stands at present and its prospects. While US thinking has evolved since the intense policy battles last year it is not yet clear whether the different elements of its approach have been aligned in terms of timelines, capacity and goals.

Year 2010 has so for been a grim year for coalition forces, with record casualties, falling public support for the war and a Taliban movement that is at its strongest since 2001. There is little consensus between or within coalition countries on how to deal with or even define the approaching Afghan endgame.

The strategic flaw in the US policy is that military action continues to define ongoing coalition efforts rather than a political strategy. There is still an aversion to negotiating with the Taliban even though virtually everyone agrees this will have to take place in order to bring an unwinnable war to an end. The belief that a political strategy can or will emerge from a change in the military balance on the battlefield is questionable on many counts but most importantly because it assumes that the surge can bring about a game changing outcome which in turn will strengthen the hand for negotiations later with the Taliban.

The Obama administration's dithering over a decision to shift gear from a military to a political strategy of accommodation with the Taliban may be explained by the compelling consideration to avoid an impression of defeat. But persisting with a failed policy does not address this dilemma. The administration may also want to avoid exposing itself to attacks from the Republicans and the right-wing ahead of critical mid-term Congressional elections in November.

This places the Obama administration in an untenable position where it knows it cannot fight indefinitely but lacks the political courage to negotiate. The only way it can extricate itself from this predicament and pave the way for an orderly withdrawal of Western forces is to pursue a negotiated political settlement and bring Afghanistan's neighbours on board to endorse such a deal. The reluctance to open a dialogue with the Taliban not only delays the inevitable but heightens the risk of a less than tidy or 'dignified' exit. The pursuit of an 'outcome' to avert an impression of defeat can lead to the very mission expansion and goal multiplication that Obama has been rightly determined to avoid. —KT

KASHMIR CONFLICT: THE EXPANDING OWNERSHIP!

IT is interesting to observe that ownership of Kashmir conflict is expanding, the stakeholders are far greater that can be visualised. Now even the non-Muslim Kashmiris are also getting on board. Kashmiri youth has taken the lead and assumed the responsibility of carrying forth the struggle to its logical conclusion. Old guard Kashmiri leaders and veterans of first generation struggle are extending full support to the youngsters. Its like a change of leadership that is in its transitional phase. Entire IOK is in a state of defiance. With death tolls exceeding psychological number of 100, the struggle sees to have entered in an irreversible phase. Secretary Generals of UN and OIC have expressed their concern over the brutalities being committed by Indian security apparatus in Kashmir.

Unable to sustain a protracted state of denial, India has, yet once again, acknowledged the disputed status of the territory. Recently, Prime Minister Singh held an emergency APC in New Delhi, which decided to send a 37-member delegation to occupied Kashmir to talk to local politicians and business groups in an effort to ease tensions. Though it was a lacklustre 'All Parties

Conference', it has kick-started a fresh political initiative by the Indian bi-partisan political leadership. While at the same time, erratic statement of Indian foreign minister in New York UN has demonstrated Indian's Machiavellian approach to the issue. Indian initiative may however be a non-starter due to the condition that talks should be held within the framework of the Indian constitution, whereas first assertion of the Kashmiri leadership is that Jammu and Kashmir is a disputed territory as such Indian Constitution does not apply here; and that India has made several promises at the international level, which ought to be fulfilled.

To coincide with the arrival of the Indian fact-finding mission in Srinagar, identical resolutions were adopted unanimously by the National Assembly and the Senate of Pakistan, condemning "state terrorism" in the region and reaffirming Pakistan's "diplomatic, political and moral support" for Kashmiris in their struggle.

Resolution adopted by the assembly expressed "grave concern on the situation in occupied Kashmir", condemned "India's state terrorism" and demanded that India "stop murder and plunder", withdraw occupying forces from the "state/urban population, cancel black laws, lift curfew, end media blackout, release Kashmiri leaders and thousands of imprisoned youth, refrain from obstructing the performance of religious duties and locking mosques and allow international human rights organisations to come to occupied Kashmir". It emphasized that Kashmiris were engaged in a "peaceful struggle for their right of self-determination in accordance with the United Nations Charter, UN resolutions, the Universal Declaration for Human Rights and resolutions of the Non-Aligned Movement as their basic right". It appealed to world nations "not to remain silent spectators of the Kashmir situation and compel India to stop injustice and repression on Kashmiris and resolve the Kashmir issue, and take practical steps for the implementation of (relevant) UN Security Council resolutions."

Kashmiri peoples' and political leadership's response to Indian parliamentary delegation clearly indicates that its not just a huge trust deficit between New Delhi and freedom fighters but a complete rejection of Indian hegemony over Kashmir. Main stream political leadership of IOK decided to abstain from directly interacting with the parliamentary delegation because they are now wary of such visits as these represent only an effort at short-term crisis management and that there is neither any clear commitment towards effective resolution of the issue nor any path finding effort for addressing the aspirations and interests of the IOK masses. However, a memorandum was addresses by the IOK political leadership to the visiting delegation, recommending a negotiation based plan of action for resolving the dispute.

Kashmiri political leadership is right in following this approach because Kashmiris have repeatedly seen in the past that it is only when a major crisis erupts that visible efforts are made by India to engage and understand peoples' aspirations; and as soon as the immediate crisis subsides, inherent political complacency and negligence is restored. IOK political leadership has made it a point to not to ask for unilateral political concessions, rather they are pursuing for a joint commitment to a meaningful process that guarantees results. They are of the opinion that this is possible only if serious efforts are made to create a conducive environment for dialogue by removal of the harsh and repressive measures, like Armed Forces Special Powers Act (AFPSA), which are in force in IOK, to suppress aspirations and fundamental democratic rights of Kashmiris.

IOK leadership has suggested that to begin with, resolution of the Kashmir dispute in accordance with aspirations of the people of Jammu and Kashmir should become a 'Common Minimum Programme' shared by all political parties in India and in Pakistan, so that such a process is transparent and is designed to deliver a negotiated solution to the Kashmir issue that is mutually worked towards by and is acceptable to all parties concerned.

Making a fresh demand for a result-oriented dialogue, the moderate faction of the All Parties Hurriyat Conference (APHC) and Jammu and Kashmir Liberation Front (JKLF) have demanded setting up of Kashmir committees in India and Pakistan to find an everlasting solution to the Kashmir issue. "We look forward to entering into a dialogue based on shared commitments... Let the Government of India establish and empower an official body, a Kashmir Committee, consisting of senior representatives of major political parties to develop and enter into a process of engagement with representatives of the people of Jammu and Kashmir," the Chairman of APHC Mirwaiz Umar Farooq and JKLF Chairman Muhammad Yasin Malik said in a joint memorandum. "We believe that a similar Kashmir Committee, bringing together all political forces, should also be established in Pakistan. We will suggest to political parties in Pakistan that this be done."

The memorandum further said, "This (setting up of Kashmir committees) will ensure that all major political forces in India and Pakistan are on board with the peace process and it will help institutionalise and sustain the process to resolve the Kashmir problem. "On our part we are ready and willing to engage and sustain a meaningful and irreversible process of dialogue designed to avoid the failures of the past and to jointly develop and implement a solution to the Kashmir dispute that is acceptable to all sides – India, Pakistan and above all the people of the State," the memorandum said.

It is unwavering determination of the people of Kashmir that has sustained the freedom struggle against the barbarity of India and its occupation forces in the face of the placatory silence of the international community, for example President Obama conveniently skipped the issue during his recent address to UNGA. It is disappointing to see what has become of 'candidate Obama' who was an ardent supporter of the cause of Kashmiris. It is UN Secretary General's legal obligation to stand for Kashmiris against Indian homicide in occupied Kashmir since the Kashmir dispute is on the agenda of UN Security Council. Moreover, being a depository of all resolutions on Kashmir dispute, UN is the rightful sponsor for undertaking a concerted campaign to throw up a viable solution to the dispute. Time has come for the UN to own the conflict, dust off archives and jump-start the process. Let's go beyond rhetoric!

INDIA AND PAKISTAN-NUCLEAR STATES IN CONFLICT

When the British withdrew from the Indian subcontinent after the second world war, it was divided, primarily on religious grounds, into the two states of India and Pakistan. At that time Kashmir was included in India, but the issue of which state it should belong to has been contested ever since, largely because Kashmir's population is predominantly Muslim. In 1947 a United Nations resolution called for a referendum in Kashmir to settle the issue on the basis of what the people wanted. It was, however never carried out and it is generally assumed that the reason for this is because the Indian government feared the popular vote would support unification with Pakistan on religious grounds. Many in Kashmir campaign for independence, a position that neither India nor Pakistan supports.

Around 30,000 people have died in Kashmir in the last 11 years. What happens in Kashmir is at the heart of the continuing tension between India and Pakistan. The possibility of the world's first direct war between two nuclear-armed states occurring is very real. The history of the conflict over Kashmir is well documented with three India/Pakistan wars taking place since 1947. But this time it would be with both sides having access to nuclear weapons. Since the attack on the Indian Parliament building in December 2001, the tension and rhetoric have grown considerably. India accused Pakistan of supporting terrorist groups. Pakistan, in turn, pledges its support for Kashmiri freedom fighters. One state's terrorist is another's freedom fighter. Since the attack in December, Pakistan has arrested around 1500 'militants' and banned five groups, two said to be sectarian, one pro-Taliban and two who have been fighting Indian rule in Kashmir. However, Gen Musharraf has pledged continued support for Kashmir.

Many people living along the border close to Kashmir have fled the area due to the large military presence being built up by both sides. From the end of 2001 there were clashes virtually every night in that border region, with sometimes one or two people being shot. There are claims that large numbers of military silos have been destroyed. In an atmosphere of increased tension and sabre-rattling rhetoric on both sides, this led to the situation in May 2002 where upwards of a million troops were gathered near the border. Any mistake or small incident runs the risk of setting off something far, far worse.

Nuclear Numbers

Estimates on actual warhead numbers vary wildly with reports that India has anywhere between 50-150 warheads and Pakistan 10-100. There is a bit more clarity, however, regarding the missile systems that would deliver them.

India:

Agni (Intermediate Range Ballistic Missile), nuclear capable and tested.

Range: 1,500 miles.

Could reach Karachi in about 14 minutes.

Prithvi (Surface to Surface Missile), nuclear capable and deployed.

Range: 90-220 miles.

Could reach Islamabad or Lahore within three minutes.

Trishul (Surface to Surface Missile), nuclear capable.

Range: 6 miles.

Pakistan:

Ghauri (Intermediate Range Ballistic Missile), nuclear capable in production.

Range: 930 miles

Could reach Bombay in 10 minutes.

One medium-range and one short-range missile, both nuclear capable, were tested in May 2002.

The Current Situation

All this, of course, is fuelled by the continuing rhetoric on both sides. Officials in both countries claimed that they would not use nuclear weapons first, but they seem remarkably keen to use them second. Given the proximity of the two states, it is clear that millions of their own people would die along with millions of their nearest neighbours. India has said that it would not use nuclear weapons first, while Pakistan has clearly stated that it would. Whilst a 'no first use' policy is an important step towards disarmament, it is all too often used as an excuse to build a large 'second use' capacity. Eventually, of course, the 'second use' becomes indistinguishable from the 'first use'. As the tension mounts, the temptation grows to get your retaliation in first. But what are the immediate reasons for the current increasing tension and the risk of war? India appears to be escalating events but its argument is that it is following the lead of the US and the west by zero tolerance of terrorist attacks. It has identified what it sees as terrorists being harboured by another state so it threatens military retaliation.

Both sides have had internal problems as well. In Pakistan, Musharraf has been promising a democratic election ever since the army took control, but there has been only a referendum. Though it was boycotted by many political parties, Musharraf claimed it as a mandate for him to continue. Meanwhile in India, the ruling BJP has lost every state election for over a year, so now uses the well-known tactic of uniting the country against an outside 'threat'. Whatever the reasons for the tensions, the crucial aim is to avoid the devastation of nuclear war.

The British Prime Minister, Tony Blair, visited the region in January 2002 to try to persuade both sides that a war was not a good idea. This took place against the background of the bombing in Afghanistan, in which Britain was an enthusiastic participant. His approach raised concerns about Western hypocrisy, as if war is fine for some countries but not others. The sincerity of Blair's mission was also in question after it transpired that his plea for peace preceded two British trade missions to Delhi in February, both designed to sell weapons to India. Defexpo is an arms fair whose promotional material pushes the weaponry on sale, with everything from small arms to missile systems. India and Pakistan have long been valuable markets for British arms manufacturers. So this arms fair, combined with the resumption of arms sales to Pakistan, as a result of its support for the war in Afghanistan, means that Britain will be arming both sides in any future war. This is, of course, not unique. A similar thing happened during the Iraq-Iran war.

So, what's the answer? The situation in south Asia shows the importance of nuclear disarmament. A war even with conventional weapons would be an appalling waste of life. But this would be turned into a complete disaster on an unimaginable scale if nuclear weapons were used. In the short term there must be more diplomatic language and there must be proper international negotiations at the UN to resolve the problem of Kashmir. Our own politicians could do more to help. How can the British Government's attempts to calm the situation be taken seriously when the Defence Minister, Geoff Hoon, appears on television saying that he would use nuclear weapons against any state if necessary? In the long term, the declared nuclear weapon states (NWS)-US, UK, France, Russia and China-must carry out their obligations under the nuclear Non-Proliferation Treaty (NPT) and get rid of their nuclear weapons. The NPT was drawn up in 1968, giving the definition of a NWS as one that tested nuclear weapons before then. Because India was preparing its nuclear programme at that time, it would not sign. Because India would not sign, neither would Pakistan. Therefore, they cannot sign the NPT as NWS and, since the nuclear testing by both sides in 1998, they cannot sign as non-nuclear weapon states. The NWS made statements at the time of the tests saying how appalled they were at this development. But after 11 September, the US lifted sanctions imposed on both sides, in order to boost its coalition in the 'War on Terrorism'.

If the NWS put the words of the NPT into action, they would be in a position to push India and Pakistan to sign the NPT themselves. After all, part of the excuse given by India and Pakistan for the 1998 nuclear tests was that those nuclear weapon states had done nothing about their NPT commitments, so if nuclear weapons were good enough for them...

Both sides need to be persuaded that nuclear weapons make the world a more dangerous, not a safer, place and to take a step back and realise that peaceful resolutions to conflict are the best way forward. This should happen through the UN. But the UN also needs to look at the continuing nuclear policies of the NWS. There are peace activists in both India and Pakistan working hard to get their views across. Their work has been particularly difficult since the nuclear tests carried out by both countries in 1998. They have the entire might of the government and military propaganda machine ranged against them. We should do all we can to support them.

AN ECOLOGICAL CRITIQUE OF PAKISTAN'S ENERGY POLICY

The most fundamental concern with Pakistan's current energy policy trajectory stems from how success is being defined by the government. There is a perception that somehow reaching our energy extraction potential is necessarily a positive indicator of development. Such definitional mistakes have led to major environmental policy concerns in yesteryears. For example, during the early decades of the twentieth century the Bureau of Reclamation in the United States had defined "conservation" of resources as harnessing every kilowatt of energy that flowed through a river. There was a perception that not harnessing such energy and letting the water flow to the ocean was "wastage." The bureau has since then realized that conservation is not synonymous with extraction but rather efficient usage of resources with minimal impact on the systems that sustain those resources in the first place.

Here are some specific metrics that appear to be misleading energy policy-makers in Pakistan, based on a recent presentation by the country's senior energy advisor to the Prime Minister:

Per capita consumption is low: Use of unrefined macro-indicator planning is pervasive in Pakistan and the country continues to consider consumption as a direct indicator of success. While there may be some correlation between higher consumption and industrial success, using this as a metric creates perverse incentives for excessive energy usage that might even be wasted. Therefore in benchmarking performance against regional economic competitors the use of "per capita consumption" is highly misleading. Indeed, if per capita consumption is low that could also be considered a measure of success in terms of efficiency of processes. For example Morocco has a lower per capita energy consumption of 372 kilograms of oil equivalent per person per year (kgoe) than Pakistan's metric of 471(kgoe). However, Morocco has a better performance than Pakistan on the human development index as well as in terms of industrialization indicators. Instead of using consumption as a metric of success, development indicators in terms of industrial output per units of investment should be used as metrics of success to prevent errant policies that artificially increase consumption.

Efficiency defined in terms of units of energy per GDP: Aggregate economic metrics such as the gross domestic product (GDP) are useful to some degree in providing a very rough gauge of economic activity in a country. However, the use of such indicators for benchmarking energy policy can again lead to skewed outcomes. For example, the Pakistani government continues to define efficiency of energy in terms of energy input divided by GDP (also referred to as energy intensity), when most countries have moved to more refined measures that take into account the climate and sectoral mix of the country in question. For example, countries in extreme climates may have a much higher energy intensity due to energy consumption for heating or air conditioning. At the same time, some countries may have a much higher contribution of the service sector than of high-energy industry in promoting GDP which would lead to low energy intensity. The ultimate policy goal from an environmental perspective should be to achieve a mix of low energy-intensive economic growth sectors. A measurement of efficiency should be based on an evaluation of how much energy is being used to produce a given industrial output or useful end product (such as lumens of light for domestic usage) and how much is being lost or wasted.

Supply-side policies driven by GDP growth targets: The aforementioned metrics of energy ultimately lead to a set of policies that have tunnel vision towards economic growth without considering whether such growth is sustainable. To make matters worse, GDP growth targets are set and then existing energy usage ratios are used to calculate what amount of energy would be required to meet those growth targets. In one set of scenarios developed for the government, conservation was the last policy scenario considered in which a modest 9% reduction through reduced demand and 15% technical savings for power generation were assumed. However, there is little attempt by policymakers to focus on how demand might be altered and made more efficient to meet the existing supply constraints. This supply-side approach stifles innovation towards environmental consciousness or energy conservation while leading to massive investments in new energy generation capacity at the expense of ecological factors. *Skewed cost-benefit analyses:* Policymakers are often presented cost-benefit analysis in a stylized objective fashion when in fact the embedded assumption in such analyses can reveal enormous inconsistencies and a departure from ecological constraints. For example, usage of high discount rates being used to calculate the benefits of environmentally beneficial projects such as solar and wind may render them uncompetitive in terms of cost even if they are likely to be more secure in the long-run. Also, there are assumptions about energy imports being more expensive than domestic production because of existing regulatory constraints. However, if the cost of production, including environmental impact are calculated, imports will not necessarily be more expensive than domestic production. This is clearly the case with natural gas imports from Central Asia being more economical as well as having much less aggregate environmental impact in project development and air pollution concerns than local coal mines. While the security of energy supplies is a vital argument against imports, geopolitical circumstances are moving towards greater interdependence between countries on matters of energy as discussed later in this essay.

THE PERIL OF PRESTIGE IN NUCLEAR POWER

The cost-benefit analyses with regard to fuel cost for nuclear energy is particularly troubling. In most cases, the capital costs are the major component of such analysis whereas operating and maintenance costs and fuel costs are frequently underestimated. The price of uranium fuel can fluctuate dramatically as we can see from observing the past five years of the price of uranium oxide which was around $6 per pound in 2001 and has jumped to over $40 per pound in 2006.[9] Furthermore the cost of appropriate disposal of nuclear wastes is frequently neglected. While reprocessing is often presented as an alternative, in reality reprocessing does not reduce waste but can only reduce the amount of mined uranium. France, among the world's leading nuclear energy users, spends about $1 billion extra per year on reprocessed plutonium fuel compared to uranium fuel. Even the relatively promising thorium reactors for which India has the second-largest ore reserves of monazite in the world, first require the thorium to be converted to fissionable uranium (233).

Plutonium fuel obtained by reprocessing (also called mixed-oxide fuel or MOX) is two to three times more costly than uranium fuel. Apart from the prestige of being a nuclear energy producer, increased investment in nuclear power makes little economic sense. By playing around with discount rates proponents of nuclear energy can sometimes come up with ostensibly cost-effective comparisons with other fuels but there is little doubt that the construction cost of a nuclear power plant is inordinately more than any other source. In a recent study by the Massachusetts Institute of Technology, the all-inclusive cost for a nuclear power plant operating over 40 years is 6.7 cents per kilowatt-hour, which is almost twice the cost for natural gas at current prices.

And all these arguments bode negatively for nuclear even without considering its environmental and human health impact. Nuclear energy is also not very reliable at this stage since plant upgrades can take years to accomplish. For example, Pakistan's only nuclear generator, the Karachi Nuclear Power Plant (KANUPP) was shut down for refurbishment in December 2002 after exhausting its 30 year design life and is still undergoing upgrades before being ready to reach capacity again.

The environmental challenges of managing radioactive mining has become evident by the recent case of the village of Baghhalchur in rural Punjab, Pakistan. From 1978 to 2000 this region provided the Pakistani Atomic Energy Commission (PAEC) with yellow cake for the country's nuclear program. The half a million tribesmen in this region near Dera Ghazi Khan, many of whom are Baluchi, have leukemia rates that are six times the national average. Even former employees of the PAEC, such as Professor Khalid Rashid of Bahria University have publicly acknowledged that there are legitimate concerns of radioactive pollution that need to be investigated. In a rare show of support for environmental enforcement the Pakistani supreme court agreed to hear the petitions of the residents of the area in March, 2006 and a decision is pending.

The ostensible benefit of nuclear energy in terms of reduced greenhouse gas emissions is also misleading since the energy required to mine uranium and the maintenance of reactors shows that there is indeed a net contribution of greenhouse gases from nuclear energy as well. While Pakistan and all other countries should keep the nuclear option open it must always be a last resort and probably requires several more decades of research on waste management solutions and cost efficiency before being viable at a large scale.

Humbling the Hysteria over Hydropower

The prestige factor with large-scale hydropower also appears to be resonating with the Pakistani government. While the advantages of dams such as Tarbela and Mangla at the time of construction are widely appreciated, the long-term viability of these projects remains questionable. In its case study on Tarbela dam, the World Commission on Dams generally concluded that the dam had made a positive contribution to the Pakistani economy, particularly the energy sector. However, what is less clear is whether the dam and other such large irreversible hydropower projects can sustain benefits over the longrun in comparison with alternative energy sources. The useful life of a dam such as Tarbela is about 100 years for which around 100,000 people were displaced, not to mention the inundation of 23,000 hectares of arable land. Even the increase in cultivable land requires further ecological study in cost-benefit analyses since in many cases mismanagement of the irrigation schemes led to salinity and water-logging and eventual loss of arable capacity in 22% of the Indus basin. Evaporation losses can greatly diminish irrigation benefits as well, and the flood control advantage of dams must be balanced with the risk of dam failure in high risk zones.

In particular seismic hazards and the vulnerability of such sources in times of armed conflict and droughts also needs to be considered, specially following the Kashmir earthquake of October

2005. The vulnerability of dams to earthquakes remains considerably high throughout this region as exemplified by numerous studies of faults in the area. A large dam failure can be utterly catastrophic as illustrated by China's experience with the collapse of the Banqiao reservoir dam in 1975 which killed over 175,000 people and displaced 11 million residents. Even though China is proceeding with the Three Gorges project on the Yangtze river, despite the refusal of the World Bank to fund, the Chinese are having second thoughts about some of their other dam projects including a moratorium on 13 proposed dams on the Nu River.

Indeed, even the positive impacts of reduced greenhouse gas emissions of large dams is being questioned since there is potential for methane generation from dam reservoirs. It is for this reason that dams above 10MW generating capacity were initially excluded from the list of eligible renewable energy sources presented by the European Union to the Intergovernmental Panel on Climate Change in 2000. While this list was subsequently not accepted by all countries, the World Bank has admitted that hydropower projects greater than 10MW have "declining commitments" from the international community. It is thus alarming that the Pakistani government is now considering five new large hydropower projects. The Bhasha (Diamir) Dam whose construction has already been inaugurated by President Musharraf would be comparable in MW capacity to Tarbela at around 3500MW. Extensive community opposition is already palpable around this project, reminiscent to earlier concerns over the Kalabagh dam, and there are growing concerns that the conflicts at the micro-level as well as distributional concerns between provinces may further destabilize the country.

As compared to large-scale hydropower, small-scale hydropower is a highly attractive renewable solution and must be encouraged across Pakistan. Such dams have the advantage of being more flexible to engineering redesign or removal if necessary as they age. There are indeed promising possibilities in this regard for smaller rivers across Pakistan such as the Kunhar, the Swat, and Chitral. While aggregate hydropower capacity from these rivers might not ostensibly match the potential from large projects, the overall efficiency in distribution systems can often make them more attractive. There is much to be gained from pursuing a sensible policy on hydropower so long as we remember that "bigger" is not always "better."

AN AGENDA FOR CHANGE

Despite the aforementioned grim critique there are some relatively quick policy interventions and compliance measures which can be undertaken to improve Pakistan's energy prospects. The country has adequate human and natural resources to meet these demands for the foreseeable future. As relations improve with its neighbors and regional security the long-term outlook can indeed be very positive as the following measures are considered domestically:

Auditing Energy Consumption

The first step to solving any technical problem to is to have a better estimate of the status quo. At present there is hardly any data available on the energy performance of Pakistan's industry. Therefore a detailed audit of industries and households in urban and rural areas is needed. A modest study of energy conservation potential including audits was performed by the government in the late eighties which included industrial units, residential and commercial buildings and appliances, turbines and tractors in agriculture and passenger and freight vehicles. Apparently there is renewed interest from the Asian Development Bank and the German development agency (GTZ) to revise this study which should subsequently be an important tool for energy policy-makers in Pakistan.

Individual studies of energy consumption, particularly in rural areas of Pakistan have revealed some counterintuitive insights which the government might also consider. For example, one doctoral study of rural energy consumption in Punjab found that electricity is only used for lighting which is a negligible proportion of the total household energy consumption, and the researcher concluded that ""a route of supply side energy policy that only encourages increasing the supply of energy resources, most often based on inaccuracies extrapolations of past growth or historic elasticity of energy supply. Food preparation, water heating and animal-warming are main demand areas in rural areas and traditional fuels continue to be preferentially used even when grid power is made available. Some of these fuels may indeed be very problematic when used in crude form, such as dung, but quite workable with small technological innovations that filter out pollutants such as inexpensive "clean" stoves that have been used in Mexico and China. A comprehensive energy audit would reveal the details necessary to implement such technological efforts and provide more effective and targeted solutions.

Creating proper economic incentives to ensure conservation behaviour on the part of consumers is an essential ingredient to effective energy policy. First there needs to be effective enforcement of energy usage to prevent theft and "free riding" of the system. The government has begun to enforce laws against such thefts but considerably more compliance assurance is needed through police action and prosecution where necessary.

Furthermore, recent analyses conducted at the Lahore University of Management Sciences has revealed that there is allocative inefficiency in Pakistan's manufacturing sector characterized by "the absence of equality between marginal rates of substitution and factor price rations." In other words the pricing of energy in Pakistan's manufacturing sector is leading firms to use resources inefficiently. Ensuring that such pricing concerns are addressed will reduce the load on the system considerably and be a win-win solution for industry as well that will have more dependable supply.

Using Technology to Overcome losses in the System

By one estimate of Pakistan's private energy systems, thermal efficiency in energy generation system tends to be around 32-35% when the global average is around 54%.24 We could thus have a 60% improvement in energy generation by simply switching to newer production technologies. Distribution losses in these systems tend to be around 23%, whereas the technical losses should be no more than 3%. By this estimate Pakistan could increase its energy availability by a staggering 80% simply through more efficient distribution systems that could be updated at a fraction of the cost of mega-energy generation projects being proposed. Furthermore, these numbers do not even account for energy conservation measures in buildings and factories that would result from proper energy audits across sectors mentioned earlier. There are some glimmers of improvement in the improvement of energy efficiency through more effective harnessing of biofuels as revealed by one comparative study of the region which compared Pakistan, India, Bangladesh and Thailand. Indeed there are many lessons on efficient technological applications, specially at the rural scale which can be gleaned from such comparisons.

Giving Precedence to Renewable Sources

Apart from natural gas, there is tremendous potential for wind and solar energy across South Asia that has hardly been explored. With funding from the Asian Development bank, Pakistan's government has set a target of generating 10 percent of its electricity needs using renewable energy resources (approximately 2,700 MW) by 2015. The government has established an Alternative Energy Development Board (AEDB) and will launch a Renewable Energy Project that will invest in developing electricity sources for rural areas. However, this target is woefully inadequate based on.

Based on comparative data from India, Pakistan as the potential for solar and wind energy that far exceeds this goal. There is tremendous potential for wind and solar energy across South Asia that has hardly been explored. According to Winrock International, less than 10 percent of India's estimated wind energy generation potential of 45,000 MW has been harnessed so far. Solar energy potential — an estimated 300 days per year of full solar exposure in many areas of the country — is enormous as well. While the Pakistani government has started to develop some wind and solar projects in Sindh and Baluchistan as highlighted by Chapter X (Pandey) in this volume, these projects continue to be relegated to the periphery rather than being given precedence over the larger infrastructure projects.

There has also been a renewed interest in mining coal in Pakistan. While coal is abundant in Baluchistan and parts of Sindh, the quality of the deposits is a matter of great concern. The contribution of coal to Pakistan's electricity generation has declined from 60% in 1947 to 8% currently but this should not be a cause for lament by the government. Some high quality coal deposits when harnessed with appropriate technologies are indeed viable. However, there must first be appropriate regulatory safeguards for safety and health in mining the coal as well as protection for sensitive ecological areas such as Kirthar National Park. At present Pakistan has not been part of numerous industry-wide efforts to improve the performance of the mining sector such as those launched by the World Business Council on Sustainable Development. Any new mining projects must adhere to such standards before being rushed through for approval.

5

Challenge of Nuclear Weapons

There are two basic types of nuclear weapon. The first type produces its explosive energy through nuclear fission reactions alone. Such fission weapons are commonly referred to as atomic bombs or atom bombs (abbreviated as A-bombs), though their energy comes specifically from the nucleus of the atom. In fission weapons, a mass of fissile material (enriched uranium or plutonium) is assembled into a supercritical mass—the amount of material needed to start an exponentially growing nuclear chain reaction—either by shooting one piece of sub-critical material into another (the "gun" method), or by compressing a sub-critical sphere of material using chemical explosives to many times its original density (the "implosion" method). The latter approach is considered more sophisticated than the former, and only the latter approach can be used if plutonium is the fissile material.

A major challenge in all nuclear weapon designs is to ensure that a significant fraction of the fuel is consumed before the weapon destroys itself. The amount of energy released by fission bombs can range between the equivalent of less than a ton of TNT upwards to around 500,000 tons (500 kilotons) of TNT.

The second basic type of nuclear weapon produces a large amount of its energy through nuclear fusion reactions. Such fusion weapons are generally referred to as thermonuclear weapons or more colloquially as hydrogen bombs (abbreviated as H-bombs), as they rely on fusion reactions between isotopes of hydrogen (deuterium and tritium). However, all such weapons derive a significant portion – and sometimes a majority – of their energy from fission (including fission induced by neutrons from fusion reactions). Unlike fission weapons, there are no inherent limits on the energy released by thermonuclear weapons. Only six countries—United States, Russia, United Kingdom, People's Republic of China, France and India—have conducted thermonuclear weapon tests. (Whether India has detonated a "true," multi-staged thermonuclear weapon is controversial.)

Thermonuclear bombs work by using the energy of a fission bomb in order to compress and heat fusion fuel. In the Teller-Ulam design, which accounts for all multi-megaton yield hydrogen bombs, this is accomplished by placing a fission bomb and fusion fuel (tritium, deuterium, or lithium deuteride) in proximity within a special, radiation-reflecting container. When the fission bomb is detonated, gamma and X-rays emitted first compress the fusion fuel, then heat it to thermonuclear temperatures. The ensuing fusion reaction creates enormous numbers of high-speed neutrons, which then can induce fission in materials which normally are not prone to it, such as depleted uranium. Each of these components is known as a "stage," with the fission bomb as the "primary" and the fusion capsule as the "secondary." In large hydrogen bombs, about half of the yield, and much of the resulting nuclear fallout, comes from the final fissioning of depleted uranium.

By chaining together numerous stages with increasing amounts of fusion fuel, thermonuclear weapons can be made to an almost arbitrary yield; the largest ever detonated (the Tsar Bomba of the USSR) released an energy equivalent to over 50 million tons (50 megatons) of TNT. Most thermonuclear weapons are considerably smaller than this, due for instance to practical constraints in fitting them into the space and weight requirements of missile warheads. There are other types of nuclear weapons as well. For example, a boosted fission weapon is a fission bomb which increases its explosive yield through a small amount of fusion reactions, but it is not a fusion bomb. In the boosted bomb, the neutrons produced by the fusion reactions serve primarily to increase the efficiency of the fission bomb. Some weapons are designed for special purposes; a neutron bomb is a thermonuclear weapon that yields a relatively small explosion but a relatively large amount of neutron radiation; such a device could theoretically be used to cause massive casualties while leaving infrastructure mostly intact and creating a minimal amount of fallout.

The detonation of a nuclear weapon is accompanied by a blast of neutron radiation. Surrounding a nuclear weapon with suitable materials (such as cobalt or gold) creates a weapon known as a salted bomb. This device can produce exceptionally large quantities of radioactive contamination. Most variety in nuclear weapon design is in different yields of nuclear weapons for different types of purposes, and in manipulating design elements to attempt to make weapons extremely small.

HISTORY OF NUCLEAR WEAPONS

The history of nuclear weapons chronicles the development of nuclear weapons. Nuclear weapons are devices that possess enormous destructive potential derived from nuclear fission or nuclear fusion reactions. Starting with the scientific breakthroughs of the 1930s which made their development possible, and continuing through the nuclear arms race and nuclear testing of the Cold War, the issues of proliferation and possible use for terrorism still remain in the early 21st century. The first fission weapons, also known as "atomic bombs," were developed jointly by the United States, Britain and Canada during World War II in what was called the Manhattan Project to counter the assumed Nazi German atomic bomb project. In August 1945 two were dropped on Japan ending the Pacific War. An international team was dispatched to help work on the project. The Soviet Union started development shortly thereafter with their own atomic bomb project, and not long after that both countries developed even more powerful fusion weapons called "hydrogen bombs."

During the Cold War, the Soviet Union and United States each acquired nuclear weapons arsenals numbering in the thousands, placing many of them onto rockets which could hit targets anywhere in the world. Currently there are at least nine countries with functional nuclear weapons. A considerable amount of international negotiating has focused on the threat of nuclear warfare and the proliferation of nuclear weapons to new nations or groups. There have been (at least) four major false alarms, the most recent in 1995, that resulted in the activation of either the US's or Russia's nuclear attack early warning protocols.

Physics and Politics in the 1930s

In the first decades of the twentieth century, physics was revolutionized with developments in the understanding of the nature of atoms. In 1898, French physicist Pierre Curie and his Polish wife Maria Sklodowska-Curie had discovered that present in pitchblende, an ore of uranium, was a substance which emitted large amounts of radioactivity, which they named radium. This raised the hopes of both scientists and lay people that the elements around us could contain tremendous amounts of unseen energy, waiting to be tapped. Experiments by Ernest Rutherford in 1911 indicated that the vast majority of an atom's mass was contained in a very small nucleus at its core, made up of protons, surrounded by a web of whirring electrons. In 1932, James Chadwick discovered that the nucleus contained another fundamental particle, the neutron, and in the same year John Cockcroft and Ernest Walton "split the atom" for the first time, the first occasion on which an atomic nucleus of one element had been successfully changed to a different nucleus by artificial means.

In 1934 the idea of chain reaction via neutron was proposed by Leó Szilárd, who patented the idea of the atomic bomb. The patent was transferred in secret to Britain's Royal Navy in 1936. In a very real sense, Szilárd was the father of the atomic bomb academically. In 1934, French physicists Irène and Frédéric Joliot-Curie discovered that artificial radioactivity could be induced in stable elements by bombarding them with alpha particles, and in the same year Italian physicist Enrico Fermi reported similar results when bombarding uranium with neutrons. In December 1938, the German chemists Otto Hahn and Fritz Strassmann sent a manuscript to *Naturwissenschaften* reporting they had detected the element barium after bombarding uranium with neutrons; simultaneously, they communicated these results to Lise Meitner. Meitner, and her nephew Otto Robert Frisch, correctly interpreted these results as being nuclear fission. Frisch confirmed this experimentally on 13 January 1939. Even before it was published, Meitner's and Frisch's interpretation of the work of Hahn and Strassmann crossed the Atlantic Ocean with Niels Bohr, who was to lecture at Princeton University. Isidor Isaac Rabi and Willis Lamb, two Columbia University physicists working at Princeton, heard the news and carried it back to Columbia. Rabi said he told Fermi; Fermi gave credit to Lamb. Bohr soon thereafter went from Princeton to Columbia to see Fermi. Not finding Fermi in his office, Bohr went down to the cyclotron area and found Herbert Anderson. Bohr grabbed him by the shoulder and said: "Young man, let me explain to you about something new and exciting in physics."

It was clear to a number of scientists at Columbia that they should try to detect the energy released in the nuclear fission of uranium from neutron bombardment. On 25 January 1939, an experimental team at Columbia University conducted the first nuclear fission experiment in the United States, which was done in the basement of Pupin Hall; the members of the team were Herbert L. Anderson, Eugene T. Booth, John R. Dunning, Enrico Fermi, G. Norris Glasoe, and Francis G. Slack. As the Nazi army marched into first Czechoslovakia in 1938, and then Poland in 1939, beginning World War II, many of Europe's top physicists had already begun to flee from the imminent conflict. Scientists on both sides of the conflict were well aware of the possibility of utilizing nuclear fission as a weapon, but at the time no one was quite sure how it could be done. In the early years of the Second World War, physicists abruptly stopped publishing on the topic of fission, an act of self-censorship to keep the opposing side from gaining any advantages.

From Los Alamos to Hiroshima

By the beginning of World War II, there was concern among scientists in the Allied nations that Nazi Germany might have its own project to develop fission-based weapons. Organized research first began in Britain as part of the "Tube Alloys" project, and in the United States a small amount of funding was given for research into uranium weapons starting in 1939 with the Uranium Committee under Lyman James Briggs. At the urging of British scientists, though, who had made crucial calculations indicating that a fission weapon could be completed within only a few years, by 1941 the project had been wrested into better bureaucratic hands, and in 1942 came under the auspices of a Military Policy Committee led by General Leslie Groves as the Manhattan Project.

Scientifically led by the American physicist Robert Oppenheimer, the project brought together the top scientific minds of the day (many exiles from Europe) with the production power of American industry for the goal of producing fission-based explosive devices before Germany could. Britain and the U.S. agreed to pool their resources and information for the project, but the other Allied power—the Soviet Union under Joseph Stalin—was not informed. A massive industrial and scientific undertaking, the Manhattan Project involved many of the world's great physicists in the scientific and development aspects. The United States made an unprecedented investment into wartime research for the project, which was spread across more than 30 sites in the U.S. and Canada. Scientific knowledge was centralized at a secret laboratory known as Los Alamos, previously a small ranch school near Santa Fe, New Mexico.

Uranium appears in nature primarily in two isotopes: uranium-238 and uranium-235. When the nucleus of uranium-235 absorbs a neutron, it undergoes nuclear fission, splitting into two "fission products" and releasing energy and 2.5 neutrons on average. Uranium-238, on the other hand, absorbs neutrons but does not split, effectively putting a stop to any ongoing fission reaction. It was discovered that an atomic bomb based on uranium would need to be made of almost completely pure uranium-235 (at least 80% pure), or else the presence of uranium-238 would quickly curtail the nuclear chain reaction. The team of scientists working on the Manhattan Project immediately realized that one of the largest problems they would have to solve was how to remove uranium-235 from natural uranium, which was composed of 99.3% uranium-238. Two methods were developed during the wartime project, both of which took advantage of the fact that uranium-

238 has a slightly greater atomic mass than uranium-235: electromagnetic separation and gaseous diffusion—methods which separated isotopes based on their differing weights. Another secret site was erected at rural Oak Ridge, Tennessee, for the large-scale production and purification of the rare isotope. It was a massive investment: at the time, one of the Oak Ridge facilities (K-25) was the largest factory under one roof. The Oak Ridge site employed tens of thousands of employees at its peak, most of whom had no idea what they were working on.

Though uranium-238 cannot be used for the initial stage of an atomic bomb, when U-238 absorbs a neutron, it transforms first into an unstable element, uranium-239, and then decays into neptunium-239, and finally the relatively stable plutonium-239, an element which does not exist in nature. Plutonium is also fissile and can be used to create a fission reaction, and after Enrico Fermi achieved the world's first sustained and controlled nuclear chain reaction in the creation of the first "atomic pile"—a primitive nuclear reactor—in a basement at the University of Chicago, massive reactors were secretly created at what is now known as Hanford Site in the state of Washington, using the Columbia River as cooling water, to transform uranium-238 into plutonium for a bomb.

For a fission weapon to operate, there must be a critical mass—the amount needed for a self-sustaining nuclear chain reaction—of fissile material bombarded with neutrons at any one time. The simplest form of nuclear weapon is a gun-type fission weapon, where a sub-critical mass of fissile material (such as uranium-235) would be shot at another sub-critical mass of fissile material. The result would be a super-critical mass which, when bombarded with neutrons, would undergo fission at a rapid rate and create the desired explosion. The weapons envisaged in 1942 were the two gun-type weapons, Little Boy (uranium) and Thin Man (plutonium), and the Fat Man plutonium implosion bomb. In early 1943 Oppenheimer determined that two projects should proceed forwards: the "Thin Man" project (plutonium gun) and the "Fat Man" project (plutonium implosion). The plutonium gun was to receive the bulk of the research effort, as it was the project with the most uncertainty involved. It was assumed that the uranium gun-type bomb could then be adapted from it.

But in April 1944 it was found by Emilio Segrè that plutonium produced by the Hanford reactors had too high a level of background neutron radiation, and underwent spontaneous fission to a very small extent, due to the presence of impurities of the Pu-240 isotope. If such plutonium were used in a "gun assembly," the chain reaction would start in the split seconds before the critical mass was assembled, blowing the weapon apart before it would have any great effect (this is known as a fizzle). So development of Fat Man, the implosion bomb, was given high priority. Chemical explosives were used to implode a sub-critical sphere of plutonium, thus increasing its density and making it into a critical mass. The difficulties with implosion were in the problem of making the chemical explosives deliver a perfectly uniform shock wave upon the plutonium sphere— if it were even slightly asymmetric, the weapon would fizzle (which would be expensive, messy, and not a very effective military device). This problem was circumvented by the use of hydrodynamic "lenses"—explosive materials of differing densities—which would focus the blast waves inside the imploding sphere, akin to the way in which an optical lens focuses light rays.

After D-Day, General Groves had ordered a team of scientists—Project Alsos—to follow eastward-moving victorious Allied troops into Europe in order to assess the status of the German nuclear program (and to prevent the westward-moving Russians from gaining any materials or scientific manpower). It was concluded that while Nazi Germany had also had an atomic bomb program, headed by Werner Heisenberg, the government had not made a significant investment in the project, and had been nowhere near success. Historians claim to have found a rough schematic showing a Nazi nuclear bomb. Research was conducted in the German nuclear energy project. In March 1945, a Nazi scientific team was directed by the physicist Kurt Diebner to develop a primitive nuclear device in Ohrdruf, Thuringia.

By the unconditional surrender of Germany on May 8, 1945, the Manhattan Project was still months away from a working weapon. That April, after the death of American President Franklin D. Roosevelt, former Vice-President Harry S. Truman was told about the secret wartime project for the first time. Because of the difficulties in making a working plutonium bomb, it was decided that there should be a test of the weapon, and Truman wanted to know for sure if it would work before his meeting with Joseph Stalin at an upcoming conference on the future of postwar Europe. On July 16, 1945, in the desert north of Alamogordo, New Mexico, the first nuclear test took place, code-named "Trinity," using a device nicknamed "the Gadget." The test, a plutonium implosion type device, released the equivalent of 19 kilotons of TNT, far mightier than any weapon ever used before. The news of the test's success was rushed to Truman, who used it as leverage at the upcoming Potsdam Conference, held near Berlin.

After hearing arguments from scientists and military officers over the possible uses of the weapons against Japan (though some recommended using them as "demonstrations" in unpopulated areas, most recommended using them against "built up" targets, a euphemistic term for populated cities), Truman ordered the use of the weapons on Japanese cities, hoping it would send a strong message which would end in the capitulation of the Japanese leadership and avoid a lengthy invasion of the island. There were suggestions to drop the atomic bomb on Tokyo, the capital of Japan, but concerns about Tokyo's cultural heritage changed the plan. On May 10–11, 1945 The Target Committee at Los Alamos, led by J. Robert Oppenheimer, recommended Kyoto, Hiroshima, Yokohama, and the arsenal at Kokura as possible targets. On August 6, 1945, a uranium-based weapon, "Little Boy", was let loose on the Japanese city of Hiroshima. Three days later, a plutonium-based weapon, "Fat Man", was dropped onto the city of Nagasaki. The atomic bombs killed at least one hundred thousand Japanese outright, most of them civilians, with the heat, radiation, and blast effects. Many tens of thousands would die later of radiation sickness and related cancers. Truman promised a "rain of ruin" if Japan did not surrender immediately, threatening to eliminate Japanese cities, one by one; Japan surrendered on August 15. Truman's threat was in fact a bluff, since the US had but one remaining uranium-gun type bomb completed.

Soviet Atomic Bomb Project

The Soviet Union was not invited to share in the new weapons developed by the United States and the other Allies. During the war, information had been pouring in from a number of volunteer spies involved with the Manhattan Project (known in Soviet cables under the code-name of *Enormoz*), and the Soviet nuclear physicist Igor Kurchatov was carefully watching the Allied weapons development.

It came as no surprise to Stalin when Truman had informed him at the Potsdam conference that he had a "powerful new weapon." Truman was shocked at Stalin's lack of interest. The Soviet spies in the U.S. project were all volunteers and none were Russians. One of the most valuable, Klaus Fuchs, was a German émigré theoretical physicist who had been a part in the early British nuclear efforts and had been part of the UK mission to Los Alamos during the war. Fuchs had been intimately involved in the development of the implosion weapon, and passed on detailed cross-sections of the "Trinity" device to his Soviet contacts. Other Los Alamos spies—none of whom knew each other—included Theodore Hall and David Greenglass. The information was kept but not acted upon, as Russia was still too busy fighting the war in Europe to devote resources to this new project.

In the years immediately after World War II, the issue of who should control atomic weapons became a major international point of contention. Many of the Los Alamos scientists who had built the bomb began to call for "international control of atomic energy," often calling for either control by transnational organizations or the purposeful distribution of weapons information to all superpowers, but due to a deep distrust of the intentions of the Soviet Union, both in postwar Europe and in general, the policy-makers of the United States worked to attempt to secure an American nuclear monopoly. A half-hearted plan for international control was proposed at the newly formed United Nations by Bernard Baruch ("The Baruch Plan"), but it was clear both to American commentators—and to the Soviets—that it was an attempt primarily to stymie Russian nuclear efforts. The Soviets vetoed the plan, effectively ending any immediate postwar negotiations on atomic energy, and made overtures towards banning the use of atomic weapons in general.

All the while, the Soviets had put their full industrial and manpower might into the development of their own atomic weapons. The initial problem for the Soviets was primarily one of resources—they had not scouted out uranium resources in the Soviet Union and the U.S. had made deals to monopolise the largest known (and high purity) reserves in the Belgian Congo. The USSR used penal labour to mine the old deposits in Czechoslovakia—now an area under their control—and searched for other domestic deposits (which were eventually found). Two days after the bombing of Nagasaki, the U.S. government released an official technical history of the Manhattan Project, authored by Princeton physicist Henry DeWolf Smyth, known colloquially as the Smyth Report. The sanitized summary of the wartime effort focused primarily on the production facilities and scale of investment, written in part to justify the wartime expenditure to the American public.

The Soviet program, under the suspicious watch of former NKVD chief Lavrenty Beria (a participant and victor in Stalin's Great Purge of the 1930s), would use the Report as a blueprint, seeking to duplicate as much as possible the American effort. The "secret cities" used for the Soviet equivalents of Hanford and Oak Ridge literally vanished from the maps for decades to come. At the Soviet equivalent of Los Alamos, Arzamas-16, physicist Yuli Khariton led the scientific effort to develop the weapon. Beria distrusted his scientists, however, and he distrusted the carefully collected espionage information. As such, Beria assigned multiple teams of scientists to the same task without informing each team of the other's existence. If they arrived at different conclusions, Beria would bring them together for the first time and have them debate with their newfound counterparts. Beria used the espionage information as a way to double-check the progress of his scientists, and in his effort for duplication of the American project even rejected more efficient bomb designs in favour of ones which more closely mimicked the tried-and-true "Fat Man" bomb used by the U.S. against Nagasaki.

Working under a stubborn and scientifically ignorant administrator, the Soviet scientists struggled on. On August 29, 1949, the effort brought its results, when the USSR tested its first fission bomb, dubbed "Joe-1" by the U.S., years ahead of American predictions. The news of the first Soviet bomb was announced to the world first by the United States, which had detected the nuclear fallout it generated from its test site in Kazakhstan. The loss of the American monopoly on nuclear weapons marked the first tit-for-tat of the nuclear arms race. The response in the U.S. was one of apprehension, fear, and scapegoating, which would lead eventually into the Red-baiting tactics of McCarthyism. Yet recent information from unclassified Venona intercepts and the opening of the KGB archives after the fall of the Soviet Union show that the USSR had useful spies that helped their program, although none were identified by the McCarthy. Before this, though, President Truman would announce his decision to begin a crash program to develop a far more powerful weapon than those which were used against Japan: the hydrogen bomb.

The First Thermonuclear Weapons

The notion of using a fission weapon to ignite a process of nuclear fusion can be dated back to 1942. At the first major theoretical conference on the development of an atomic bomb hosted by J. Robert Oppenheimer at the University of California, Berkeley, participant Edward Teller directed the majority of the discussion towards Enrico Fermi's idea of a "Super" bomb which would utilize the same reactions which powered the Sun itself. It was thought at the time that a fission weapon would be quite simple to develop and that perhaps work on a hydrogen bomb would be possible to complete before the end of the Second World War. However, in reality the problem of a "regular" atomic bomb was large enough to preoccupy the scientists for the next few years, much less the more speculative "Super." Only Teller continued working on the project—against the will of project leaders Oppenheimer and Hans Bethe.

After the atomic bombings of Japan, many scientists at Los Alamos rebelled against the notion of creating a weapon thousands of times more powerful than the first atomic bombs. For the scientists the question was in part technical—the weapon design was still quite uncertain and unworkable—and in part moral: such a weapon, they argued, could only be used against large civilian populations, and could thus only be used as a weapon of genocide. Many scientists, such as Bethe, urged that the United States should not develop such weapons and set an example towards the Soviet Union. Promoters of the weapon, including Teller, Ernest Lawrence, and Luis Alvarez, argued that such a development was inevitable, and to deny such protection to the people of the United States—especially when the Soviet Union was likely to create such a weapon themselves—was itself an immoral and unwise act.

Oppenheimer, who was now head of the General Advisory Committee of the successor to the Manhattan Project, the Atomic Energy Commission, presided over a recommendation against the development of the weapon. The reasons were in part because the success of the technology seemed limited at the time (and not worth the investment of resources to confirm whether this was so), and because Oppenheimer believed that the atomic forces of the United States would be more effective if they consisted of many large fission weapons (of which multiple bombs could be dropped on the same targets) rather than the large and unwieldy predictions of massive super bombs, for which there were a relatively limited amounts of targets of the size to warrant such a development.

Furthermore, were such weapons developed by both the U.S. and the USSR, they would be more effectively used against the U.S. than by it, as the U.S. had far more regions of dense industrial and civilian activity which would serve as ideal targets for the large weapons than the Soviet Union did.

In the end, President Truman made the final decision, looking for a proper response to the first Soviet atomic bomb test in 1949. On January 31, 1950, Truman announced a crash program to develop the hydrogen (fusion) bomb. At this point, however, the exact mechanism was still not known: the "classical" hydrogen bomb, whereby the *heat* of the fission bomb would be used to ignite the fusion material, seemed highly unworkable. However, an insight by Los Alamos mathematician Stanislaw Ulam showed that the fission bomb and the fusion fuel could be in separate parts of the bomb, and that *radiation* of the fission bomb could first work in a way to *compress* the fusion material before igniting it.

Teller pushed the notion further, and used the results of the boosted-fission "George" test (a boosted-fission device using a small amount of fusion fuel to boost the yield of a fission bomb) to confirm the fusion of heavy hydrogen elements before preparing for their first true multi-stage, Teller-Ulam hydrogen bomb test. Many scientists initially against the weapon, such as Oppenheimer and Bethe, changed their previous opinions, seeing the development as being unstoppable. The first fusion bomb was tested by the United States in *Operation Ivy* on November 1, 1952, on Elugelab Island in the Enewetak (or Eniwetok) Atoll of the Marshall Islands, code-named "Mike". "Mike" used liquid deuterium as its fusion fuel and a large fission weapon as its trigger. The device was a prototype design and not a deliverable weapon: standing over 20 ft (6 m) high and weighing at least 140,000 lb (64 t) (its refrigeration equipment added an additional 24,000 lb as well), it could not have been dropped from even the largest planes.

Its explosion yielded 10.4 megatons of energy—over 450 times the power of the bomb dropped onto Nagasaki— and obliterated Elugelab, leaving an underwater crater 6240 ft (1.9 km) wide and 164 ft (50 m) deep where the island had once been. Truman had initially tried to create a media blackout about the test—hoping it would not become an issue in the upcoming presidential election—but on January 7, 1953, Truman announced the development of the hydrogen bomb to the world as hints and speculations of it were already beginning to emerge in the press. Not to be outdone, the Soviet Union exploded its first thermonuclear device, designed by the physicist Andrei Sakharov, on August 12, 1953, labeled "Joe-4" by the West. This created concern within the U.S. government and military, because, unlike "Mike," the Soviet device was a deliverable weapon, which the U.S. did not yet have. This first device though was arguably not a "true" hydrogen bomb, and could only reach explosive yields in the hundreds of kilotons (never reaching the megaton range of a "staged" weapon). Still, it was a powerful propaganda tool for the Soviet Union, and the technical differences were fairly oblique to the American public and politicians.

Following the "Mike" blast by less than a year, "Joe-4" seemed to validate claims that the bombs were inevitable and vindicate those who had supported the development of the fusion program. Coming during the height of McCarthyism, the effect was most pronounced by the security hearings in early 1954 which revoked former Los Alamos director Robert Oppenheimer of his security clearance, on the grounds that he was unreliable, had not supported the American hydrogen bomb program, and had made long-standing, left-wing ties in the 1930s. Edward Teller participated in the hearing as the only major scientist to testify against Oppenheimer, a role which resulted in his virtual expulsion from the physics community. On February 28, 1954, the U.S. detonated its first deliverable thermonuclear weapon (which used isotopes of lithium as its fusion fuel), known as the "Shrimp" device of the "Castle Bravo" test, at Bikini Atoll, Marshall Islands. The device yielded 15 megatons of energy, over twice its expected yield, and became the worst radiological disaster in U.S. history. The combination of the unexpectedly large blast and poor weather conditions caused a cloud of radioactive nuclear fallout to contaminate over 7,000 square miles, including Marshall Island natives and the crew of a Japanese fishing boat, as a snow-like mist. The contaminated islands were evacuated (and are still uninhabitable), but the natives received enough of a radioactive dose that they suffered far elevated levels of cancer and birth defects in the years to come.

The crew of the Japanese fishing boat, *Lucky Dragon 5*, returned to port suffering from radiation sickness and skin burns. Their cargo, many tons of contaminated fish, managed to enter into the market before the cause of their illness was determined. When a crew member died from the sickness and the full results of the contamination were made public by the U.S., Japanese concerns were reignited about the hazards of radiation and resulted in a boycott on eating fish (a main staple of the island country) for some weeks. The hydrogen bomb age had a profound effect on the thoughts of nuclear war in the popular and military mind. With only fission bombs, nuclear war could be considered something which could easily be "limited." Dropped by planes and only able to destroy the most built up areas of major cities, it was possible to consider fission bombs simply a technological extension of previous wartime bombing (such as the extensive firebombing which took place against Japan and Germany during World War II), and claims that such weapons could lead to worldwide death or harm were easily brushed aside as grave exaggeration.

Even the decades before the development of fission weapons there had been speculation about the possibility for human beings to end all life on the planet by either accident or purposeful maliciousness, but technology had never allowed for such a capacity. The far greater power of hydrogen bombs made this seem ever closer. The "Castle Bravo" incident itself raised a number of questions about the survivability of a nuclear war. Government scientists in both the U.S. and the USSR had insisted that fusion weapons, unlike fission weapons, were "cleaner" as fusion reactions did not result in the dangerously radioactive by-products as did fission reactions. While technically true, this hid a more gruesome point: the last stage of a multi-staged hydrogen bomb often used the neutrons produced by the fusion reactions to induce fissioning in a jacket of natural uranium, and provided around half of the yield of the device itself.

This fission stage made fusion weapons considerably more "dirty" than they were made out to be, a fact made evident by the towering cloud of deadly fallout which followed the "Bravo" test. When the Soviet Union tested its first megaton device in 1955, the possibility of a limited nuclear war seemed even more remote in the public and political mind: even if a city or country was not the direct target of a nuclear attack, the clouds of fallout and harmful fission products would disperse along with normal weather patterns and embed themselves in the soil and water of non-targeted areas of the planet as well. Speculation began to look towards what would happen as the fallout and dust created by a full-scale nuclear exchange would affect the world as a whole, rather than just the cities and countries which had been directly involved. In this way, the fate of the world was now tied to the fate of the bomb-wielding superpowers.

Deterrence and Brinkmanship

Throughout the 1950s and the early 1960s a number of trends were enacted between the U.S. and the USSR as they both endeavored in a tit-for-tat approach to disallow the other power from acquiring nuclear supremacy. This took form in a number of ways, both technologically and politically, and had massive political and cultural effects during the Cold War. The first atomic bombs dropped on Hiroshima and Nagasaki were large, custom-made devices, requiring highly trained personnel for their arming and deployment. They could be dropped only from the largest bomber planes—at the time the B-29 Superfortress—and each plane could only hold a single bomb in its hold.

The first hydrogen bombs were similarly massive and complicated. This ratio of one plane to one bomb was still fairly impressive in comparison with conventional, non-nuclear weapons, but against other nuclear-armed countries it was considered to be a grave danger. In the immediate postwar years, the U.S. expended much effort on making the bombs "G.I.-proof"—capable of being used and deployed by members of the U.S. Army, rather than Nobel Prize–winning scientists, and in the 1950s a program of nuclear testing was undertaken in order to improve the nuclear arsenal. Starting in 1951, the Nevada Test Site (in the Nevada desert) became the primary location for all U.S. nuclear testing (in the USSR, Semipalatinsk Test Site in Kazakhstan served a similar role). Tests were divided into two primary categories: "weapons related" (verifying that a new weapon worked or looking at exactly how it worked) and "weapons effects" (looking at how weapons behaved under various conditions or how structures behaved when subjected to weapons).

In the beginning, almost all nuclear tests were either "atmospheric" (conducted above ground, in the atmosphere) or "underwater" (such as some of the tests done in the Marshall Islands). Testing was used as a sign of both national and technological strength, but also raised questions about the safety of the tests, which released nuclear fallout into the atmosphere (most dramatically with the Castle Bravo test in 1954, but in more limited amounts with almost all atmospheric nuclear testing). Because testing was seen as a sign of technological development (the ability to design usable weapons without some form of testing was considered dubious), halts on testing were often called for as stand-ins for halts in the nuclear arms race itself, and many prominent scientists and statesmen lobbied for a ban on nuclear testing. In 1958, the U.S., USSR, and the United Kingdom (a new nuclear power) declared a temporary testing moratorium for both political and health reasons, but by 1961 the Soviet Union had broken the moratorium and both the USSR and the U.S. began testing with great frequency.

As a show of political strength, the Soviet Union tested the largest-ever nuclear weapon in October 1961, the massive Tsar Bomba, which was tested in a reduced state with a yield of around 50 megatons—in its full state it was estimated to have been around 100 Mt. The weapon was largely impractical for actual military use, but was hot enough to induce third-degree burns at a distance of 62 mi (100 km) away. In its full, "dirty" design, it would have increased the amount of worldwide fallout since 1945 by 25%. In 1963, all nuclear and many non-nuclear states signed the Limited Test Ban Treaty, pledging to refrain from testing nuclear weapons in the atmosphere, underwater, or in outer space. The treaty permitted underground tests.

Most tests were considerably more modest, and worked for direct technical purposes as well as their potential political overtones. Weapons improvements took on two primary forms. One was an increase in efficiency and power, and within only a few years fission bombs were being developed which were many times more powerful than the ones created during World War II. The other was a program of miniaturization, reducing the size of the nuclear weapons themselves. Smaller bombs meant that bombers could carry more of them, and thus become even more of a threat against even the most rigorous air defenses, and they could also be used in conjunction with the development in rocketry during the 1950s and 1960s. U.S. rocket efforts had received a large boost in the postwar years, largely from the acquiring of engineers who had worked on the Nazi rocketry program during the war, such as Wernher von Braun, who had been involved in the design and manufacture of the V-2 rockets which were launched across the English Channel. An American program, Project Paperclip, had endeavored to move scientists of this sort into American hands (and kept out of Soviet hands) and put them to work on projects for the U.S.

Weapons Improvement

The first nuclear-tipped rockets, such as the MGR-1 Honest John, first deployed by the U.S. in 1953, were surface-to-surface missiles with relatively short ranges (around 15 mi/25 km maximum) with yields around twice the size of the first fission weapons. The limited range of these weapons meant that they could only be used in certain types of potential military situations—the U.S. rocket weapons could not, for example, threaten the city of Moscow with the threat of an immediate strike, and could only be used as "tactical" weapons (that is, for small-scale military situations). For "strategic" weapons—weapons which would serve to threaten an entire country—for the time being, only long-range bombers capable of penetrating deep into enemy territory would work. In the U.S. this resulted in the creation of the Strategic Air Command in 1946, a system of bombers headed by General Curtis LeMay (who had previously presided over the firebombing of Japan during WWII), which kept a number of nuclear-armed planes in the sky at all times, ready to receive orders to attack Moscow whenever commanded.

These technological possibilities enabled nuclear strategy to develop a logic considerably different than previous military thinking had allowed. Because the threat of nuclear warfare was so awful, it was first thought that it might make any war of the future impossible. President Dwight D. Eisenhower's doctrine of "massive retaliation" in the early years of the Cold War was a message to the USSR, saying that if the Red Army attempted to invade the parts of Europe not given to the Eastern bloc during the Potsdam Conference (such as West Germany), nuclear weapons would be used against the Soviet troops and potentially the Soviet leaders. With the development of more rapid-response technologies (such as rockets and long-range bombers), this policy began to shift. If the Soviet Union also had nuclear weapons and a policy of "massive retaliation" was carried out, it was reasoned, then any Soviet forces not killed in the initial attack, or launched while the attack was ongoing, would be able to serve their own form of nuclear "retaliation" against the U.S. Recognizing this to be an undesirable outcome, military officers and game theorists at the RAND think tank developed a nuclear warfare strategy that would eventually become known as Mutually Assured Destruction (MAD).

MAD divided potential nuclear war into two stages: first strike and second strike. A first strike would be the first use of nuclear weapons by one nuclear-equipped nation against another nuclear-equipped nation. If the attacking nation did not prevent the attacked nation from a nuclear response, then a second strike could be deployed against the attacking nation. In this situation, whether the U.S. first attacked the USSR or the USSR first attacked the U.S., the end result would be that both nations would be damaged perhaps to the point of utter social collapse. According to game theory, because starting a nuclear war would be suicidal, no logical country would willfully enter into a nuclear war. However, if a country were capable of launching a first strike which would utterly destroy the ability of the attacked country to respond in kind, then the balance of power would be disturbed and nuclear war could then be safely undertaken.

MAD played on two seemingly opposed modes of thought: cold logic and emotional fear. The phrase by which MAD was often known, "nuclear deterrence", was translated as "dissuasion" by the French and "terrorization" by the Russians. This apparent paradox of nuclear war was summed up by British Prime Minister Winston Churchill as "the worse things get, the better they are"—the greater the threat of mutual destruction, the safer the world would be. This philosophy made a number of technological and political demands on participating nations. For one thing, it said that it should always be assumed that an enemy nation may be trying to acquire "first strike capability," something which must always be avoided. In American politics this translated into demands to avoid "missile gaps" and "bomber gaps" where the Soviet Union could potentially "out shoot" American efforts (most of these supposed "gaps" proved to be political figments, but this hardly mattered at the time). It also encouraged the production of thousands of nuclear weapons by both the U.S. and the USSR, far more than would be needed to simply destroy the major civilian and military infrastructures of the opposing country.

These policies and strategies were satirized in the 1964 Stanley Kubrick film Dr. Strangelove, in which the Soviets, unable to keep up with the US's first strike capability, instead plan for MAD by building a Doomsday Machine, and thus, after a (literally) mad US General orders a nuclear attack on the USSR, the end of the world is brought about. The policy also encouraged the development of the first early warning systems. Conventional war, even at its fastest, was fought over time scales of days and weeks. With long-range bombers, the time from the start of an attack to its conclusion was reduced to mere hours. With rockets, it could be reduced to minutes. It was reasoned that conventional command and control systems could not be expected to adequately respond to a nuclear attack, and so great lengths were taken to develop the first computers which could look for enemy attacks and direct rapid responses. In the U.S., massive funding was poured into the development of SAGE, a system which would track and intercept enemy bomber aircraft using information from remote radar stations, and was the first computer system to feature real-time processing, multiplexing, and display devices—the first "general" computing machine, and a direct predecessor of modern computers.

ANTI-NUCLEAR

Bombers and short-range rockets were not reliable: planes could be shot down, and earlier nuclear missiles could cover only a limited range— for example, the first Soviet rockets' range limited them to targets in Europe. However, by the 1960s, both the United

States and the Soviet Union had developed intercontinental ballistic missiles, which could be launched from extremely remote areas far away from their target; and submarine-launched ballistic missiles, which had less range but could be launched from submarines very close to the target without any radar warning. This made any national protection from nuclear missiles increasingly impractical. The military realities made for a precarious diplomatic situation. The international politics of brinkmanship led leaders to exclaim their willingness to participate in a nuclear war rather than concede any advantage to their opponents, feeding public fears that their generation may be the last. Civil defence programs undertaken by both superpowers, exemplified by the construction of fallout shelters and urging civilians about the "survivability" of nuclear war, did little to ease public concerns.

The climax of brinksmanship came in early 1962, when an American U-2 spy plane photographed a series of launch sites for medium-range ballistic missiles being constructed on the island of Cuba, just off the coast of the southern United States, beginning what became known as the Cuban Missile Crisis. The U.S. administration of John F. Kennedy concluded that the Soviet Union, then led by Nikita Khrushchev, was planning to station Russian nuclear missiles on the island, which was under the control of Communist Fidel Castro. On October 22, Kennedy announced the discoveries in a televised address, and declared that a naval quarantine would be put around Cuba to turn back any Soviet nuclear shipments, and warned that the military was prepared "for any eventualities."

The missiles would have a range of 2,400 miles (4,000 km), and allow the Soviet Union to easily destroy many major American cities on the Eastern Seaboard if a nuclear war were started. The leaders of the two superpowers stood nose to nose, seemingly poised over the beginnings of a third world war. Khrushchev's ambitions for putting the weapons on the island were motivated in part by the fact that the U.S. had stationed similar weapons in Britain, Italy, and nearby Turkey, and had previously attempted to sponsor an invasion of Cuba the year before in the failed Bay of Pigs Invasion.

On October 26, an offer was sent from Khrushchev to Kennedy offering to withdraw all missiles if Kennedy would commit to a policy of no future invasions of Cuba. Khrushchev worded the threat of assured destruction eloquently: "You and I should not now pull on the ends of the rope in which you have tied a knot of war, because the harder you and I pull, the tighter the knot will become. And a time may come when this knot is tied so tight that the person who tied it is no longer capable of untying it, and then the knot will have to be cut. What that would mean I need not explain to you, because you yourself understand perfectly what dreaded forces our two countries possess."

A day later, however, the Russians put forward another offer, this time demanding that the U.S. remove its missiles from Turkey before any missiles would be withdrawn from Cuba. On the same day, a U-2 plane was shot down over Cuba and another was almost intercepted over Russia, and Soviet merchant ships were nearing the quarantine zone. Kennedy responded by accepting the first deal publicly, and sending his brother Robert to the Soviet embassy to accept the second deal in private. On October 28, the Soviet ships stopped at the quarantine line and, after some hesitation, turned back towards the Soviet Union. Khrushchev announced that he had ordered the removal of all missiles in Cuba, and U.S. Secretary of State Dean Rusk was moved to comment, "We went eyeball to eyeball, and the other fellow just blinked."

The Crisis was later seen as the closest the U.S. and the USSR ever came to nuclear war and had been narrowly averted by last-minute compromise by both superpowers. Fears of communication difficulties led to the installment of the first hotline, a direct link between the superpowers which would allow them to more easily discuss future military activities and political maneuverings. It had been made clear that with their missiles, bombers, submarines, and computerized firing systems, the escalation of any situation to Armageddon could be done far more easily than anybody desired. After stepping so close to the brink, both the U.S. and the USSR worked to reduce their nuclear tensions in the years immediately following. The most immediate culmination of this work was the signing of the Partial Test Ban Treaty in 1963, in which the U.S. and USSR agreed to no longer test nuclear weapons in the atmosphere, underwater, or in outer space. Testing underground continued, allowing for further weapons development, but the worldwide fallout risks were purposefully reduced, and the era of using massive nuclear tests as a form of saber-rattling ended.

In December 1979, NATO decided to deploy cruise and Pershing II missiles in Western Europe in response to Soviet deployment of intermediate range mobile missiles, and in the early 1980s, a "dangerous Soviet-US nuclear confrontation" arose. In New York on June 12, 1982, one million people gathered to protest nuclear weapons, and to support the second UN Special Session on Disarmament. As the nuclear abolitionist movement grew, there were many protests at the Nevada Test Site. For example, on February 6, 1987, nearly 2,000 demonstrators, including six members of Congress, protested against nuclear weapons testing and more than 400 people were arrested. Four of the significant groups organizing this renewal of anti-nuclear activism were Greenpeace, The American Peace Test, The Western Shoshone, and Nevada Desert Experience.

Initial Proliferation

The United Kingdom had been an integral part of the Manhattan Project following the Quebec Agreement in 1943. The passing of the McMahon Act by the United States in 1946 unilaterally broke this partnership and prevented the passage of any further information to the United Kingdom. The British Government under Clement Attlee determined that it would be essential for there to be a British Bomb. Because of the involvement in the Manhattan Project Britain had extensive knowledge in some areas, but not in others.

An improved version of 'Fat Man' was developed, and on 26 February 1952, Prime Minister Winston Churchill announced that the United Kingdom also had an atomic bomb and a successful test took place on the 3rd October 1952. At first these were free-fall bombs and then there was a missile, Blue Steel, and a later-canceled MRBM, Blue Streak. Anglo-American cooperation on

Nuclear weapons was restored by the 1958 US-UK Mutual Defence Agreement. As a result of this and the Polaris Sales Agreement, the United Kingdom has bought United States designs for submarine missiles and fitted its own warheads. It retains full independent control over the use of the missiles. It no longer possesses any free-fall bombs. France had been heavily involved in nuclear research before World War II through the work of the Joliot-Curies. This was discontinued after the war because of the instability of the Fourth Republic and the lack of finance available. However, in the 1950s a civil nuclear research program was started, a byproduct of which would be plutonium.

In 1956 a secret Committee for the Military Applications of Atomic Energy was formed and a development program for delivery vehicles started. With the return of Charles de Gaulle to the presidency of France in 1958 the final decisions to build a bomb were taken, and a successful test took place in 1960. Since then France has developed and maintained its own nuclear deterrent. In 1951 China and the Soviet Union signed an agreement whereby China would supply uranium ore in exchange for technical assistance in producing nuclear weapons. In 1953 China had established a research program under the guise of civilian nuclear energy. Throughout the 1950s the Soviet Union provided large amounts of equipment, but as the relations between the two countries worsened, the amount of assistance was reduced, and in 1959 the donation of a bomb for copying purposes was refused. Despite this, rapid progress was made with the test of an atomic bomb on the 16th October 1964 at Lop Nur, a nuclear missile on 25 October 1966, and of a hydrogen bomb on the 14th June 1967. Nuclear warheads were produced from 1968 and thermonuclear warheads from 1974. It is also thought that Chinese warheads have been successfully miniaturised from 2200 kg to 700 kg through the use of designs obtained by espionage from the United States. The current number of weapons is unknown owing to strict secrecy, but it is thought that up to 2000 warheads may have been produced, though far fewer may be available for use. China is the only nuclear weapons state to have guaranteed the non-first use of nuclear weapons.

Cold War

After World War II, the balance of power between the Eastern and Western blocs, resulting in the fear of global destruction, prevented the further military use of atomic bombs. This fear was even a central part of Cold War strategy, referred to as the doctrine of Mutually Assured Destruction ("MAD" for short). So important was this balance to international political stability that a treaty, the Anti-Ballistic Missile Treaty (or ABM treaty), was signed by the U.S. and the USSR in 1972 to curtail the development of defences against nuclear weapons and the ballistic missiles which carry them. This doctrine resulted in a large increase in the number of nuclear weapons, as each side sought to ensure it possessed the firepower to destroy the opposition in all possible scenarios and against all perceived threats. Early delivery systems for nuclear devices were primarily bombers like the United States B-29 Superfortress and Convair B-36, and later the B-52 Stratofortress. Ballistic missile systems, based on Wernher von Braun's World War II designs (specifically the V2 rocket), were developed by both United States and Soviet Union teams (in the case of the U.S., effort was directed by the German scientists and engineers although the Soviet Union also made extensive use of captured German scientists, engineers, and technical data).

These systems, after testing, were used to launch satellites, such as Sputnik, and to propel the Space Race, but they were primarily developed to create the capability of Intercontinental Ballistic Missiles (ICBMs) with which nuclear powers could deliver that destructive force anywhere on the globe. These systems continued to be developed throughout the Cold War, although plans and treaties, beginning with the Strategic Arms Limitation Treaty (SALT I), restricted deployment of these systems until, after the fall of the Soviet Union, system development essentially halted, and many weapons were disabled and destroyed. There have been a number of potential nuclear disasters. Following air accidents U.S. nuclear weapons have been lost near Atlantic City, New Jersey (1957); Savannah, Georgia (1958); Goldsboro, North Carolina (1961); off the coast of Okinawa (1965); in the sea near Palomares, Spain (1966); and near Thule, Greenland (1968). Most of the lost weapons were recovered, the Spanish device after three months' effort by the DSV Alvin and DSV Aluminaut.

The Soviet Union was less forthcoming about such incidents, but the environmental group Greenpeace believes that there are around forty non-U.S. nuclear devices that have been lost and not recovered, compared to eleven lost by America, mostly in submarine disasters. The U.S. has tried to recover Soviet devices, notably in the 1974 Operation Jennifer using the specialist salvage vessel *Hughes Glomar Explorer*. On January 27, 1967, more than 60 nations signed the Outer Space Treaty, banning nuclear weapons in space.

The end of the Cold War failed to end the threat of nuclear weapon use, although global fears of nuclear war reduced substantially. In a major move of symbolic de-escalation, Boris Yeltsin, on January 26, 1992, announced that Russia planned to stop targeting United States cities with nuclear weapons.

Second Nuclear Age

Although it had started before the end of the Cold War, the *second nuclear age*-proliferation of nuclear weapons among lesser powers and for reasons other than the American-Soviet rivalry-really began with the end of the Cold War. India's first atomic-test explosion was in 1974 with Smiling Buddha, which it described as a "peaceful nuclear explosion". India tested fission and perhaps fusion devices in 1998, and Pakistan successfully tested fission devices that same year, raising concerns that they would use nuclear weapons on each other. All of the former Soviet bloc countries with nuclear weapons returned their warheads to Russia by 1996.

In January 2004, Pakistani metallurgist and weapons scientist Abdul Qadeer Khan confessed to having been a part of an international proliferation network of materials, knowledge, and machines from Pakistan to Libya, Iran, and North Korea. South Africa also had an active program to develop uranium-based nuclear weapons, but dismantled its nuclear weapon program in the 1990s. It is not believed that it actually tested such a weapon though it later claimed to have constructed several crude devices which it eventually dismantled. In the late 1970s American spy satellites detected a "brief, intense, double flash of light near the southern tip of Africa." Known as the Vela Incident, it was speculated to have been a South African or possibly Israeli nuclear weapons test, though some feel that it may have been caused by natural events.

Israel is widely believed to possess an arsenal of potentially up to several hundred nuclear warheads, but this has never been officially confirmed or denied (though the existence of their Dimona nuclear facility were confirmed by Mordechai Vanunu in 1986). North Korea announced in 2003 that it also had several nuclear explosives though it has not been confirmed and the validity of this has been a subject of scrutiny amongst weapons experts. The first detonation of a nuclear weapon by the Democratic People's Republic of Korea was the 2006 North Korean nuclear test, conducted on October 9, 2006. On the 25th of May 2009 North Korea continued nuclear testing, violating United Nations Security Council Resolution 1718.

In Iran, Ayatollah Ali Khamenei issued a fatwa forbidding the production, stockpiling and use of nuclear weapons on August 9, 2005. The full text of the fatwa was released in an official statement at the meeting of the International Atomic Energy Agency (IAEA) in Vienna. Despite this, however, there is mounting concern in many nations about Iran's refusal to halt its nuclear power program, which many (including some members of the US Government) fear is a cover for weapons development.

NUCLEAR WEAPONS IN THE TWENTY-FIRST CENTURY

Nuclear weapons played a pivotal role in international security during the latter half of the twentieth century. Despite rapid increases in communications, transportation, and weapons technology, there has been no large-scale strategic conflict since the Second World War. Nuclear weapons, as the most destructive instruments ever invented, had a stabilizing effect on superpower relations by making any conflict unacceptably costly. However, geopolitical change and the evolution of military technology suggest that the composition of our nuclear forces and our strategy for their employment may be different in the twenty-first century. The time is right for a fundamental rethinking of our expectations and requirements for these unique weapons.

Nuclear weapons are one component of an integrated defence strategy that includes diplomacy and conventional forces. The principal role of nuclear weapons was and continues to be that of deterring any potential adversaries from an attack on America or our vital interests. This role is expected to continue for as long as nuclear weapons hold the appellation of ýÿsupreme" instruments of military force. However, this does not mean that their role in military planning will not change at all. Changes in the geopolitical environment and the inexorable advance of military technology here and abroad suggest that the position of nuclear weapons in national security policy will evolve with time. Given the unique destructive power of nuclear weapons, it is essential that this evolution be planned, to the extent possible, with due consideration of the integration of strategic nuclear forces into a consistent and comprehensive policy for national security.

Even with the dramatic changes that have occurred in the world during the past decade, nuclear warplanning today is similar in many respects to what it was during the Cold War. The Single Integrated Operational Plan (SIOP) is focused on a massive counterattack strategy that aims to eliminate the ability of an adversary to inflict further damage to American interests. Nuclear weapons provide an assured retaliatory capability to convince any adversary that aggression or coercion would be met with a response that would be certain, overwhelming, and devastating. It is often, but not universally, thought that nuclear weapons would be used only in extremis, when the nation is in the gravest danger. While there has been some discussion of "single weapon" strikes against isolated targets, such as sites of weapons of mass destruction, most of the attention in nuclear strategy has been and is directed toward large-scale engagements. This may not be true in the future.

The advance of conventional weapons technology may result in the ability of conventional weapons to perform some of the missions currently assigned to nuclear weapons. For example, take the case of a road mobile ballistic missile. If one knows the location of such a target and if one can place a conventional weapon on that target with meter-scale accuracy, then it can be destroyed without a nuclear weapon. On the other hand, if one does not know the location of the target to within many kilometers then even a nuclear weapon may not destroy it. The key parameters required for target destruction are intelligence and precision delivery, not the explosive force of the weapon. However, even if a weapon is precisely delivered to the correct target point, countermeasures as simple as steel netting, boulder fields, or decoys complicate reliance on conventional weapons with limited radii of destruction.

The role of nuclear weaponry as the ultimate deterrent to aggression and the ultimate destructive force in combat will likely lead to the retention of at least some nuclear forces for decades to come. However, the composition of our nuclear arsenal may undergo significant modification to respond to changing conditions, changing military needs, and changes in our confidence in our ability to maintain credible nuclear forces without nuclear testing or large-scale weapons production. Options for precision delivery of nuclear weapons may reduce the requirement for high yield. Lower yield weapons could be produced as modifications of existing weapons designs, or they could employ more rugged and simpler designs that might be developed and maintained with high confidence without nuclear testing and with a smaller nuclear weapons complex than we envision is required to maintain our current nuclear forces.

To the role that nuclear weapons might play in the twenty-first century, starting about 2020. A twenty-year horizon was chosen because over this time scale it is possible to make reasonable projections of technology and some assumptions about the probable threat situation. It takes about twenty years for substantially new weapons technologies to be developed and fielded into dependable military systems.

Since this is true for other countries as well as the United States, one can project the development of potential adversarial capabilities to some degree. Of course, changes in governments could occur quickly compared to this time scale, but the technology that would be employed against the United States would proceed more slowly. This chapter focuses on state-to-state defence and does not explicitly consider terrorism or the rapid evolution of entirely new state threats. It is unlikely that an emergent power would be able to develop the technology necessary to confront the United States on a time scale faster than two decades without some obvious indicators that would enable our technological or diplomatic response.

Why is this an important issue now? Current plans call for the deployment of the "next generation" of strategic forces in about 2020, including replacements for intercontinental ballistic missiles (ICBMs), the Ohio-class ballistic missile submarine, and perhaps even the venerable B52 bomber. This strategic modernization will be expensive, and it is not too soon to begin the debate over what kinds of strategic forces are needed to meet future needs.

It takes at least a decade to deploy a new technology, and if research and development are required, additional time may be needed. For such a key component of national defence, it is not sufficient to merely demonstrate that new systems work. There must be sufficient time to shake out the inevitable problems associated with new systems so as to make them dependable beyond reasonable doubt of our own government and the governments of potential adversaries. Time must also be allowed for the negotiation of treaties or other international agreements that support the new force structure and that preclude the marginalization of our forces by either a massive breakout or any other action that would reduce the effectiveness of our forces. Finally, the twentieth century repeatedly demonstrated that sweeping geopolitical changes occur on a short time scale compared to our ability to respond with new technologies or doctrines. It is imperative to consider the widest range of potential options before a crisis develops and to maintain a sufficiently robust research and development base to enable a response at that time.

The development of naval air power during the 1930s is a prime example of the need to evaluate the role of new technologies well before any anticipated engagement. The development of radar and ballistic missiles during the 1940s is an example of technologies developed during a conflict using preexisting foundations of research and technology. Some investment in thinking about future strategic forces now could reap significant dividends in the future.

Planning for future strategic defence is a highly complex affair that requires the consideration of many possible contingencies. This chapter is not intended to be a complete analysis of such a complex topic. Rather, its purpose is to stimulate thinking about changes in the international environment and technology that might be expected to influence the makeup of our strategic warfighting capability.

In order to set the stage, I first present a brief overview of the geopolitical situation that might reasonably be expected to influence defence strategy in 2020. The weapons technology might be available to the United States and other countries. Some force structures, including weapons and supporting infrastructure, that might satisfy future defence needs. The chapter concludes with a summary and suggestions for further work.

THE INTERNATIONAL SITUATION IN THE TWENTY-FIRST CENTURY

Before one can rationally future defence needs, it is necessary to know what one is defending against. The past decade has demonstrated the difficulty and danger of predicting the geopolitical future, but there are some forecasts that can be made with reasonable confidence.

Strategic Threats to U.S. National Security in the Twenty-First Century

Future national security threats to the United States might be divided into three major categories: major power conflicts, especially those involving Russia and China; regional conflicts, including potential nuclear states such as Iran, Iraq, or North Korea; and conflicts involving terrorist groups and other nonstate organizations. Only the first two major categories will be considered here, since it is arguable whether there is any role for strategic nuclear forces in dealing with terrorism and substate threats. However, strategic conflicts can be sparked by terrorist acts, as was the case in the First World War and other conflicts.

Russia – During the past 200 years European Russia has sustained a series of catastrophes including the invasion of Napoleon, the Crimean War, the First World War, the Revolution, the Second World War, and now the transition from a communist state to something else. In each case the country recovered within a generation. Even after the Second World War, when the country was essentially in ruins, it came back to launch Sputnik within twelve years. While one cannot predict what will happen in a country so volatile as Russia, it is not unreasonable to assume that it will endeavour to return to a conventional military power while continuing to rely on a significant nuclear capability. It is clear from Russia's investment in conventional military technology that it wishes to reassert its status in this area and to continue a lucrative business in the international arms trade.

China – China's international aims are in development, but their long stated intention to "reunify" Taiwan into the mainland and their territorial moves in the South China Sea indicate that they plan to play a broader role on the international stage. China has a small nuclear arsenal but one capable of inflicting unacceptable damage on American territory and interests. It is unclear at present what, if any, impact alleged Chinese nuclear espionage will have on the modernization of its nuclear arsenal. However, it is worth noting that China has several nuclear weapons systems in the advanced development stage including a new cruise missile, which presumably can carry a nuclear warhead, and new land-launched and sea-launched ballistic missiles. Road mobile nuclear capable missiles add a degree of survivability to China's limited nuclear arsenal. The desire to develop an operational ballistic missile submarine is another suggestion that China is concerned about the survivability of its nuclear forces and perhaps is a comment on its future goals of power projection outside of the immediate Pacific area.

Other Countries ýÿ The nuclear tests of India and Pakistan again demonstrate that countries will act in their own perceived national interests, sometimes in direct opposition to the wishes of the United States or to previous treaty commitments or arrangements. Continued tensions in South Asia, including Sino-

Indian tensions, bear close monitoring, but they may not directly involve the United States. The Middle East will continue to be a problem area due to the misalignment of ethnic, cultural, and national borders. The prospects for Arab or Islamic unification do not appear imminent at present, but historically this unification has relied on a charismatic leader, whose advent is difficult to predict. Continued problems in the Balkans and elsewhere in the world may tax American and allied conventional capabilities, but such conflicts are not expected to assume a nuclear dimension in the foreseeable future. North Korea is presumed to have at least some nuclear capability and has demonstrated remarkable progress in ballistic missile technology, despite its perilous economic condition. Japan and South Korea look upon North Korea's nuclear ambitions with concern and could pursue their own nuclear programs if they felt uncertainty in the American nuclear umbrella. Similar concerns could apply to Taiwan in light of recent statements made by the People's Republic of China.

Nuclear engagement scenarios are not necessarily binary. Third countries may feel compelled to intervene in disputes between nuclear states or in conflicts involving weapons of mass destruction that could spill over into their territory or interests. For example, China may feel a need to act in a nuclear exchange between India and Pakistan. Similarly, Israel may feel a need to act in a major conflict of its neighbours that involved weapons of mass destruction.

FOREIGN WEAPONS TECHNOLOGY IN THE TWENTY-FIRST CENTURY

Trends evident today suggest that by 2020 many countries in the world will have access to several important technologies.

- Weapons of mass destruction: India and Pakistan graphically demonstrated the ability of midlevel technology states to construct or obtain nuclear weapons. Chemical and biological weapons are assumed to be within the reach of many countries today.
- Long-range ballistic missile technology: It is apparent that countries like North Korea, Iran, India, Pakistan, and other

countries have or will soon have the capability to project force at intercontinental distances. The developing international marketplace in these technologies may make long-range missiles available to almost any country that has the money and the basic technical capability to acquire and use them. Although such missiles may lack the precision of current U.S. weapons, they might be entirely adequate for the delivery of weapons of mass destruction.

- Space imaging: Commercial services already provide high-resolution images from space. The technical capability to provide these images in real time to customers around the world should be expected to develop. Whether international agreements will be enacted to prevent collection against sensitive sites remains to be seen. At some point, Third World countries will have the capability to launch their own intelligence satellites or will pay others to launch them, thus bypassing the need for commercial services.
- Russian weapons technology: Despite its economic troubles, Russia is committing significant resources to the research and development of advanced conventional weapons. Part of the reason for this is certainly to provide a credible defence of Russia and its vital interests. However, Russia also sees a lucrative international arms market that appreciates the low cost and operational simplicity of its weapons. One might expect more countries to have access to "last generation" but quite capable Russian military technology including missiles, air defenses, submarines, tanks, and other systems.
- Advanced communications and computer technology: The spread of communications and computer technology will serve as a force multiplier for a growing number of countries. The ability to effectively employ a small number of electronic weapons against a technologically and/or numerically superior enemy is a cost-effective force-levelling tactic.

The United States will enjoy superiority in conventional and nuclear weapons as long as adequate investments are made in research and development and in the deployment of the resulting weapons systems. However, we should expect other countries to employ many of our ideas in their own defence strategy including the simple copying of our technology and doctrines, or the use of our technology to develop weapons systems of their own. They may also attempt to exploit weaknesses in our advanced technology through means such as electromagnetic weapons, chemical and/ or biological weapons, and other "asymmetric means."

U.S. DEFENCE TECHNOLOGIES IN THE TWENTY-FIRST CENTURY

Conventional Military Technology

Advances in military technology have been much discussed in the literature and are said to be leading toward a revolution in military affairs. Relevant to the present discussion, there are several advances in conventional weapons technology that deserve mention.

- Advanced precision munitions: It is already possible for cruise missiles to deliver payloads to targets hundreds of miles from their launch point with few meter accuracy. High precision for intercontinental missiles, either land- or sea-launched, is also possible. Given that ballistic missile reentry vehicles arrive on target with velocities of thousands of meters per second, it is not necessary to have explosive payloads to destroy some classes of targets.
- Advanced real-time imagery and data fusion: Data collection from satellites and from unmanned forward platforms will enable real-time remote battle management, including the direction of precision munitions to distant, even mobile, targets.
- Antiballistic missile technology will mature if the appropriate investment is made, enabling some defence against limited missile attacks. Analogous defenses could be developed against cruise missiles and aircraft, although these threats are in many ways a tougher problem due to the greater number of potential entry points and the availability of stealth technology.

- Information warfare may develop in such a fashion to enable the United States to interdict enemy command, control, and communications.

There has been much discussion of other advanced conventional technologies including unmanned aircraft, sensor technology, beam weapons, and so on. In this chapter we will focus on those technologies that could have a strategic impact and that are related to the changing role of nuclear weapons. The importance of considering future defence against ballistic missiles, cruise missiles, and aircraft cannot be overestimated. The inexorable advance of technology will eventually make such defenses feasible and will put them within the grasp of any country that wishes to have them. Such is the case now with reasonably sophisticated air defenses. Long range strategic planners must at least consider the return of a traditional "armour /antiarmor" competition even for strategic forces. Stealth technologies, advanced countermeasures, and new technologies will affect these trades but will not change the fundamental ability of defence technologies to influence strategic thinking.

Nuclear Weapons—Related Technology

Nuclear weapons pack incredible destructive force into a small, deliverable package. In addition to their psychological deterrent value, they are the only current means of holding at risk several classes of targets.

- Mobile targets, such as road mobile and rail mobile missiles
- Fixed moderately hard targets, such as missile silos
- Distributed targets, such as airfields or naval bases
- Hard targets, such as deeply buried command structures
- Superhard targets, such as facilities located beneath mountains

Conventional weapons might be able to address some of the missions currently assigned to nuclear weapons, but not all of them. Some targets, like missile silos and command and control structures, are sufficiently hard that no conventional weapon will have the energy to defeat them.

Other targets, such as airfields and naval bases, are sufficiently dispersed that a massive amount of conventional explosives would be required for their destruction. Even though conventional weapons could damage or destroy such targets, they could do so today only over an extended time frame and with the use of limited resources that may be required in other theatres of operation. Future conventional weapons designs may change this, but there are still limits on the amount of damage that can be caused with a given quantity of high explosive. For these and other reasons, nuclear weapons are expected to continue to play a role in strategic doctrine, independent of their role as a psychological deterrent to aggression.

The United States employs a counterforce strategy that targets military assets that could inflict damage to our national interests. We do not threaten cities or populations as in a countervalue policy, although there is an implicit threat of doing so that is a potent element of the deterrent calculus. American nuclear weapons systems are designed to hold specific classes of targets at risk, using the minimum explosive forces necessary to accomplish the mission. However, a sizable factor governing the explosive force required to defeat a target of given hardness is the precision with which weapons can be delivered. The evolution of accurate delivery systems could change engagement strategies for nuclear weapons, in some cases reducing the required yield or even eliminating the need for an explosion at all.

Once again, the use of conventional weapons presumes a level of detailed information on the location and characteristics of the target that has so far eluded military planners. A reliance on precision conventional munitions for some strategic missions presumes a major investment in intelligence collection and analysis tools, including accurate means of assessing target damage following an attack. This is particularly important for strategic targets such as mobile missiles or weapons of mass destruction that could, if they survive, inflict significant damage.

Advances in military technology may change the makeup and use of our strategic forces in several ways.

- Some important classes of targets, such as mobile missiles, might be effectively dealt with by long-range precision conventional weapons. One can envision submarine-launched ballistic missiles (SLBMs) and intercontinental ballistic missiles (ICBMs), loaded with such precision weapons, which could be directed by real-time intelligence to targets anywhere on the planet within 30 minutes. Maneuvering reentry vehicles could enable these weapons to follow and destroy moving targets.
- A 5-kiloton (kt) nuclear explosive detonated on a 30-foot-thick missile silo door will vaporize that door, destroying the missile inside. With precision delivery many hard targets might be able to be defeated with nuclear explosives having lower yield than we might currently employ. Such lower-yield weapons could use simpler and/or more robust designs than we have in our current arsenal. Simpler, more robust designs, in turn, might allow the nuclear arsenal to be maintained with a smaller maintenance and production complex than is required to support the sophisticated, highly optimized weapons in our stockpile. As in the case of advanced conventional weapons, the use of lower-yield nuclear weapons against hardened targets could be made problematic through the use of relatively simple countermeasures. In the example of a silo door, shielding could be used to separate the blast from the door area, reducing the effectiveness of the weapon.
- Widely dispersed targets require energy (yield) for assured destruction. Several dispersed lower-yield weapons will produce the same effect as a single higher-yield weapon. Using multiple weapons on a single target assumes that fratricide effects can be dealt with in planning multiple nuclear bursts in a single target area. Such an approach also requires a larger number of weapons, a factor that would be more challenging if deep cuts in weapons numbers are negotiated. A benefit of lower-yield weapons is that the collateral damage sustained by the near-target area may be reduced, an important factor in attacks near urban areas.

- Some very hard targets require high yield to destroy them. No application of conventional explosives or even lower-yield nuclear explosives will destroy such targets, which might include hardened structures buried beneath hundreds of feet of earth or rock. For such purposes it might be desirable to retain a small number of higher-yield nuclear weapons in the arsenal as deterrents against enemy confidence in the survival of such targets.
- Superhard targets, such as those found under certain Russian mountains, may not be able to be defeated reliably by even high-yield nuclear weapons. In this case, one might use a different strategy such as "functional defeat" in which power, communications, or other vital functions are eliminated or denied without the physical destruction of the main target. Alternately, one might use negotiations to eliminate a target, bargaining away a limited set of special targets for concessions on our part.

These proposals are a departure from conventional thinking on nuclear issues. For example, our ability to negotiate away superhard targets would be very difficult at best. Others, such as the ability of precision advanced conventional munitions to hold at risk mobile and other soft-point targets, are more realistic and require only projections of current technology. In the latter case, a challenge may come from arms control concerns of other countries that see their own nuclear forces made marginal. Also, potential adversaries may use "asymmetric means" to counter our advanced technology.

An important consideration in thinking about lower-yield nuclear forces for most of our strategic nuclear requirements is that such weapons could be much simpler than our current highly optimized nuclear designs. Given sufficient throw-weight on our missiles, we could use gun-assembled or other simple, rugged designs that might be maintained with high confidence without nuclear testing. Such designs would require a significantly smaller industrial plant for their maintenance than our current forces. If based on uranium weapons designs, a much smaller plutonium infrastructure would be required. Other technologies specific to high-yield nuclear weapons could be placed in a standby mode rather than a production mode. Finally, simpler weapons might be maintained with higher confidence for longer periods by a weapons staff that has little or no direct experience with nuclear testing. However, should the country elect to follow such a path it will still be necessary to retain expertise in more sophisticated nuclear designs as a hedge against changing conditions in the future. There is an additional, nontechnical, consideration that will influence future nuclear policy. Given current and projected scientific capabilities, it is difficult or impossible to confidently field a new, highly optimized, nuclear warhead design without nuclear testing. For this and other reasons, the United States intends to maintain its existing nuclear designs into the indefinite future. This is a fundamental change in how we maintain our arsenal. Recent concerns about espionage in the weapons program raise questions about our ability to keep weapons designs secret over many decades. Some in the intelligence community contend that a fixed target, such as our nuclear designs, will be compromised by a determined adversary given sufficient time. Information about our designs could provide important guidance to countries that wish to improve their own nuclear arsenals. Such information would also be advantageous to countries attempting to optimize some future ballistic missile defence system of their own for use against our systems. Finally, it could assist potential adversaries in deploying their strategic forces in a manner designed to make it difficult for us to assure their destruction.

Planners need to consider what we will do when, and not if, the details of our nuclear forces become known by a potential adversary. There are several paths that could be employed here, including disinformation, counterintelligence, etc. One path that has been proven to work has been to change our forces on a regular basis in response to evolving military requirements and technology options. The certification of substantially new nuclear weapons designs is difficult or impossible to do with high confidence without underground nuclear testing. However, the United States has a large archive of previously tested designs that might be fielded with reasonable confidence to meet evolving military needs. In addition, the current stockpile has significant flexibility for modification for new requirements. Such flexibility was most recently evidenced by the modification of the B61 bomb to provide earth-penetrating capability. A move toward a mixed force of long-range conventional and lower-yield nuclear weapons with improved accuracy would be another means of meeting this need. Such decisions need not be exclusive. It may be wisest to employ multiple technologies, both nuclear and nonnuclear, to create a robust future strategic posture.

STRATEGIC FORCES TO MEET FUTURE DEFENCE NEEDS

Planning strategic forces is a highly complicated affair that must include technical, geopolitical, and military considerations. A full analysis is not attempted here. The purpose of this section is to suggest some broad options that can be used as starting points for more detailed treatment. Although this section concentrates on strategic forces, it is worth noting that several countries possess potent "nonstrategic" nuclear forces that are designed for tactical engagements. Nonstrategic forces include nuclear artillery shells, atomic demolition munitions, short-range missiles, and air-delivered bombs. While such weapons are typically lower in yield than most strategic bombs and warheads, they are still nuclear explosives with destructive power vastly greater than conventional weapons. One might expect the division between "tactical" and "strategic" weapons to blur in the future, especially if significant reductions in strategic arsenals occur.

Status Quo

Nuclear weapons represent the ultimate defence of the nation, a deterrent against any and all potential adversaries. Combined with diplomacy and conventional military capabilities, nuclear weapons have helped to avoid a large-scale conflict between leading world powers for over fifty years. This is an astonishing achievement given the acceleration in communications and transportation that took place during this time. When the Cold War ended, the U.S. nuclear stockpile consisted of a set of highly optimized warheads and bombs on highly reliable missiles and aircraft. These weapons systems were designed primarily to counter the massive Soviet threat. They were and are the most advanced of their kind in the world. Current plans call for them to be retained essentially indefinitely. There are several good reasons for this.

- These weapons are safe, reliable, and meet performance requirements.
- We have nuclear test data that support our understanding of their operation.
- New warheads of comparable capability are difficult or impossible to field without nuclear testing.
- They can be modified in many ways to respond to changing military requirements, as was done when the B61 bomb was modified to give it an earth-penetrating capability.

This scenario maintains a triad of ICBMs, SLBMs, and bombers. More than one type of weapon is maintained in each leg of the triad to provide backup capability should one weapon type encounter a problem. This strategy served us well during the Cold War. Given the rapidity with which the geopolitical situation can change, there is merit in following a prudent and conservative path for future nuclear forces. There are several potential disadvantages to maintaining the existing stockpile indefinitely. Over time such highly optimized systems may be less well suited to military requirements. Refurbishment and other changes will be made to aging warheads and bombs, changes that might be difficult to certify without nuclear testing. Also, the cost of maintaining these weapons is high for both DoD and DOE. In the case of DOE, an extensive infrastructure of laboratories and plants is required for the Stockpile Stewardship program, including a new manufacturing capability for plutonium pits. Finally, the current stockpile may not be credible against some set of potential adversaries. For example, if a national emergency were to develop that involved the imminent use of weapons of mass destruction against American interests, would an adversary consider our threat of a multiwarhead attack by the Peacekeeper ICBM or a Trident SLBM as overkill and hence not a realistic threat? Such a reliance on high-yield strategic weapons could lead to "self-deterrence," a limitation on strategic options, and consequently a lessening of the stabilizing effect of nuclear weapons.

Reduced Stockpile of Existing Designs

This scenario assumes that arms control initiatives have make it advantageous to the United States to greatly reduce our stockpile of existing nuclear weapons. It is similar to Scenario 1 with lower force levels. One can debate the merit of eliminating one arm of the strategic triad or the nonstrategic (i.e. tactical) nuclear forces under such circumstances, depending on the depth of the reductions. Cost savings associated with reduced numbers are not directly proportional to the number of weapons since a significant infrastructure is required to support any type of modern nuclear design. The cost advantage would be in the size of the required production plant and not in the diversity of technical capabilities that are required.

At very low stockpile numbers it may be useful to explicitly consider a "flexible stockpile" strategy that takes advantage of the flexibility inherent in current nuclear weapon designs. The United States could have a mixed force of weapons based upon current types suitably modified to meet evolving military needs. Special consideration might be given to maneuvering reentry vehicles that can deal effectively with enemy defenses. One could consider tailored output weapons for special applications such as those that produce an enhanced electromagnetic pulse for the disabling of electronics or those that produce enhanced radiation for the destruction of chemical or biological weapons with minimum collateral damage. (There is serious doubt in the nuclear weapons community as to whether such systems could be introduced into the stockpile without additional nuclear testing.) Careful consideration must be given to single-point failure in a reduced stockpile. For example, the use of a common missile or a common warhead for ICBMs and SLBMs would save money but would introduce a potential single-point failure in the majority of strategic forces.

In selecting weapons that would be maintained in a smaller force structure, consideration might be given to those that are the most rugged, the easiest and cheapest to maintain, and the most flexible. Highly optimized weapons may be more efficient, but efficiency can come at the cost of complexity of maintenance.

Without nuclear testing, small changes caused by natural aging or required component replacements will introduce some uncertainty into the stockpile, uncertainty that must be figured into military strategy. Understanding such uncertainty is especially important if the number of weapons types is reduced, admitting the possibility of single-point failure of a large part of the force. It may be advisable to view ruggedness and ease of maintenance as principal criteria for the selection of the types and distribution of weapons within a reduced stockpile. Given the uncertainty of future military needs, the ability of a weapon to be maintained, modified, and/or certified without nuclear testing may also be an important element in the decision process.

Mixed Conventional and Nuclear Strategic Forces

Reasonable assumptions about the development of advanced conventional munitions leads to a scenario where the strategic workload is carried by a combination of nuclear and nonnuclear forces. It is possible to envision nonnuclear components to each of the arms of the strategic triad. Using conventional ICBMs and SLBMs, or their projected replacements, one could design reentry warheads to achieve high accuracy. These warheads would contain "smart" guidance systems that would receive intelligence handoffs from satellites or other sources before and/or during flight. Such systems would know that a target exists in a general area, be aware of its potential movement and signatures, and be able to home in on it. Given the kinetic energy of a reentering warhead, it might not be necessary for the system to contain high explosives. Hitting the target might be sufficient to destroy it. Similar warheads could be developed for cruise missiles that could be launched from bombers, submarines, or surface warships. In the case of cruise missiles, the lower velocity of delivery would require a high-explosive warhead.

A nonnuclear long-range weapon would be especially useful against limited numbers of time-urgent weapons of mass destruction targets such as biological weapons warheads that were in preparation for use against U.S. forces. Long-range nonnuclear weapons would enable such targets to be destroyed without causing the United States to be the first to employ nuclear weapons in a conflict. The use of nonnuclear strategic weapons against Russia, China, or other nuclear states would require care, since the appearance of such a weapon on long-range sensors might be indistinguishable from a nuclear attack by the United States.

A word of caution is needed on the use of precision munitions for high-value strategic targeting: The Kosovo conflict demonstrated very clearly that just the ability to place a weapon on the designated aim point is not enough to ensure mission success. Inaccurate target coordinates provided to pilots sometimes resulted in weapons being delivered very precisely to the wrong spot. Effective utilization of precision munitions demand that a premium be placed on the collection and the analysis of target information. This includes postattack damage assessments that determine the need for follow-on attacks and the ability of the adversary to use its weapons for offense or defence. The nuclear component in this scenario could take one of several forms. First, one could employ a small number of existing weapons designs to retain a traditional counterforce deterrent strategy. Second, one could modify existing designs to reduce their yield, relying on precision delivery to help achieve military objectives.

In this case one could use existing reentry warheads or develop new ones with the precision guidance necessary to destroy moderately-hard-point targets with low yield. Third, one could design and deploy a new set of nuclear weapons that do not require nuclear testing to be certified. Such weapons might be, but do not need to be, based on simple gun-assembled uranium designs that do not require a plutonium infrastructure and that do not require the same sophistication in nuclear weapons science and engineering as our current stockpile. However, nothing comes for free, and one must recognize that such simple weapons have important, perhaps fatal, tactical limitations that would preclude their use in some engagement scenarios. Also, such simple devices would be based on a very limited nuclear test database and would require extensive and expensive flight testing to assure that they could be delivered with the required precision. Fourth, one could consider a combination of new or modified low-yield warheads and some existing higher-yield designs to be retained against the possibility of unexpected developments in adversaries' defenses or of the need to hold very hard targets at risk. In this case one would need to retain much of the infrastructure of the current stockpile to ensure the continued performance of these highly optimized weapons. Savings could be achieved in the size of the plant complex required to remanufacture components and complete weapons.

Prospects for Wholly Nonnuclear Strategic Forces

It is almost impossible to conceive of technological and political developments that would enable the United States to meet its defence needs in 2020 without nuclear weapons. There are several reasons for this. First, nuclear weapons continue to play a vital role in deterring other countries from launching significant military strikes against America, our allies, or our vital interests. The real threat of not just military defeat but national annihilation is a potent deterrent now and should be expected to remain so for at least the next few decades. Second, it does not appear possible with current or projected technology to assure ourselves that there are no—and never will be any nuclear weapons in the hands of potential adversaries. Given the unique destructive power of nuclear weapons, an asymmetry of this kind should be unacceptable to American military planners. Third, the development of antiballistic missile defence is encouraging, but the assumption that a leak-proof shield can be fielded by 2020 is debatable. Fourth, some targets will not be able to be held at risk by any type of conventional weapon because of their extreme hardness. Fifth, the ability of an adversary to deliver a nuclear weapon by aircraft, cruise missile, naval vessel, or by clandestine insertion into this country are additional concerns beyond the long-range ballistic missile threat. Lacking the ability to deter such threats and to respond in kind would open up the country to blackmail.

It is critical in any discussion of strategic forces to consider the overall stability provided by technology and policy. Such calculations have become considerably more complex in the multipolar world that is expected to persist at least over the time scale addressed in this chapter.

The future is unpredictable, but we can count on it to be dynamic. Strategic thinking must be flexible and must consider the evolution of several possible futures, each of which has branches that are contingent on the geopolitical situation and technological capabilities here and abroad. Countries will respond to technology and policy developments in the United States and elsewhere. We must be careful that any changes to our strategic position make the overall situation better and not worse.

Russia has already promised that it will use "asymmetric means" to counter advanced U.S. technology. Official Chinese publications indicate that China will likely follow a similar strategy. The capabilities of their own research and development complex should not be underestimated. While Russia cannot yet match the United States in the most sophisticated technology, it has shown a remarkable ability to achieve military objectives through cleverness and sometimes through brute force. Finally, the development of advanced conventional strategic weapons could push the Russians to an even greater reliance on high-yield nuclear weapons. Rather than an evolution toward some fixed strategy, strategic thinking should be done along a flexible time line that recognizes changes in the world and in military technology. What may work at one time may not work at another time when the situation has substantially changed.

One "asymmetric" counter to advanced technology is cyber-warfare, including non-explosive weapons that could disable or render ineffective advanced conventional or even nuclear munitions. Precision kill requires sophisticated electronics, and electronics can be affected by various means such as radio frequency or microwave weapons. Russia's electromagnetic weapons program is perhaps the most advanced in the world, and at least some of this technology has been shared with China. Given the uncertainty in future advanced weapons technology, the United States may wish to retain some higher-yield nuclear weapons as hedges against the development of potent point or area defenses. The development of antisatellite weapons would create a similar complication to the United States if we were to rely on advanced conventional weapons that require precise targeting information to be effective.

Arms control initiatives will play an important role in the planning of future strategic forces. Proposed deep reductions in nuclear stockpiles may be a motivation for using conventional weapons as part of the strategic weapons mix. Such a decision will strongly depend on whether warheads or launchers are the counted quantity. If nuclear warheads and not delivery vehicles are the counted quantity, then existing or new launchers can be equipped with advanced conventional warheads. If missiles and aircraft are the counted quantity, we will need to be careful about treaties that allow only one warhead, nuclear or conventional, on a missile. Maintaining an effective deterrent requires a minimum number of nuclear weapons, and the dilution of our forces with conventional weapons could drive us from a counterforce strategy (military targets) to a countervalue strategy (cities) with attendant ethical and perhaps legal problems.

Arms control agreements can assist in strategic planning by restricting certain classes of weapons or targets. If, in some scenario, our weapons are particularly susceptible to nuclear interceptors, then we may wish to negotiate the elimination of nuclear interceptors in return for some other concession. If we are unable to destroy one or more targets by any weapon in our arsenal, we may want to attempt to negotiate away the target in return for assurances that we will not construct similarly hard targets in the United States. Such negotiations are by nature complex because they involve giving up different commodities on each side. However, the advantages of reduced reliance on nuclear weapons, with their large radii of destruction, might be an incentive. Also, the development of new conventional strategic weapons, the use of which might be incorporated into nonnuclear war planning and that will not necessarily lead to national destruction, should be considered with care.

One of the features of nuclear weapons is that they are so destructive that their use is reserved for only the most extreme cases. Making strategic weapons more "usable" could start the United States on a path of escalation that could exacerbate and not reduce the potential for war. Conversely, lowering the threshold for using nuclear weapons in response to a strategic situation could raise the level of care with which countries interact. This points to the need for a detailed stability analysis to be performed as a prelude to any arms control negotiations. Such an analysis must explicitly include the balance of nuclear forces, the state and projected future of ballistic missile defenses, and the ability of advanced conventional weapons to perform missions formerly assigned to nuclear weapons. The weapons research and development programs of potential adversaries will provide input to this analysis by providing pointers to future defence capabilities. And, of course, any analysis of future strategic weapons needs must necessarily consider the possible geopolitical situation that will be present at the time of their deployment. Finally, the distinction between tactical and strategic nuclear weapons will fade for small stockpiles. Both types of weapons must be included in negotiations for overall stability to be maintained.

Another important consideration in planning future strategic forces is cost. Nuclear weapons systems are sometimes considered expensive to maintain due to their complexity, their unique characteristics, and the lack of private industry support of some components of their infrastructure. In fact, nuclear weapons are cheaper to develop and to maintain than very large conventional force structures. This was the reason why NATO chose to rely on nuclear weapons as a principal part of its defence against the massive Soviet conventional threat in Europe. Nuclear weapons are considered expensive today because they are primarily strategic in nature and we are in the midst of a ýÿstrategic pause" that has lessened the perceived need for strategic weapons.

For the DoD, costs include operations, maintenance, and the development of next generation capabilities that will replace current systems upon their obsolescence. For the DOE, costs include the operation of the weapons laboratories and production plants and the material costs associated with weapons refurbishment. To first order, the cost of maintaining the DOE nuclear weapons complex is independent of the number of weapons in the stockpile. Some capability in uranium, plutonium, and other special materials is required. Scientific capabilities must be maintained, especially in those classified areas unique to nuclear weapons, to enable informed decisions to be made on weapons aging, component replacements, and future modifications. Tritium has some variable cost, as it must be produced to support some fixed number of weapons. Plutonium pit production can be maintained at a small rate at Los Alamos, but any stockpile above about one thousand weapons will require the construction of a new large production plant to replace the Rocky Flats facility, which ceased production in 1989. Should the country go to a precision low-yield nuclear force that is based on uranium rather than plutonium, the cost of the large pit-production facility could be avoided, and the remaining high-yield weapons that did employ plutonium pits could be supported by a modified Los Alamos plutonium facility.

The end of the Cold War, the evolution of new regional threats to international security, and the stated desire of many countries to reduce or eliminate their nuclear arsenals suggest that the time is right for a fundamental rethinking of the role of nuclear weapons in national security. Nuclear weapons, as the most destructive instruments yet invented, must be considered as part of a coordinated national security program that employs diplomacy, arms control initiatives, and conventional forces to optimize stability and peace in the world.

Technology assessments suggest that advanced conventional weapons delivered by ballistic or cruise missiles could defeat many targets that are presently targeted by nuclear weapons. Precision delivery of nuclear weapons would enable some classes of hard targets to be defeated with much lower yields than are currently employed. Some number of current nuclear weapons designs might be retained in order to address very hard targets or for traditional deterrent roles. Simple, rugged nuclear weapons designs that might be maintained at relatively low cost and without the need for nuclear testing might be a part of such a strategy.

Nuclear weapons cannot be uninvented. Nor can we assume that their role in strategic deterrence will never change. Prudent thought given to the role of nuclear weapons in the twenty-first century will reap handsome dividends for the national security of the United States and for the stability of the whole world.

6

Nuclear Non-Proliferation Treaty

The Treaty on the Non-Proliferation of Nuclear Weapons, also Nuclear Non-Proliferation Treaty (NPT or NNPT) is a treaty to limit the spread (proliferation) of nuclear weapons. The treaty came into force on 5 March 1970 and currently there are 189 states party to the treaty, five of which are recognized as nuclear weapon states: the United States, Russia, the United Kingdom, France, and China (also the five permanent members of the United Nations Security Council). Four non-parties to the treaty are known or believed to possess nuclear weapons. India, Pakistan and North Korea have openly tested and declared that they possess nuclear weapons, while Israel has had a policy of opacity regarding its own nuclear weapons program. North Korea acceded to the treaty, violated it, and withdrew from it in 2003.

The treaty was proposed by Ireland and Finland and they were the first to sign. The NPT consists of a preamble and eleven articles. Although the concept of "pillars" appears nowhere in the NPT, the treaty is nevertheless sometimes interpreted as a *three pillar* system, with an implicit balance among them:

1. *non-proliferation,*
2. *disarmament,* and
3. *the right to peacefully use nuclear technology.*

The treaty is reviewed each five years in meetings called Review Conferences of the Parties to the Treaty of Non-Proliferation of Nuclear Weapons. In addition, Sessions of the Preparatory Committee for the Review Conference take place on the intermediate years. Simultaneously, many events organized by independent institutions, groups of experts, think tanks and NGO's take place worldwide in order to provide reports and recommendations that compliment the Preparatory Committees. Even though the treaty was originally conceived with a limited duration of 25 years, the signing parties decided by consensus to extend the treaty indefinitely and without conditions during the Review Conference in New York City on May 11, 1995.

TREATY "PILLARS"

The NPT is commonly described as having three main "pillars": non-proliferation, disarmament, and peaceful use. This "pillars" concept has been questioned by some who believe that the NPT is, as its name suggests, principally about nonproliferation, and who worry that "three pillars" language misleadingly implies that the three elements have equivalent importance.

Non-proliferation

Five states are recognized by the NPT as nuclear weapon states (NWS): China (signed 1992), France (1992), the Soviet Union (1968; obligations and rights now assumed by the Russian Federation), the United Kingdom (1968), and the United States (1968) (The U.S., UK, and Soviet Union were the only states openly possessing such weapons among the original ratifiers of the treaty, which entered into force in 1970). These five nations are also the five permanent members of the United Nations Security Council. These five NWS agree not to transfer "nuclear weapons or other nuclear explosive devices" and "not in any way to assist, encourage, or induce" a non-nuclear weapon state (NNWS) to acquire nuclear weapons. NNWS parties to the NPT agree not to "receive," "manufacture" or "acquire" nuclear weapons or to "seek or receive any assistance in the manufacture of nuclear weapons". NNWS parties also agree to accept safeguards by the International Atomic Energy Agency (IAEA) to verify that they are not diverting nuclear energy from peaceful uses to nuclear weapons or other nuclear explosive devices.

The five NWS parties have made undertakings not to use their nuclear weapons against a non-NWS party except in response to a nuclear attack, or a conventional attack in alliance with a Nuclear Weapons State. However, these undertakings have not been incorporated formally into the treaty, and the exact details have varied over time. The U.S. also had nuclear warheads targeted at North Korea, a non-NWS state, from 1959 until 1991. The previous United Kingdom Secretary of State for Defence, Geoff Hoon, has also explicitly invoked the possibility of the use of the country's nuclear weapons in response to a non-conventional attack by "rogue states". In January 2006, President Jacques Chirac of France indicated that an incident of state-sponsored terrorism on France could trigger a small-scale nuclear retaliation aimed at destroying the "rogue state's" power centres.

Disarmament

The NPT's preamble contains language affirming the desire of treaty signatories to ease international tension and strengthen international trust so as to create someday the conditions for a halt to the production of nuclear weapons, and treaty on general and complete disarmament that liquidates, in particular, nuclear weapons and their delivery vehicles from national arsenals.

The wording of the NPT's Article VI arguably imposes only a vague obligation on all NPT signatories to move in the general direction of nuclear and total disarmament, saying, "Each of the Parties to the Treaty undertakes to pursue negotiations in good faith on effective measures relating to cessation of the nuclear arms race at an early date and to nuclear disarmament, and on a treaty on general and complete disarmament." Under this interpretation, Article VI does not strictly require all signatories to actually conclude a disarmament treaty. Rather, it only requires them "to negotiate in good faith."

On the other hand, some governments, especially non-nuclear-weapon states belonging to the Non-Aligned Movement, have interpreted Article VI's language as being anything but vague. In their view, Article VI constitutes a formal and specific obligation on the NPT-recognized nuclear-weapon states to disarm themselves of nuclear weapons, and argue that these states have failed to meet their obligation. Some government delegations to the Conference on Disarmament have put forth proposals for a complete and universal disarmament, but no disarmament treaty has emerged from these proposals. Critics of the NPT-recognized nuclear-weapon states sometimes argue that what they view as the failure of the NPT-recognized nuclear weapon states to disarm themselves of nuclear weapons, especially in the post-Cold War era, has angered some non-nuclear-weapon NPT signatories of the NPT. Such failure, these critics add, provides justification for the non-nuclear-weapon signatories to quit the NPT and develop their own nuclear arsenals.

Other observers have suggested that the linkage between proliferation and disarmament may also work the other way, i.e., that the failure to resolve proliferation threats in Iran and North Korea, for instance, will cripple the prospects for disarmament. No current nuclear weapons state, the argument goes, would seriously consider eliminating its last nuclear weapons without high confidence that other countries would not acquire them. Some observers have even suggested that the very progress of disarmament by the superpowers—which has led to the elimination of thousands of weapons and delivery systems —could eventually make the possession of nuclear weapons more attractive by increasing the perceived strategic value of a small arsenal. As one U.S. official and NPT expert warned in 2007, "logic suggests that as the number of nuclear weapons decreases, the 'marginal utility' of a nuclear weapon as an instrument of military power increases. At the extreme, which it is precisely disarmament's hope to create, the strategic utility of even one or two nuclear weapons would be huge."

Peaceful use of Nuclear Energy

The third pillar allows for and agrees upon the transfer of nuclear technology and materials to NPT signatory countries for the development of civilian nuclear energy programs in those countries, as long as they can demonstrate that their nuclear programs are not being used for the development of nuclear weapons. Since very few of the states with nuclear energy programs are willing to abandon the use of nuclear energy, the third pillar of the NPT under Article IV provides other states with the possibility to do the same, but under conditions intended to make it difficult to develop nuclear weapons.

The treaty recognizes the inalienable right of sovereign states to use nuclear energy for peaceful purposes, but restricts this right for NPT parties to be exercised "in conformity with Articles I and II" (the basic nonproliferation obligations that constitute the "first pillar" of the Treaty).

As the commercially popular light water reactor nuclear power station uses enriched uranium fuel, it follows that states must be able either to enrich uranium or purchase it on an international market. Mohamed ElBaradei, Director General of the International Atomic Energy Agency, has called the spread of enrichment and reprocessing capabilities the "Achilles' heel" of the nuclear nonproliferation regime.

As of 2007 13 states have an enrichment capability. Because the availability of fissile material has long been considered the principal obstacle to, and "pacing element" for, a country's nuclear weapons development effort, it was declared a major emphasis of U.S. policy in 2004 to prevent the further spread of uranium enrichment and plutonium reprocessing (a.k.a. "ENR") technology. Countries possessing ENR capabilities, it is feared, have what is in effect the option of using this capability to produce fissile material for weapons use on demand, thus giving them what has been termed a "virtual" nuclear weapons program.

The degree to which NPT members have a "right" to ENR technology notwithstanding its potentially grave proliferation implications, therefore, is at the cutting edge of policy and legal debates surrounding the meaning of Article IV and its relation to Articles I, II, and III of the Treaty.

Countries that have signed the treaty as Non-Nuclear Weapons States and maintained that status have an unbroken record of not building nuclear weapons. However, Iraq was cited by the IAEA and sanctioned by the UN Security Council for violating its NPT safeguards obligations; North Korea never came into compliance with its NPT safeguards agreement and was cited repeatedly for these violations, and later withdrew from the NPT and tested multiple nuclear devices; Iran was found in non-compliance with its NPT safeguards obligations in an unusual non-consensus decision because it "failed in a number of instances over an extended period of time" to report aspects of its enrichment program; and Libya pursued a clandestine nuclear weapons program before abandoning it in December 2003.

In 1991 Romania reported previously undeclared nuclear activities by the former regime and the IAEA reported this non-compliance to the Security Council for information only.

In some regions, the fact that all neighbours are verifiably free of nuclear weapons reduces any pressure individual states might feel to build those weapons themselves, even if neighbours are known to have peaceful nuclear energy programs that might otherwise be suspicious. In this, the treaty works as designed.

In 2004, Mohamed ElBaradei, the then Director General of the International Atomic Energy Agency (IAEA), said that by some estimates thirty-five to forty states could have the knowledge to develop nuclear weapons.

Key Articles

Article I: Each nuclear-weapons state (NWS) undertakes not to transfer, to any recipient, nuclear weapons, or other nuclear explosive devices, and not to assist any non-nuclear weapon state to manufacture or acquire such weapons or devices.

Article II: Each non-NWS party undertakes not to receive, from any source, nuclear weapons, or other nuclear explosive devices; not to manufacture or acquire such weapons or devices; and not to receive any assistance in their manufacture.

Article III: Each non-NWS party undertakes to conclude an agreement with the IAEA for the application of its safeguards to all nuclear material in all of the state's peaceful nuclear activities and to prevent diversion of such material to nuclear weapons or other nuclear explosive devices.

Article IV: 1. Nothing in this Treaty shall be interpreted as affecting the inalienable right of all the Parties to the Treaty to develop research, production and use of nuclear energy for peaceful purposes without discrimination and in conformity with Articles I and II of this Treaty.

2. All the Parties to the Treaty undertake to facilitate, and have the right to participate in, the fullest possible exchange of equipment, materials and scientific and technological information for the peaceful uses of nuclear energy. Parties to the Treaty in a position to do so shall also co-operate in contributing alone or together with other States or international organizations to the further development of the applications of nuclear energy for peaceful purposes, especially in the territories of non-nuclear-weapon States Party to the Treaty, with due consideration for the needs of the developing areas of the world.

Article VI. The states undertake to pursue "negotiations in good faith on effective measures relating to cessation of the nuclear arms race at an early date and to nuclear disarmament", and towards a "Treaty on general and complete disarmament under strict and effective international control".

Article X. Establishes the right to withdraw from the Treaty giving 3 months' notice. It also establishes the duration of the Treaty (25 years before 1995 Extension Initiative).

History

The impetus behind the NPT was concern for the safety of a world with many nuclear weapon states. It was recognized that the cold war deterrent relationship between just the United States and Soviet Union was fragile. More nuclear players reduced security for all, multiplying the risks of miscalculation, accident or unauthorized use, or through the escalation of a small nuclear conflict.

The NPT process was launched by Frank Aiken, Irish Minister for External Affairs, in 1958. It was opened for signature in 1968, with Finland the first State to sign. By 1992 all five then-declared nuclear powers had signed the treaty, and the treaty was renewed in 1995 (and followed by the Comprehensive Test Ban Treaty in 1996). Several NPT signatories have given up nuclear weapons or nuclear weapons programs.

South Africa undertook a nuclear weapons program, allegedly with the assistance of Israel in the 1970s, and may have conducted a nuclear test in the Atlantic ocean in 1979, but has since renounced its nuclear program and signed the treaty in 1991 after destroying its small nuclear arsenal. Several former Soviet Republics destroyed or transferred to Russia the nuclear weapons inherited from the Soviet Union.

7

Nuclear Explosions

The effects of a nuclear explosion depend in part to the height of the detonation. There five general classifications of bursts: air, high-altitude, underwater, underground, and surface bursts.

An air burst is defined as one in which the explosion occurs in the air at an altitude below 100,000 feet (30,480 meters), but at such a height that the fireball does not touch the surface of the earth. A detontation above that altitude is generally refered to as a high-altitude burst.

A nuclear explosion that occurs at or slightly above the actual surface of the land or water is known as a surface burst. If the explosion happens beneath the surface of the land or water, then it is known as underground or underwater respectively. The design of Robust Nuclear Earth Penetrator (RNEP) uses the charaterastics of an underground burst in an attempt to destroy buried targets.

One of the greatest results of the type of burst is the amount of radioactive debris and fallout, and the force of the blast wave.

THE BLAST WAVE

A fraction of a second after a nuclear explosion, the heat from the fireball causes a high-pressure wave to develop and move outward producing the blast effect. The front of the blast wave, i.e., the shock front, travels rapidly away from the fireball, a moving wall of highly compressed air.

The air immediately behind the shock front is accelerated to high velocities and creates a powerful wind. These winds in turn create dynamic pressure against the objects facing the blast. Shock waves cause a virtually instantaneous jump in pressure at the shock front.

The combination of the pressure jump (called the overpressure) and the dynamic pressure causes blast damage.

Both the overpressure and the dynamic pressure reach to their maximum values upon the arrival of the shock wave.

They then decay over a period ranging from a few tenths of a second to several seconds, depending on the blast's strength and the yield.

Overpressure

Blast effects are usually measured by the amount of overpressure, the pressure in excess of the normal atmospheric value, in pounds per square inch (psi).

After 10 seconds, when the fireball of a 1-megaton nuclear weapon has attained its maximum size (5,700 feet across), the shock front is some 3 miles farther ahead. At 50 seconds after the explosion, when the fireball is no longer visible, the blast wave has traveled about 12 miles. It is then traveling at about 784 miles per hour, which is slightly faster than the speed of sound at sea level.

Peak overpressure	*Maximum Wind Speed*
50 psi	934 mph
20 psi	502 mph
10 psi	294 mph
5 psi	163 mph
2 psi	70 mph

As a general guide, city areas are completely destroyed by overpressures of 5 psi, with heavy damage extending out at least to the 3 psi contour.

These many different effects make it difficult to provide a simple rule of thumb for assessing the magnitude of injury produced by different blast intensities. A general guide is given below:

Overpressure	*Physical Effects*
20 psi	Heavily built concrete buildings are severely damaged or demolished.
10 psi	Reinforced concrete buildings are severely damaged or demolished.
	Most people are killed.
5 psi	Most buildings collapse.
	Injuries are universal, fatalities are widespread.
3 psi	Residential structures collapse.
	Serious injuries are common, fatalities may occur.
1 psi	Window glass shatters
	Light injuries from fragments occur.

Blast Effects on Humans

Blast damage is caused by the arrival of the shock wave created by the nuclear explosion. Humans are actually quite resistant to the direct effect of overpressure. Pressures of over 40 psi are required before lethal effects are noted.

The danger from overpressure comes from the collapse of buildings that are generally not as resistant. Urban areas contain many objects that can become airborne, and the destruction of buildings generates many more. The collapse of the structure above can crush or suffocate those caught inside. Serious injury or death can also occur from impact after being thrown through the air.

The blast also magnifies thermal radiation burn injuries by tearing away severely burned skin. This creates raw open wounds that readily become infected.

The Mach Stem

If the explosion occurs above the ground, when the expanding blast wave strikes the surface of the earth, it is reflected off the ground to form a second shock wave traveling behind the first. This reflected wave travels faster than the first, or incident, shock wave since it is traveling through air already moving at high speed due to the passage of the incident wave. The reflected blast wave merges with the incident shock wave to form a single wave, known as the Mach Stem. The overpressure at the front of the Mach wave is generally about twice as great as that at the direct blast wave front.

At first the height of the Mach Stem wave is small, but as the wave front continues to move outward, the height increases steadily. At the same time, however, the overpressure, like that in the incident wave, decreases because of the continuous loss of energy and the ever-increasing area of the advancing front. After about 40 seconds, when the Mach front from a 1-megaton nuclear weapon is 10 miles from ground zero, the overpressure will have decreased to roughly 1 psi.

Thermal Radiation

A primary form of energy from a nuclear explosion is thermal radiation. Initially, most of this energy goes into heating the bomb materials and the air in the vicinity of the blast. Temperatures of a nuclear explosion reach those in the interior of the sun, about 100,000,000° Celsius, and produce a brilliant fireball.

Two pulses of thermal radiation emerge from the fireball. The first pulse, which lasts about a tenth of a second, consists of radiation in the ultraviolet region. The second pulse which may last for several seconds, carries about 99 percent of the total thermal radiation energy. It is this radiation that is the main cause of skin burns and eye injuries suffered by exposed individuals and causes combustible materials to break into flames.

Thermal radiation damage depends very strongly on weather conditions. Clouds or smoke in the air can considerably reduce effective damage ranges versus clear air conditions.

The Fireball

The fireball, an extremely hot and highly luminous spherical mass of air and gaseous weapon residues, occurs within less than one millionth of one second of the weapon's detonation. Immediately after its formation, the fireball begins to grow in size, engulfing the surrounding air. This growth is accompanied by a decrease in temperature because of the accompanying increase in mass. At the same time the fireball rises, like a hot-air balloon. Within seven-tenths of one millisecond from the detonation, the fireball from a 1-megaton weapon is about 440 feet across, and this increases to a maximum value of about 5,700 feet in 10 seconds. It is then rising at a rate of 250 to 350 feet per second. After a minute, the fireball has cooled to such an extent that it no longer emits visible radiation. It has then risen roughly 4.5 miles from the point of burst.

The Mushroom Cloud

As the fireball increases in size and cools, the vapors condense to form a cloud containing solid particles of the weapon debris, as well as many small drops of water derived from the air sucked into the rising fireball.

Depending on the height of burst, a strong updraft with inflowing winds, called "afterwinds," are produced. These afterwinds can cause varying amounts of dirt and debris to be sucked up from the earth's surface into the cloud. In an air burst with a moderate (or small) amount of dirt and debris drawn up into the cloud, only a relatively small proportion become contaminated with radioactivity. For a burst near the ground, however, large amounts of dirt and debris are drawn into the cloud during formation.

The color of the cloud is initially red or reddish brown, due to the presence of nitrous acid and oxides of nitrogen. As the fireball cools and condensation occurs, the color changes to white, mainly due to the water droplets (as in an ordinary cloud).

The cloud consists chiefly of very small particles of radioactive fission products and weapon residues, water droplets, and larger particles of dirt and debris carried up by the afterwinds.

The eventual height reached by the radioactive cloud depends upon the heat energy of the weapon and upon the atmospheric conditions. If the cloud reaches the tropopause, about 6-8 miles above the Earth's surface, there is a tendency for it to spread out. But if sufficient energy remains in the radioactive cloud at this height, a portion of it will ascend into the more stable air of the stratosphere.

The cloud attains its maximum height after about 10 minutes and is then said to be "stabilized." It continues to grow laterally, however, to produce the characteristic mushroom shape. The cloud may continue to be visible for about an hour or more before being dispersed by the winds into the surrounding atmosphere where it merges with natural clouds in the sky.

Thermal Pulse Effects

One of the important differences between a nuclear and conventional weapon is the large proportion of a nuclear explosion's energy that is released in the form of thermal energy. This energy is emitted from the fireball in two pulses. The first is quite short, and carries only about 1 percent of the energy; the second pulse is more significant and is of longer duration (up to 20 seconds).

The energy from the thermal pulse can initiate fires in dry, flammable materials, such as dry leaves, grass, old newspaper, thin dark flammable fabrics, etc. The incendiary effect of the thermal pulse is also substantially affected by the later arrival of the blast wave, which usually blows out any flames that have already been kindled. However, smoldering material can reignite later.

The major incendiary effect of nuclear explosions is caused by the blast wave. Collapsed structures are much more vulnerable to fire than intact ones. The blast reduces many structures to piles of kindling, the many gaps opened in roofs and walls act as chimneys, gas lines are broken open, storage tanks for flammable materials are ruptured. The primary ignition sources appear to be flames and pilot lights in heating appliances (furnaces, water heaters, stoves, etc.). Smoldering material from the thermal pulse can be very effective at igniting leaking gas.

Thermal radiation damage depends very strongly on weather conditions. Cloud cover, smoke, or other obscuring material in the air can considerably reduce effective damage ranges versus clear air conditions.

Thermal radiation also affects humans both directly - by flash burns on exposed skin - and indirectly - by fires started by the explosion.

Firestorms

Under some conditions, the many individual fires created by a nuclear explosion can coalesce into one massive fire known as a "firestorm." The combination of many smaller fires heats the air and causes winds of hurricane strength directed inward toward the fire, which in turn fan the flames. For a firestorm to develop:

- There must be at least 8 pounds of combustibles per square foot.
- At least one-half of the structures in the area are on fire simultaneously.
- There is initially a wind of less than 8 miles per hour.
- The burning area is at least 0.5 square miles.

In Hiroshima, a firestorm did develop and about 4.4 square miles were destroyed. Although there was some damage from uncontrolled fires at Nagasaki, a firestorm did not develop. One reason for this was the difference in the terrain. Hiroshima is relatively flat, while Nagasaki has uneven terrain. Firestorms can also be caused by conventional bombing. During World War II, the cities of Dresden, Hamburg, and Tokyo all suffered the effects of firestorms.

Flash Burns

Flash burns are one of the serious consequences of a nuclear explosion. Flash burns result from the absorption of radiant energy by the skin of exposed individuals. A distinctive feature of flash burns is the fact they are limited to exposed areas of the skin facing the explosion.

A 1-megaton explosion can cause first-degree burns (a bad sunburn) at a distance of about 7 miles, second-degree burns (producing blisters and permanent scars) at distances of about 6 miles, and third-degree burns (which destroy skin tissue) at distances up to 5 miles. Third-degree burns over 24 percent of the body, or second-degree burns over 30 percent, will result in serious shock, and will probably prove fatal unless prompt, specialized medical care is available.

It has been estimated that burns caused some 50 percent of the deaths at Hiroshima and Nagasaki.

Flash blindness

Flash blindness is caused by the initial brilliant flash of light produced by the nuclear detonation. The light is received on the retina than can be tolerated, but less than is required for irreversible injury. The retina is particularly susceptible to visible and short wavelength infrared light. The result is a bleaching of visual pigment and temporary blindness. Vision is completely recovered as the pigment is regenerated. During the daylight hours, flash blindness does not persist for more than 2 minutes, but generally lasts a few seconds. At night, when the pupil is dilated, flashblindness will last for a longer period of time.

A 1-megaton explosion can cause flash blindness at distances as great as 13 miles on a clear day, or 53 miles on a clear night. If the intensity is great enough, a permanent retinal burn will result. Retinal injury is the most far-reaching injury effect of nuclear explosions, but it is relatively rare since the eye must be looking directly at the detonation. Retinal injury results from burns in the area of the retina where the fireball image is focused.

Nuclear Radiation

The release of radiation is a phenomenon unique to nuclear explosions. There are several kinds of radiation emitted; these types include gamma, neutron, and ionizing radiation, and are emitted not only at the time of detonation (initial radiation) but also for long periods of time afterward (residual radiation).

INITIAL NUCLEAR RADIATION

Initial nuclear radiation is defined as the radiation that arrives during the first minute after an explosion, and is mostly gamma radiation and neutron radiation.

The level of initial nuclear radiation decreases rapidly with distance from the fireball to where less than one roentgen may be received five miles from ground zero. In addition, initial radiation lasts only as long as nuclear fission occurs in the fireball. Initial nuclear radiation represents about 3 percent of the total energy in a nuclear explosion.

Though people close to ground zero may receive lethal doses of radiation, they are concurrently being killed by the blast wave and thermal pulse. In typical nuclear weapons, only a relatively small proportion of deaths and injuries result from initial radiation.

Residual Nuclear Radiation

The residual radiation from a nuclear explosion is mostly from the radioactive fallout. This radiation comes from the weapon debris, fission products, and, in the case of a ground burst, radiated soil. There are over 300 different fission products that may result from a fission reaction. Many of these are radioactive with widely differing half-lives. Some are very short, i.e., fractions of a second, while a few are long enough that the materials can be a hazard for months or years. Their principal mode of decay is by the emission of beta particles and gamma radiation.

Radiation Effects on Humans

Certain body parts are more specifically affected by exposure to different types of radiation sources. Several factors are involved in determining the potential health effects of exposure to radiation. These include:

- The size of the dose (amount of energy deposited in the body)
- The ability of the radiation to harm human tissue
- Which organs are affected

The most important factor is the amount of the dose - the amount of energy actually deposited in your body. The more energy absorbed by cells, the greater the biological damage. Health physicists refer to the amount of energy absorbed by the body as the radiation dose.

The absorbed dose, the amount of energy absorbed per gram of body tissue, is usually measured in units called rads. Another unit of radiation is the rem, or roentgen equivalent in man. To convert rads to rems, the number of rads is multiplied by a number that reflects the potential for damage caused by a type of radiation. For beta, gamma and X-ray radiation, this number is generally one. For some neutrons, protons, or alpha particles, the number is twenty.

Hair

The losing of hair quickly and in clumps occurs with radiation exposure at 200 rems or higher.

Brain

Since brain cells do not reproduce, they won't be damaged directly unless the exposure is 5,000 rems or greater. Like the heart, radiation kills nerve cells and small blood vessels, and can cause seizures and immediate death.

Thyroid

The certain body parts are more specifically affected by exposure to different types of radiation sources. The thyroid gland is susceptible to radioactive iodine. In sufficient amounts, radioactive iodine can destroy all or part of the thyroid. By taking potassium iodide can reduce the effects of exposure.

Blood System

When a person is exposed to around 100 rems, the blood's lymphocyte cell count will be reduced, leaving the victim more susceptible to infection. This is often refered to as mild radiation sickness. Early symptoms of radiation sickness mimic those of flu and may go unnoticed unless a blood count is done.According to data from Hiroshima and Nagaski, show that symptoms may persist for up to 10 years and may also have an increased long-term risk for leukemia and lymphoma. For more information, visit Radiation Effects Research Foundation.

Heart

Intense exposure to radioactive material at 1,000 to 5,000 rems would do immediate damage to small blood vessels and probably cause heart failure and death directly.

Gastrointestinal Tract

Radiation damage to the intestinal tract lining will cause nausea, bloody vomiting and diarrhea. This is occurs when the victim's exposure is 200 rems or more. The radiation will begin to destroy the cells in the body that divide rapidly. These including blood, GI tract, reproductive and hair cells, and harms their DNA and RNA of surviving cells.

Long Term Effects on Humans

Long after the acute effects of radiation have subsided, radiation damage continues to produce a wide range of physical problems. These effects- including leukemia, cancer, and many others- appear two, three, even ten years later.

Blood Disorders

According to Japanese data, there was an increase in anemia among persons exposed to the bomb. In some cases, the decrease in white and red blood cells lasted for up to ten years after the bombing.

Reproductive Tract

Because reproductive tract cells divide rapidly, these areas of the body can be damaged at rem levels as low as 200. Long-term, some radiation sickness victims will become sterile.

Dose-rem	*Effects*
5-20	Possible late effects; possible chromosomal damage.
20-100	Temporary reduction in white blood cells.
100-200	Mild radiation sickness within a few hours: vomiting, diarrhea, fatigue; reduction in resistance to infection.
200-300	Serious radiation sickness effects as in 100-200 rem and hemorrhage; exposure is a Lethal Dose to 10-35% of the population after 30 days (LD 10-35/30).
300-400	Serious radiation sickness; also marrow and intestine destruction; LD 50-70/30.
400-1000	Acute illness, early death; LD 60-95/30.
1000-5000	Acute illness, early death in days; LD 100/10.

Cataracts

There was an increase in cataract rate of the survivors at Hiroshima and Nagasaki, who were partly shielded and suffered partial hair loss.

Malignant Tumors

All ionizing radiation is carcinogenic, but some tumor types are more readily generated than others. A prevalent type is leukemia.

The cancer incidence among survivors of Hiroshima and Nagasaki is significantly larger than that of the general population, and a significant correlation between exposure level and degree of incidence has been reported for thyroid cancer, breast cancer, lung cancer, and cancer of the salivary gland.

Often a decade or more passes before radiation-caused malignancies appear.

Keloids

Beginning in early 1946, scar tissue covering apparently healed burns began to swell and grow abnormally. Mounds of raised and twisted flesh, called keloids, were found in 50 to 60 percent of those burned by direct exposure to the heat rays within 1.2 miles of the hypocenter. Keloids are believed to be related to the effects of radiation.

Radioactive Fallout

Fallout is the radioactive particles that fall to earth as a result of a nuclear explosion. It consists of weapon debris, fission products, and, in the case of a ground burst, radiated soil. Fallout particles vary in size from thousandths of a millimeter to several millimeters. Much of this material falls directly back down close to ground zero within several minutes after the explosion, but some travels high into the atmosphere. This material will be dispersed over the earth during the following hours, days (and) months. Fallout is defined as one of two types: early fallout, within the first 24 hours after an explosion, or delayed fallout, which occurs days or years later.

Most of the radiation hazard from nuclear bursts comes from short-lived radionuclides external to the body; these are generally confined to the locality downwind of the weapon burst point. This radiation hazard comes from radioactive fission fragments with half-lives of seconds to a few months, and from soil and other materials in the vicinity of the burst made radioactive by the intense neutron flux.

Most of the particles decay rapidly. Even so, beyond the blast radius of the exploding weapons there would be areas (*hot spots*) the survivors could not enter because of radioactive contamination from long-lived radioactive isotopes like strontium 90 or cesium 137. For the survivors of a nuclear war, this lingering radiation hazard could represent a grave threat for as long as 1 to 5 years after the attack.

Predictions of the amount and levels of the radioactive fallout are difficult because of several factors. These include; the yield and design of the weapon, the height of the explosion, the nature of the surface beneath the point of burst, and the meteorological conditions, such as wind direction and speed.

An air burst can produce minimal fallout if the fireball does not touch the ground. On the other hand, a nuclear explosion occurring at or near the earth's surface can result in severe contamination by the radioactive fallout.

Fallout Particles

Many fallout particles are especially hazardous biologically. Some of the principal radioactive elements are as follows:

Strontium 90 is very long-lived with a half-life of 28 years. It is chemically similar to calcium, causing it to accumulate in growing bones. This radiation can cause tumors, leukemia, and other blood abnormalities.

Iodine 131 has a half-life of 8.1 days. Ingestion of it concentrates in the thyroid gland. The radiation can destroy all or part of the thyroid. Taking potassium iodide can reduce the effects.

The amount of tritium released varies by bomb design. It has a half-life of 12.3 years and can be easily ingested, since it can replace a hydrogen in water. The beta radiation can cause lung cancer.

Cesium 137 has a half-life of 30 years. It does not present as large a biological threat as Strontium 90. It behaves similar to potassium, and will distribute fairly uniformly thoughout the body. This can contribute to gonadal irradiation and genetic damage.

When a plutonium weapon is exploded, not all of the plutonium is fissioned. Plutonium 239 has a half-life of 24,400 years. Ingestion of as little as 1 microgram of plutonium, a barely visible speck, is a serious health hazard causing the formation of bone and lung tumors.

The Fallout Pattern

The details of the actual fallout pattern depend on wind speed and direction and on the terrain. The fallout will contain about 60 percent of the total radioactivity. The largest particles will fall within a short distance of ground zero. Smaller particles will require many hours to return to earth and may be carried hundreds of miles. This means that a surface burst can produce serious contamination far from the point of detonation.

From the 15-megaton thermonuclear device tested at Bikini Atoll on March 1, 1954 - the BRAVO shot of Operation CASTLE - the fallout caused substantial contamination over an area of more than 7,000 square miles. The contaminated region was roughly cigar-shaped and extended more than 20 miles upwind and over 350 miles downwind.

Fallout can also enter into the stratosphere. In this stable region, radioactive particles can remain from 1 to 3 years before returning to the surface.

The OTA Study

The Office of Technology Assessment (1979) estimated the effects of a large-scale nuclear attack on U.S. military and economic targets. This scenario assumes a direct attack on 250 U.S. cities, with a total yield of 7,800 megatons. The most immediate effects would be the loss of millions of human lives, accompanied by similar incomprehensible levels of injuries, and the physical destruction of a high percentage of U.S. economic and industrial capacity. The full range of effects resulting from several thousand warheads - most having yields of a megaton or greater - impacting on or near U.S. cities can only be discussed in terms of uncertainty and speculation. It is estimated that 100 million to 165 million people would be killed.

Although this type of attack is less likely than during the Cold War, the risk of a limited nuclear strike by one of the smaller nuclear powers still remains a possibility.

Electromagnetic Pulse

Electromagnetic pulse (EMP) is an electromagnetic wave similar to radio waves, which results from secondary reactions occurring when the nuclear gamma radiation is absorbed in the air or ground. It differs from the usual radio waves in two important ways. First, it creates much higher electric field strengths. Whereas a radio signal might produce a thousandth of a volt or less in a receiving antenna, an EMP pulse might produce thousands of volts. Secondly, it is a single pulse of energy that disappears completely in a small fraction of a second. In this sense, it is rather similar to the electrical signal from lightning, but the rise in voltage is typically a hundred times faster. This means that most equipment designed to protect electrical facilities from lightning works too slowly to be effective against EMP.

There is no evidence that EMP is a physical threat to humans. However, electrical or electronic systems, particularly those connected to long wires such as power lines or antennas, can undergo damage. There could be actual physical damage to an electrical component or a temporary disruption of operation.

An attacker might detonate a few weapons at high altitudes in an effort to destroy or damage the communications and electric power systems. It can be expected that EMP would cause massive disruption for an indeterminable period, and would cause huge economic damages. On July 8, 1962, the EMP from the high altitude (250 miles above Johnston Island) "Starfish Prime" test (1.4 Mt) turned off 300 streetlights in Oahu, Hawaii (740 miles away).

Ozone Depletion

When a nuclear weapon explodes in the air, the surrounding air is subjected to great heat, followed by relatively rapid cooling. These conditions are ideal for the production of tremendous amounts of nitric oxides. These oxides are carried into the upper atmosphere, where they reduce the concentration of protective ozone. Ozone is necessary to block harmful ultraviolet radiation from reaching the Earth's surface.

The nitric oxides produced by the weapons could reduce the ozone levels in the Northern Hemisphere by as much as 30 to 70 percent. Such a depletion might produce changes in the Earth's climate, and would allow more ultraviolet radiation from the sun through the atmosphere to the surface of the Earth, where it could produce dangerous burns and a variety of potentially dangerous ecological effects.

It has been estimated that as much as 5,000 tons of nitric oxide is produced for each megaton of nuclear explosive power.

Nuclear Winter

In 1983, R.P. Turco, O.B. Toon, T.P. Ackerman, J.B. Pollack, and Carl Sagan (referred to as TTAPS) published a paper entitled "Global Atmospheric Consequences of Nuclear War" which is the foundation on which the nuclear winter theory is based on.

Theory states that nuclear explosions will set off firestorms over many cities and forests within range. Great plumes of smoke, soot, and dust would be sent aloft from these fires, lifted by their own heating to high altitudes where they could drift for weeks before dropping back or being washed out of the atmosphere onto the ground. Several hundred million tons of this smoke and soot would be shepherded by strong west-to-east winds until they would form a uniform belt of particles encircling the Northern Hemisphere.

These thick black clouds could block out all but a fraction of the sun's light for a period as long as several weeks. The conditions of semidarkness, killing frosts, and subfreezing temperatures, combined with high doses of radiation from nuclear fallout, would interrupt plant photosynthesis and could thus destroy much of the Earth's vegetation and animal life. The extreme cold, high radiation levels, and the widespread destruction of industrial, medical, and transportation infrastructures along with food supplies and crops would trigger a massive death toll from starvation, exposure, and disease.

It is not certain that a nuclear war would produce a nuclear winter effect. However, it remains a possibility and the TTAPS study concluded: "...the possibility of the extinction of Homo Sapiens cannot be excluded."

EFFECTS OF NUCLEAR EXPLOSIONS

The basic differences in the mechanisms of energy production and related characteristics of conventional as compared with nuclear detonations. In this chapter that discussion will be extended to consider the forms in which the energy produced in such detonations affects the surrounding environment.

The location of the point of detonation in the environment is as important as the yield in determining the way the energy is distributed, and this factor will be discussed in some detail.

GENERAL EFFECTS OF NUCLEAR EXPLOSIONS

a. While the destructive action of conventional explosions is due almost entirely to the transmission of energy in the form of a blast wave with resultant mechanical damage, the energy of a nuclear explosion is transferred to the surrounding medium in three distinct forms: blast; thermal radiation; and nuclear radiation. The distribution of energy among these three forms will depend on the yield of the weapon, the location of the burst, and the characteristics of the environment. For a low altitude atmospheric detonation of a moderate sized weapon in the kiloton range, the energy is distributed roughly as follows:

(1) 50% as blast;

(2) 35% as thermal radiation; made up of a wide range of the electromagnetic spectrum, including infrared, visible, and ultraviolet light and some soft x-ray emitted at the time of the explosion; and

(3) 15% as nuclear radiation; including 5% as initial ionizing radiation consisting chiefly of neutrons and gamma rays emitted within the first minute after detonation, and 10% as residual nuclear radiation. Residual nuclear radiation is the hazard in fallout.

b. Considerable variation from this distribution will occur with changes in yield or location of the detonation. This is best shown by comparing the ranges of damage due to these effects of weapons of different size yields.

c. The distribution of weapon energy yield is altered significantly by the enhanced radiation nuclear warhead. In simplest terms an enhanced radiation warhead is designed specifically to reduce the percentage of energy that is dissipated as blast and heat with a consequent increase in the percentage yield of initial radiation. Approximate percentage energies are 30% blast; 20% thermal; 45% initial radiation; and 5% residual radiation.

INITIAL ENERGY TRANSFER AND FORMATION OF FIREBALL

a. Because of the tremendous amounts of energy liberated per unit mass in a nuclear detonation, temperatures of several tens of million degrees centigrade develop in the immediate area of the detonation. This is in marked contrast to the few thousand degrees of a conventional explosion. At these very high temperatures the nonfissioned parts of the nuclear weapon are vaporized. The atoms do not release the energy as kinetic energy but release it in the form of large amounts of electromagnetic radiation. In an atmospheric detonation, this electromagnetic radiation, consisting chiefly of soft x-ray, is absorbed within a few meters of the point of detonation by the surrounding atmosphere, heating it to extremely high temperatures and forming a brilliantly hot sphere of air and gaseous weapon residues, the so-called fireball. Immediately upon formation, the fireball begins to grow rapidly and rise like a hot air balloon. Within a millisecond after detonation, the diameter of the fireball from a 1 megaton (Mt) air burst is 150 m. This increases to a maximum of 2200 m within

10 seconds, at which time the fireball is also rising at the rate of 100 m/sec. The initial rapid expansion of the fireball severely compresses the surrounding atmosphere, producing a powerful blast wave, discussed below.

b. The fireball itself emits enormous amounts of electromagnetic radiation, similar in its spectrum to sunlight. This is usually termed thermal radiation. The visible light component accounts for the blinding flash seen upon detonation as well as the subsequent brightness of the fireball, while the infrared component results in widespread burns and incendiary effects.

c. As it expands toward its maximum diameter, the fireball cools, and after about a minute its temperature has decreased to such an extent that it no longer emits significant amounts of thermal radiation. The combination of the upward movement and the cooling of the fireball gives rise to the formation of the characteristic mushroom-shaped cloud. As the fireball cools, the vaporized materials in it condense to form a cloud of solid particles. Following an air burst, condensed droplets of water give it a typical white cloudlike appearance. In the case of a surface burst, this cloud will also contain large quantities of dirt and other debris which are vaporized when the fireball touches the earth's surface or are sucked up by the strong updrafts afterwards, giving the cloud a dirty brown appearance. The dirt and debris become contaminated with the radioisotopes generated by the explosion or activated by neutron radiation and fall to earth as fallout.

d. The cloud rises for a period of approximately 10 minutes to a stabilized height which depends on the thermal output of the weapon and atmospheric conditions. It will continue to grow laterally assuming the familiar mushroom shape and may remain visible for an hour or more under favorable conditions. For example, the nuclear cloud from a 1 Mt surface burst will stabilize at an altitude of over 20 kilometers (km) and will have a mean lateral diameter of 35 km.

TYPES OF BURSTS

The relative effects of blast, heat, and nuclear radiation will largely be determined by the altitude at which the weapon is detonated. Nuclear explosions are generally classified as air bursts, surface bursts, subsurface bursts, or high altitude bursts.

a. *Air Bursts.* An air burst is an explosion in which a weapon is detonated in air at an altitude below 30 km but at sufficient height that the fireball does not contact the surface of the earth. After such a burst, blast may cause considerable damage and injury. The altitude of an air burst can be varied to obtain maximum blast effects, maximum thermal effects, desired radiation effects, or a balanced combination of these effects. Burns to exposed skin may be produced over many square kilometers and eye injuries over a still larger area. Initial nuclear radiation will be a significant hazard with smaller weapons, but the fallout hazard can be ignored as there is essentially no local fallout from an air burst. The fission products are generally dispersed over a large area of the globe unless there is local rainfall resulting in localized fallout. In the vicinity of ground zero, there may be a small area of neutron-induced activity which could be hazardous to troops required to pass through the area. Tactically, air bursts are the most likely to be used against ground forces.

b. *Surface Burst.* A surface burst is an explosion in which a weapon is detonated on or slightly above the surface of the earth so that the fireball actually touches the land or water surface. Under these conditions, the area affected by blast, thermal radiation, and initial nuclear radiation will be less extensive than for an air burst of similar yield, except in the region of ground zero where destruction is concentrated. In contrast with air bursts, local fallout can be a hazard over a much larger downwind area than that which is affected by blast and thermal radiation.

c. *Subsurface Burst.* A subsurface burst is an explosion in which the point of the detonation is beneath the surface of land or water. Cratering will generally result from an underground burst, just as for a surface burst. If the burst does not penetrate the surface, the only other hazard will be from ground or water shock. If the burst is shallow enough to penetrate the surface, blast, thermal, and initial nuclear radiation effects will be present, but will be less than for a surface burst of comparable yield. Local fallout will be very heavy if penetration occurs.

d. *High Altitude Burst.* A high altitude burst is one in which the weapon is exploded at such an altitude (above 30 km) that initial soft x-rays generated by the detonation dissipate energy as heat in a much larger volume of air molecules. There the fireball is much larger and expands much more rapidly. The ionizing radiation from the high altitude burst can travel for hundreds of miles before being absorbed. Significant ionization of the upper atmosphere (ionosphere) can occur. Severe disruption in communications can occur following high altitude bursts. They also lead to generation of an intense electromagnetic pulse (EMP) which can significantly degrade performance of or destroy sophisticated electronic equipment. There are no known biological effects of EMP; however, indirect effects may result from failure of critical medical equipment.

BLAST

Formation of Blast Wave

a. As a result of the very high temperatures and pressures at the point of detonation, the hot gaseous residues move outward radially from the center of the explosion with very high velocities. Most of this material is contained within a relatively thin, dense shell known as the hydrodynamic front. Acting much like a piston that pushes against and compresses the surrounding medium, the front transfers energy to the atmosphere by impulse and generates a steep-fronted, spherically expanding blast or shock wave. At first, this shock wave lags behind the surface of the developing fireball. However, within a fraction of a second after detonation, the rate of expansion of the fireball decreases to such an extent that the shock catches up with and then begins to move ahead of the fireball. For a fraction of a second, the dense shock front will obscure the fireball, accounting for the characteristic double peak of light seen with a nuclear detonation.

b. As it expands, the peak pressures of the blast wave diminish and the speed of propagation decreases from the initial supersonic velocity to that of sound in the transmitting medium. However, upon reflection from the earth's surface, the pressure in the wave will be reinforced by the fusion of the incident and the reflected wave (the Mach effect) described below.

c. A large part of the destruction caused by a nuclear explosion is due to blast effects. Objects within the path of the blast wave are subjected to severe, sharp increases in atmospheric pressure and to extraordinarily severe transient winds. Most buildings, with the exception of reinforced or blast-resistant structures, will suffer moderate to severe damage when subjected to overpressures of only 35.5 kiloPascals (kPa) (0.35 Atm). The velocity of the accompanying blast wind may exceed several hundred km/hr. Most materiel targets are drag- or wind-sensitive.

d. The range for blast effects increases significantly with the explosive yield of the weapon. In a typical air burst, these values of overpressure and wind velocity noted above will prevail at a range of 0.7 km for 1 kiloton (Kt) yield; 3.2 km for 100Kt; and 15.0 km for 10 Mt.

Propagation of Blast Wave in Air

During the time the blast wave is passing through the superheated atmosphere in the fireball, it travels at supersonic velocities. After it leaves the vicinity of the fireball, it slows down to the normal speed of sound in the atmosphere. As long as the blast wave is expanding radially, its intensity decreases approximately as the square of the distance. When the expanding blast wave from a nuclear air burst strikes the surface of the earth, however, it is reflected, and the reflected wave reinforces and intensifies the primary wave.

a. Targets in the vicinity of ground zero may actually be subjected to two blast waves: the initial or incident wave, followed slightly later by a secondary reflected wave. This limited region close to ground zero in which the incident and reflected waves are separate is known as the region of regular reflection.

b. Beyond the area of regular reflection as it travels through air which is already heated and compressed by the incident blast wave, the reflected wave will move much more rapidly and will very quickly catch up with the incident wave. The two then fuse to form a combined wave front known as the Mach stem. The height of the Mach stem increases as the blast wave moves outward and becomes a nearly vertical blast front. As a result, blast pressures on the surface will not decrease as the square of the distance, and most direct blast damage will be horizontally directed, e.g., on the walls of a building rather than on the roof.

c. As the height of burst for an explosion of given yield is decreased, or as the yield of the explosion for a given height of burst is increased, Mach reflection commences nearer to ground zero and the overpressure near ground zero becomes larger. However, as the height of burst is decreased, the total area of coverage for blast effects is also markedly reduced. The choice of height of burst is largely dependent on the nature of the target. Relatively resistant targets require the concentrated blast of a low altitude or surface burst, while sensitive targets may be damaged by the less severe blast wave from an explosion at a higher altitude. In the latter case a larger area and, therefore, a larger number of targets can be damaged.

d. A surface burst results in the highest possible overpressures near ground zero. In such a burst, the shock front is hemispherical in form, and essentially all objects are subjected to a blast front similar to that in the Mach region described above. A subsurface burst produces the least air blast, since most of the energy is dissipated in the formation of a crater and the production of a ground shock wave.

STATIC OVERPRESSURE AND DYNAMIC PRESSURE

a. Two distinct though simultaneous phenomena are associated with the blast wave in air:

   (1) Static overpressure, i.e., the sharp increases in pressure due to compression of the atmosphere. These pressures are those which are exerted by the dense wall of air that comprises the wave front. The magnitude of the overpressure at any given point is directly proportional to the density of the air in the wave.

   (2) Dynamic pressures, i.e., drag forces exerted by the strong transient blast winds associated with the movement of air required to form the blast wave. These forces are termed dynamic because they tend to push, tumble, and tear apart objects and cause their violent displacement.

b. In general, the static overpressure rises very abruptly from normal atmospheric in the unaffected air in front of the blast wave to a sharp peak. It then decreases behind the front. As the blast wave moves out from ground zero, the peak overpressure of the front diminishes while the decay of overpressure behind the front becomes more gradual. After traveling a sufficient distance from the fireball, the pressure behind the front actually drops below normal atmospheric pressure, the so-called negative phase of the blast wave.

c. In passing through the atmosphere, the blast wave imparts its energy to the molecules of the surrounding air, setting them into motion in the direction of the advancing shock front. The motion of these air molecules is manifested as severe transient winds, known as "blast winds," which accompany the blast wave. The destructive force associated with these winds is proportional to the square of their velocity and is measured in terms of dynamic pressure. These winds constitute decay forces which produce a large number of missiles and tumbling of objects. These dynamic forces are highly destructive.

d. Most of the material damage caused by a nuclear air burst is caused by a combination of the high static overpressures and the dynamic or blast wind pressures. The relatively long duration of the compression phase of the blast wave is also significant in that structures weakened by the initial impact of the wave front are literally torn apart by the forces and pressures which follow. The compression and drag force phases together may last several seconds or longer, during which forces many times greater than those in the strongest hurricane are present. These persist even through the negative phase of a blast wave when a partial vacuum is present because of the violent displacement of air.

e. It is of practical value to examine the variation in pressure at a fixed location as a function of time. For a short period of time after a nuclear air burst, there will be no increase in pressure since it takes a finite time for the shock front to reach a given point. This arrival time, which may range from a few seconds to minutes, will depend primarily on the distance of the location from the center of burst and to a lesser extent on the yield of the explosion. Initially, the speed of the shock front is many times the speed of sound because it is traveling through superheated air, but as it travels away from the fireball it slows down to the speed of sound, 330 m/sec, in normal atmospheres. With high yield detonations, the early velocity of the shock front and the distance traveled through superheated air is greater. Therefore, time is somewhat less. Upon arrival of the shock front, both the static overpressure and the dynamic pressure increase almost immediately from zero to their maximum values. The peak values of pressure will, of course, depend on the distance from ground zero, the height of burst, and the yield and will be further modified by differences in terrain and meteorological conditions. With passage of the blast front, both the static and dynamic pressures decay, though at slightly different rates. Most blast damage will be experienced during the positive or compression phase of the wave. The duration of this positive phase increases with yield and distance from ground zero and ranges from 0.2 to 0.5 sec for a 1 KT nuclear air burst to 4 to 10 sec for a 10 Mt explosion. This compares with only a few hundredths of a second for the duration of a blast wave from a conventional high-explosive detonation.

f. Because of the much longer duration of the blast wave from a nuclear explosion, structures are subjected to maximum loading for correspondingly longer periods of time, and damage will be much more extensive for a given peak overpressure than might otherwise be expected. During the negative phase, which is generally of even longer duration, the static pressure will drop below normal atmospheric pressure and the blast winds will actually reverse direction and blow back towards ground zero. Damage sustained during the negative phase is generally minor, however, because the peak values of underpressure and wind velocity are relatively low.

Blast Loading

When a blast wave strikes the surface of a hard target, such as a building, the reflected wave will reinforce the incident wave, and the face of the building will be subjected to overpressures 2 to 8 times that of the incident wave alone. The severity of this additional stress depends on many factors, including the peak overpressure of the incident blast wave, as well as the angle at which the wave strikes the building. As the shock front advances, it bends or diffracts around the building, and the pressure on the front wall decreases rapidly.

However, during the brief interval in which the blast wave has not yet engulfed the entire structure, a considerable pressure gradient exists from front to rear that places a severe stress on the building. For small objects, this period of so-called diffraction loading is so small that no significant stress is encountered. For large buildings, however, the stress of diffraction loading will be considerable.

Even after the shock front has passed across the building, the structure will still be subjected to a severe compression force and to severe drag forces from the transient winds. The actual overpressures required to produce severe damage to diffraction sensitive targets are actually quite low. Table 3-II depicts failure of sensitive structural elements when exposed to overpressure blast loading.

Drag Loading

All objects in the path of the blast wave, regardless of size or structure, will be subject to the dynamic pressure loading or drag forces of the blast winds. Drag loading is influenced to a moderate degree by the shape of the target. Round objects are relatively unaffected by the winds, while flat or recessed surfaces offer great resistance and hence are subjected to increased impact pressure and probability of damage.

The effect of dynamic pressure is generally dependent on the peak value of dynamic pressure and its duration. While the dynamic pressure at the face of a building is generally less than the peak overpressure due to the blast wave and its reflection, the period of dynamic loading is much longer than that of diffraction loading, and hence the damage to frame-type buildings, bridges, and other structures will be considerable.

Equipment and personnel are relatively resistant to static overpressures but highly vulnerable to dynamic pressure. For example, military vehicles, from jeeps to tanks, are most likely to suffer damage when pushed, overturned, and thrown about by the blast winds. Likewise, blast winds are the cause of most blast injuries. Because of the violence of the winds associated with even low values of overpressure, mechanical injuries due to missiles sent into motion by the winds or to violent bodily translation will far outnumber direct blast injuries due to actual compression of the organism.

SHOCK WAVES IN OTHER MEDIA

a. In surface and subsurface bursts, a sizable portion of the yield is transmitted in the form of ground or water shock waves. In the case of a surface burst on land, a crater is formed at ground zero, the size of which depends primarily upon yield. Relatively little damage beyond a distance of approximately three crater radii will occur due to ground shock. Most damage will be due to the accompanying air blast wave. In subsurface bursts the crater will be formed either by ejection of material as in a shallow explosion or by the collapse of ground into the cavity formed by a deeper explosion. Since the overpressure in a ground shock wave decreases very rapidly with distance, shock damage will again be confined to a region close to the point of detonation.

b. Ground shock waves will also be induced as a result of an air burst. If the overpressure in the blast wave is very large, the ground shock will penetrate some distance into the ground and may damage underground structures and buried utilities, etc.

c. Because of the density and relative incompressibility of water, shock waves in that medium have very high peak overpressures and velocities of propagation. The peak overpressure at a distance of 1 km from a 10 Kt underwater burst is approximately 6080 kPa (60 atm (atmospheres of pressure)), while the peak overpressure in air at the same distance from an air burst is only 111.4 kPa (1.1 atm). The resulting surface waves at this distance will be approximately 10 m in height. The shock front will also travel at approximately five times the speed of the blast wave in air. Severe damage to naval vessels may result from the shock wave produced by an underwater or water surface burst. Although the major portion of the shock energy is propagated in the water, a significant amount is also transferred through the surface as a typical air blast. This blast wave could probably be the principal source of damage to land targets if the explosion occurred in a coastal area.

THERMAL RADIATION

Formation of Thermal Radiation

Large amounts of electromagnetic radiation in the visible, infrared, and ultraviolet regions of the electromagnetic spectrum are emitted from the surface of the fireball within the first minute or less after detonation. This thermal radiation travels outward from the fireball at the speed of light, 300,000 km/sec. The chief hazard of thermal radiation is the production of burns and eye injuries in exposed personnel. Such thermal injuries may occur even at distances where blast and initial nuclear radiation effects are minimal. Absorption of thermal radiation will also cause the ignition of combustible materials and may lead to fires which then spread rapidly among the debris left by the blast. The range of thermal effects increases markedly with weapon yield.

Propagation of Thermal Energy

a. Most of the energy released in the fission or fusion processes is initially in the form of the kinetic energy of the products of the reactions (e.g., fission fragments, etc.). Within millionths of a second after detonation, numerous inelastic collisions of these vaporized atoms give rise to a plasma of intensely hot weapon residues. Since the temperature of this system is of several tens of million degrees centigrade, it emits enormous quantities of energy in the form of electromagnetic radiation. This radiation is subsequently absorbed by the surrounding atmosphere, which is heated to extremely high temperatures, causing it to emit additional radiation of slightly lower energy. This complex process of radiative transfer of energy is the basic mechanism by which the fireball is formed and expands.

b. Because this thermal radiation travels at the speed of light, and its mean free path (distance between point of emission and point of absorption) is relatively long, the initial expansion of the fireball is extremely rapid, much more so than the outward motion of gaseous material from the center of the burst responsible for production of the blast wave. Consequently, the blast wave front at first lags behind the radiative front (surface of the fireball).

c. However, as the fireball expands and its energy is deposited in an ever-increasing volume its temperature decreases and the transfer of energy by thermal radiation becomes less rapid. At this point, the blast wave front begins to catch up with the surface of the fireball and then moves ahead of it, a process called hydrodynamic separation. Due to the tremendous compression of the atmosphere by the blast wave, the air in front of the fireball is heated to incandescence. Thus, after hydrodynamic separation, the fireball actually consists of two concentric regions: the hot inner core known as the isothermal sphere; and an outer layer of luminous shock-heated air.

d. The outer layer initially absorbs much of the radiation from theisothermal sphere and hence the apparent surface temperature of the fireball and the amount of radiation emitted from it decreases after separation. But, as the shock front advances still farther, the temperature of the shocked air diminishes and it becomes increasingly transparent. This results in an unmasking of the still incandescent isothermal region and an increase in the apparent surface temperature of the fireball. This phenomena is referred to as breakaway.

Rate of Thermal Emission

a. The rate of thermal emission from the fireball is governed by its apparent surface temperature. From the foregoing discussion, it should be apparent that the thermal output of a nuclear air burst will then occur in two pulses (Figure 3-IV), an initial pulse, consisting primarily of ultraviolet radiation, which contains only about 1% of the total radiant energy of the explosion and is terminated as the shock front moves ahead of the fireball, and a second pulse which occurs after breakaway.

b. The thermal radiation emitted from the fireball surface during the second thermal pulse is responsible for most of the thermal effects. It consists chiefly of radiation in the infrared, visible, and ultraviolet regions of the electromagnetic spectrum. Thermal exposure (measured in joules per unit area of exposed surface) will be less farther from the center of the explosion because the radiation is spread over a greater area and is attenuated in passing through the intervening air. Since the fireball is very close to a point source of thermal radiation, the quantity of thermal radiation at any given point varies approximately with the square of the distance from the explosion. The inverse square law does not apply exactly because thermal radiation, particularly ultraviolet, will also be absorbed and scattered by the atmosphere. The degree of atmospheric visibility affects the attenuation of thermal energy with distance to a limited degree, but less than would be expected from the purely absorptive properties of the atmosphere, because the decrease in transmission is largely compensated by an increase in scattered radiation.

Shielding

Since thermal radiation travels in straight lines from the fireball (unless scattered) any opaque object interposed between the fireball and the target will act as a shield and provide significant protection from thermal radiation. If a significant amount of scattering is present, as is the case when visibility is poor, thermal radiation will be received from all directions and shielding will be less effective.

Yield and Altitude

a. *Yield.* The total amount of thermal radiation, the period of time during which it is emitted, and the range for thermal effects increase with the yield of the nuclear explosion.
b. *Altitude Effects.* The thermal radiation intensity at a given point will depend on the altitude and the type of burst. In general, the thermal hazard is greatest in the case of a low altitude air burst. General thermal effects will be less for surface bursts and frequently nonexistent for subsurface bursts. In surface bursts a large part of the thermal energy is absorbed by the ground or water around ground zero. In addition, shielding due to terrain irregularities of dust, moisture, and various gases in the air near the surface of the earth will tend to reduce the amount of thermal energy

reaching a target. In subsurface bursts without appreciable penetration, most of the thermal energy is absorbed and dissipated in heating and vaporizing soil and water below the surface.

c. *High Altitude Effects.* In high altitude air bursts (above 30 km), the low density of the atmosphere alters the nature of the thermal radiation process because the primary thermal radiation is absorbed in a much larger volume of air, and the temperature of the system is correspondingly less. While a greater percentage of the yield of the explosion appears in the form of thermal radiation, much of the radiation is emitted so slowly that it is ineffective. About 25-35% of the total yield is emitted in a single pulse of very short duration. Moreover, because of the relatively great distance between the center of the burst and the earth's surface, the intensity of thermal radiation at ground level is generally low.

Thermal Effects

a. When thermal radiation strikes an object, part will be reflected, part will be transmitted, and the rest will be absorbed. The fraction of the incident radiation that is absorbed depends on the nature and color of the material. A thin material may transmit a large part of the radiant energy striking it. A light colored object may reflect much of the incident radiation and thus escape damage. Thermal damage and injury is due to the absorption of large amounts of thermal energy within relatively short periods of time. The absorbed thermal radiation raises the temperature of the absorbing surface and results in scorching, charring, and possible ignition of combustible organic materials, such as wood, paper, fabrics, etc. If the target material is a poor thermal conductor, the absorbed energy is largely confined to a superficial layer of the material.

b. The radiation exposure (# Joules/sq/cm) required for the ignition of materials and other thermal effects increases with the yield of the weapon. This is so because increased thermal energy is required to compensate for energy lost via conduction and convection during the longer thermal pulse of higher yield weapons. For lower yield weapons, the thermal pulse is so short that there is not much time for these processes to cool the exposed surface. Hence, a much higher percentage of the deposited thermal energy is effective in producing thermal damage. This increased thermal requirement does not mean that the thermal hazard is less significant for higher yields. On the contrary, the total thermal energy released during a nuclear explosion increases markedly with yield, and the effects extend over much greater distances. Therefore, although more thermal energy is required to produce a given thermal response for a large yield explosion, the effective range to which this level extends is very much greater.

c. Actual ignition of materials exposed to thermal radiation is highly dependent on the width of the thermal pulse (which is dependent on weapon yield) and the nature of the material, particularly its thickness and moisture content. At locations close to ground zero where the radiant thermal exposure exceeds 125 Joules/sq cm, almost all ignitable materials will flame, although burning may not be sustained. On the other hand, at greater distances only the most easily ignited materials will flame, although charring of exposed surfaces may occur. The probability of significant fires following a nuclear explosion depends on the density of ignition points, the availability and condition of combustible material, wind, humidity, and the character of the surrounding area. Incendiary effects are compounded by secondary fires started by the blast wave effects such as from upset stoves and furnaces, broken gas lines, etc. In Hiroshima, a tremendous fire storm developed within 20 minutes after detonation. A fire storm burns in upon itself with great ferocity and is characterized by gale force winds blowing in towards the center of the fire from all points of the compass. It is not, however, a phenomenon peculiar to nuclear explosions, having been observed frequently in large forest fires and following incendiary raids during World War II.

MILITARY BALANCE OF SOUTH ASIA

China's military spending was approximated at US$ 77.95 billion in 2010, and is expected to grow by 12.7% to US$ 91.5 billion by 2012. Estimates of China's military budget have always different, and according to various standards, may either range between the range of US$ 35-60 billion, or may even be as high as US$ 200 billion. The US DoD, SIPRI, RAND, CIA and DIA all have different estimates of China's military budget, according to different sources as well as different standards. Due to China's incomparable economic growth, it state services and military apparatus have achieved quantum leaps during the last two decades. Perceived designs of China's political economy paint it as a hegemonic power that seeks to destabilize its neighbors and usurp the resources and riches of the region that is in its reach.

Sino-Japanese confrontations and other engagements in South China sea – especially around the disputed Spratly Islands – have been painted as aggressive maneuvers where China was to blame; in reality, it was China's awesome military capacity in the tactical dimension, coupled with tough diplomatic engagement in the strategic dimension, that helped China achieve her objectives, regardless of how the international media shaped public opinion about it. The so-called string of pearls that China is creating in the Pacific and Indian oceans is also a globalist theory that is designed to push Japan, South Korea, Taiwan (or the disputed Republic of China, rather), the Philippines, Malaysia, Indonesia, and even India, closer to the American perception of China's military 'designs'. Despite such concerns, China's military modernization and secretive development is unparalleled; the People's Liberation Army, Navy and Air Force operate at the cutting edge of military technology, and are significantly developing their conventional capabilities through research, development, testing and improvement.

China is also blamed for many cases of industrial espionage that were not just economic, but also military, in nature. Many of China's military technologies resemble those used, developed and deployed by the US, Russia, Japan, and European nations – however, China has the capacity to manufacture its weapons and weapons systems indigenously. China has also been the focus of cyber-warfare allegations, after hacking and online sabotage operations severely affected US military networks and software systems, weeks after prominent global commercial organizations and banks came under the same kind of hacking attacks and network-centric warfare. Despite these allegations, many analysts agree that hacking has become a non-state act, as the internet phenomenon of "Anonymous" has yet to be identified (and eliminated, if possible) and the perpetrators of the Stuxnet attack on Iran have yet to be ascertained (even though some blame the US and Israel for targeting Iran's nuclear program with the virus).

The People's Republic of China has modernized, capable and strategically defensive armed forces, even though they appear – or are made to appear – hostile and aggressive in tactical engagements. China also looks to strike a better balance in its relations with India and Pakistan, and will focus on improving relations with its neighbors according to its next Five-Year Plan period for 2011-15. This balance will be akin to China's relations with both countries in the 1950's, meaning that China wants to have the same kind of cooperation with India as it currently does with Pakistan – this will definitely reduce tensions in the region, and have ripple effects across the entire continent. However, such plans for greater cooperation and understanding might stall because of enhanced US-India engagement, and such ties might make China more cautious, since Indo-US collaboration is construed primarily in terms of China's containment.

India military spending stands at US$ 36.03 billion at 2012, and this is the official declassified estimate. An actual figure which includes the current program of defense expansion and modernization, of weapons imports, of operations planning and deployment, and the military scope for next ten years, would be much higher – some say it would be closer to China's official declassified estimate, while others stipulate it to be much higher. India's perception of China, and of Pakistan, continues to monopolize the attention of its defence establishment.

Since the last ten years, India has begun to focus more on China than on Pakistan, and many analysts and defense experts continue to say that India's view of the "Chinese threat" is not careful enough. However, the Mumbai attack shocked India into realizing two enemies in its neighbourhood, and may lead it to cultivate its own kind of asymmetric warriors in the form of Hindu zealots of the VHP – whose affiliate elements are already terrorizing Muslim and Christian minorities inside India. India's last army chief, General Deepak Kapoor, developed military strategies and doctrines on the basis of a scenario where India faces a two-front war with Pakistan and China under what he called a nuclear "overhang" – which basically means that India will be hard-pressed to pre-emptively use its nuclear weapons against two nuclear powers who can collectively outweigh India's conventional military forces.

This required the development of a "Cold Start" doctrine (to start preparing for military operations while the political leadership tries out diplomacy to make its mind and come to a decision – which is when South Block will have dynamic and implementable options to execute) and holding a number of exercises every year to keep the military ready and alert. To make this possible and tactically effective, the Indian Army developed Independent Battle Groups, or IBGs, in a unique warfare methodology where military units across the services can combine forces to achieve tactical and strategic objectives. As such, elements of the Army can collaborate with those of the Air Force in select operations, or under specified circumstances – in the recently held Vijayee Bhava exercises, troop formations of more than 20,000 soldiers and 200 tanks (this being a figure revised for the media) from the 21st Strike Corps of the Southern Command took part along with elements of the Air Force. Network centric warfare techniques were practiced along with massive mechanized mobilization maneuvers that included, for instance, battalion-to-squadron support, regiment-to-group support, corps-to-wing support, etc. Since the overall central command would be in one place, delays in analysis of inputs and decision-making would not deter ground forces from reacting effectively and timely to the situation(s) they face. Essentially, India's doctrinal direction and indigenous development is designed to make its military function like independent-yet-centrally-controlled task forces, which can achieve India's diplomatic, military, political, and most importantly economic, objectives using both conventional and nuclear assets. Just because India is in the process of achieving this strategic 'decentralization' of its entire armed forces, its military augmentation cannot be possible without using foreign resources – which means weapons support – purchase, development and refurbishment – along with combined training exercised and joint deployments with the US, Russia and Israel, from which India collectively imports about 70% of its weapons requirements. On that note, India is also the world's largest weapons importer, accounting for about 9-10% of all global arms imports.

The 123 agreement and the NSG 'waiver' situation were watersheds in India's goals of becoming a superpower by obtaining unconventional technology of the highest international standards whose outputs could be used for both peaceful and military designs. Increased nuclear trade with India – which is justified because of a 'vast market' for such technologies and its civilian outputs – has also enabled quantum leaps in India's secret development of nuclear weapons, both in WMD and plutonium weapon. It has also enabled India to explore other non-peaceful purposes such as radiation warfare tools and suitcase nukes. India's civilian nuclear matrix – except for those plants explicitly built with foreign funds and technology – has not been able to accommodate benefits from global nuclear trade, but India's military establishment and strategic nuclear arsenal has been sufficiently augmented, thanks to the de-listing of India's strategic defence industries, especially DRDO, from organizations whom the US could not share such technology with. India is currently moving to build a US$ 2.2 billion dedicated, highly secure and state-of-the-art optical fiber cable (OFC) network for the Army, Navy and Air Force. Utilizing a variety of firewalls and cryptograph layers of security software and coding, this will be one of the world's largest closed user group (CUG) networks for exclusive use by the 1.32 million active personnel of the Indian armed forces. Policy circles are currently deliberating whether the 2.17 million reserve personnel should be granted access to the CUG or not, and cases like Wikileaks are definitely deterring South Block from expanding the security clearance of electronic data so wide. The Indian Armed Forces plan to have an active military space program – and are putting both communications and military satellites into space – and are also currently developing a missile defense shield and nuclear triad capability to deal with what India perceives as immediate regional threats – China and Pakistan. India's development cooperation with Russia on critical military projects such as on the Fifth Generation Fighter Aircraft (FGFA), Multirole Transport Aircraft (MTA), and others might come under strain because India has potential sellers from Europe and the US as well, and Russia's recent MiG-29 crash showed how India would flinch at not getting the right weapon for the price. And while India's defense modernization and upgradation may give it a definitive edge over Pakistan and its methods of asymmetric warfare, India still has a long road to travel before it can match what China's military has to offer on its southern perimeters. Arunachal Pradesh and Aksai Chin continue to remain a geographical and territorial dispute between the two Asian powers, making them unable to overcome suspicion as they try to engage each other's economies.

Pakistan's military budget was estimated at US$ 6.41 billion for 2010-11. Pakistan's defense spending faces frequent fluctuations and increases, despite the fact that the military budget (official and declassified, of course) actually decreases year-by-year in terms of purchasing power parity because of the weakness of the Pak Rupee.

Pakistan's military forces are divided between two geographical sectors – in the West, ground troops and the Air Force are engaging TTP insurgents and Al Qaeda affiliates in the northern parts of the country, whereas in the south, they are dealing with a fiery insurgency in Balochistan, being run by Bramdagh Bugti and Harbiyar Marri, self-exiled separatist warlords of the Baloch people.

In the eastern part of the country, troops that were usually deployed against arch enemy India are now stationed inside urban areas to protect against terrorist attacks and to deter suicide bombers from attaining free passage. Troops are also deployed throughout major communications arteries and road routes, and the countryside, to hinder insurgent logistics. After a unilateral strike by the US in Abbottabad to kill Osama bin Laden, and after the dastardly attack on PNS Mehran, vocal calls by opposition politicians and civil society for more accountability of military spending is constituted as impediments of delay rather than meddling, and may serve to Pakistan's benefit if it can account for a strategic reorientation towards internal threats, and towards consolidating territorial security.

Pakistan's military, especially its Army, is under severe pressure because of public opinion home and abroad, and this is considered to be a unique kind of fourth-generation psychological warfare tactic that is succeeding because of broad-based support to the anti-Pakistan narrative by major globalist organizations (or self-proclaimed research think tanks, which are heavily staffed if not "infiltrated" by Indian and Israeli analysts inimical to Pakistan) and by world powers that seek to either destabilize Pakistan, or keep it crippled. This globalist psy-op may intensify based on future projects, but Pakistan's intelligence community is divided between dealing with the problem of the existential threat (terrorists and militant extremists in the host society) or with retaliating to this psychological warfare with strategic propaganda and motivation tactics. Pakistan's political and military leadership needs to develop a workable counter-terror strategy, because the US – which itself is reconfiguring its strategies on a quarterly basis, but still faces criticisms and mistakes – claims that Pakistan does not have a robust methodology to deal with terrorists. Despite being deployed on a multidimensional front in the War on Terror, Pakistan's primary military doctrine has been tested in the Azm-e-Nau exercises, which has tested battle concepts based on integration of force components and different quantums. These exercises and their doctrines were developed from the tactical and operational lessons learned from pitched battles in Swat, South Waziristan, Bajaur and other fronts, and were also designed to train the Armed Forces for any kind of "international aggression", an obvious allusion to India.

The US coalition support fund (CSF) and other counter insurgency funds do not support Pakistan's military operations as much as they should, and, in hindsight, they are effectively views as impediments or "strings" attached to Pakistan's government that force it to follow "dictations from America". The Friends of

Democratic Pakistan (FoDP) forum is also not forthcoming in support Pakistan's military operations either, as a perception of corrupt governance deters donors from giving Pakistan economic aid as well as much needed political and military assistance. Causing delays in disbursing these funds after time-consuming accountability and audit processes has caused great problems for Pakistan, and indirectly, it will lead to even more problems for the US and its NATO allies in Afghanistan – who, as history has shown, will turn around and blame Pakistan. Facing both TTP and Al Qaeda as a frontline state, Pakistan is hard pressed for friends: Al Qaeda targets it for being allied to the US, while the US, NATO, India and others allege Pakistan to support the terrorists who threaten to destroy world peace. This situation leads Pakistan to – like the US – behave unilaterally, and sometimes, follow its own strategic national interest (whatever that may be, and however it is designed and implemented) without regard for the interests and objectives of other regional stakeholders. The revelations by the late Asia Times bureau chief Saleem Shahzad proved to be damning for Pakistan and even more worrisome for Al Qaeda as its roots, reach and doctrine became exposed as a result of "Inside Al Qaeda and the Taliban". Extremism, or sympathy for radical religious elements, in Pakistan's Armed Forces is an issue that has been continuously dealt with by the Military Intelligence as well as counter-intelligence units of the ISI – isolated incidents should not be painted as the norm, and they should also not be used to portray the Pakistani military as a 'hotbed of anti-US anti-Indian militant extremism' when they professional soldiers already are suffering the most because of the War on Terror.

However, modern neo-extremist organizations such as Hizb-ut-Tahrir, Lashkar-e-Toiba, and the deceased Ilyas Kashmiri's Harkat ul Mujahideen al Alami (which became a crucial component of Al Qaeda Lashkar-e-Zil when Kashmiri became Al Qaeda's military commander) are focusing more on Pakistan than on America, not just because of Pakistan's nuclear weapons – which are quite hard to obtain, and even harder to use or deploy – but also because it is their strategic doctrine to get control of a Muslim nation state through which they can attack oppressive non-Muslim powers. This is how Ayman al Zawahiri – Al Qaeda's new commander – sees the future of Islamic militancy and its ultimate success, and operations to achieve this goal are being undertaken by AQIM in Yemen as well as Al Shabab in Somalia.

Despite the fact that Pakistan is suffering the most out of any country engaged in the War on Terror, Pakistan is not deterred by internal demoralization or by international voices that raise more suspicion than concern, and Pakistan's security forces continue to fight terrorist elements on a daily basis. International forces that point more fingers than they point out problems should know that Pakistan's people are not happy with daily suicide bombings, or kidnappings, or terror attacks, and that Pakistan's security forces and civilians have suffered the most casualties in the War on Terror – this automatically means that Pakistan is fighting the terrorists, not harboring them (despite what American media outlets will continue to say after May 2nd) and an effective media campaign built on dissemination of evidence and calculated propaganda is necessary for Pakistan to make its case truthfully plain and clear to the international community.

Pakistan's civilian government needs to immediately draft and enact a suitable counter-extremism doctrine as well, because such evidence only makes it more important for Pakistan to rationalize the brand of political Islam that is prevalent among its people, and it must draw on principles of democracy, pluralism, peace and non-violence in order to actually achieve security for its people. Only definitions of counter-extremism can help Pakistan differentiate between friend and foe, and it can help rehabilitate internal enemies and support those citizens and individuals who are non-violent and exhort the principles of peace and brotherhood.

However, Pakistan is – as US estimates state – deficient and ill-equipped to deal with the militants in terms of weapons and financial support. US estimates also stated that Pakistani elements might be in collusion with Al Qaeda and the Taliban – that is only because of recurrent evidence of ex-military and ex-policemen being either caught or killed along with Al Qaeda. More often than not, Pakistan's incapacity and incapability is confused with deceit and treachery, even though such information also indicates that the evident threat is neutralized. Pakistan desperately needs night-vision equipment, specialized weapons and ammunition for counter-terrorist forces (both military and police), and it also needs state-of-the-art stun grenades, body armor, communications and surveillance equipment, and once it has that, it can develop modern tactics and strategies to deal with terrorist threats – pre-emptively as well.

This is why Pakistan's option of a limited and calculated strike against selective targets in North Waziristan is better than a full-scale military assault that creates a vast displaced population (within which terrorist elements can find refuge and shelter, and also infiltrate Pakistan's urban centers). Pakistan already seems to be deploying such a strategy in Kurram agency. Pakistan's military engagement with China, coupled with a US$ 60 billion dollar package deal signed with China last year, is looked at with a lot of hope, and may start delivering within a couple of years. Pakistan is developing the agile and multirole JF-17 Thunder aircraft with China, and also developing indigenous weapons for small-scale and medium-scale use.

For better or for worse, a debilitated state of security in the country has caused the mushrooming of both private security firms as well as security tools such as scanners, bullet-proof vests and glasses, etc. Weapons procurement has been made extremely difficult because of government regulations, but illegal firearms can still be procured despite unconventional checks and balances being placed on them by the intelligence community. The economy of drugs and guns pervades Afghanistan and Pakistan, and in a nutshell, this is what the United States (and its last two presidents) calls the "Af-Pak" region. In a way, Afghanistan is the Mexico of Central Asia.

President Karzai, with or without the legitimacy he has or does not have, must know that no Afghan President can ever acknowledge the Durand line as the border of Afghanistan and Pakistan – he must also understand that in this situation, he must be the first Afghan President to acknowledge and decree the border of Afghanistan and Pakistan, to settle this border dispute once and for all, otherwise this frontier will see the same kind of tension that is seen on the Arunachal Pradesh and Aksai Chin borders. If Pakistan and Afghanistan are conjoined twins, then the issue of a border is immaterial, and such misconceptions and historical roots of hatred must be overcome. Pakistan's military engagement in Afghanistan is expected to decrease, and it may be replaced with enhanced diplomatic and economic engagement as the US withdraws – Pakistan's counter-terrorism activities will focus to the east of the Durand line, as it hopes that Afghan security forces will be able to deal with insurgents, militants and radical extremists on the Western side of the border. But many important questions for the "Af-Pak" region remain unanswered: Does Pakistan need to protect itself as a strategic gateway (a status it enjoys in both political and economic terms)? Does it need to provide sovereign protection for economic routes that run both ways – between the Middle East and Central Asia, and India, China and the Far East? What does Pakistan need to do about Balochistan, and has it really become for Pakistan what Kashmir is for India?

Many experts believe that the panacea to Pakistan's problems lies in economic growth; that development and creation of opportunities will be able to mainstream those people who are marginalized and who fall into the trap of the extremist fringe. Political stability, enforcement of the rule of law, and employment opportunities may give Pakistan a fighting chance against all kinds of extremists – homegrown or otherwise, religious or otherwise. The Pakistani military has done as much as it can – it can be asked to do it again and again, whenever and wherever need be, but is such repetitive deployment to Pakistan's benefit? Repeating the same ineffective policy will only waste Pakistan's time and resources, as its enemy would regroup and reinvigorate itself to fight the Pakistani state.

Afghanistan, under President Hamid Karzai, has developed a 167,000 strong Afghan National Army which is expected to reach 260,000 by 2014, and a civilian counterpart in the form of the Afghan National Police, which is staffed by 115,000 members and will grow to 160,000. However, despite massive security assistance, training and support (both to deployed active troops and troops in combat), Afghan security forces remain mired in allegations of corruption, moral turpitude, and misuse of power, along with rampant drug abuse that is unbecoming of officers of the state, let alone personnel of security forces. Fiscal pressures and expectations of a financial meltdown only compound the fact that the Afghan people are not fully able to govern themselves as yet, and that the Afghan government is ill-equipped to deal with the problems it faces – if it faces them alone. The Taliban remain a potent enemy not only for the Afghan government and security forces, but also for US troops and the NATO-ISAF contingent that has begun drawing down from the country. The current Afghan dispensation has started talks with the Taliban, but in the absence of any overt sign by Mullah Omar and the central leadership (whether it is based in Quetta, or Karachi, or Kandahar) means that President Karzai is talking to some Taliban while some other Taliban (and Al Qaeda) are fighting them and the "Americans", which the composite narrative for the oppressor being used by both radical and mainstream Islamic conservatives in the so-called "Af-Pak" region.

Afghanistan needs to reorient itself for sovereign security, and deal with a Taliban insurgency that is gaining the momentum as President Obama hastens the withdrawal of US troops, and by implication, that of NATO-ISAF presence in Afghanistan. British PM David Cameron has made similar statements. And both countries' militaries have said that they are stupefied by the political leadership – Admiral Mullen and General Petraeus termed the withdrawal orders a bit "aggressive", while the British defence high command has also made cautious noises about the overall withdrawal plan. There have been hints by the highest echelons of the US defense establishment that there will be continued US presence in Afghanistan beyond 2014-15, but is that for ensuring Afghan sovereignty? Or controlling Al Qaeda and Taliban influence? Is it to keep an eye on Pakistan, and on China as well? Afghanistan needs to understand the ground reality of its national and territorial sovereignty, and take neighbors into confidence. Leaving Afghanistan alone and incapable of dealing with its problems will automatically lead to a situation where neighbors and regional powers will have to step in – this time, they must do so in order to help, and by respecting Afghan sovereignty and the security and safety of the Afghan people.

India should focus on internal threats, as should Pakistan. India needs to deal with issues of equitable economic development, lest it run into the same problems that developing economies like Tunisia, Egypt, Bahrain and Libya are facing. Militancy threatens both Pakistan and India – for the former, it is religious or right-wing extremist militancy, and for the latter, it is Naxalite or left-wing extremist militancy (except for Kashmir, which is a nationalist insurrection inherited from its colonial past).

They can be dealt with militarily as well, but long-term panacea's to these kinds of militancy lies in the establishment of social safety needs, the equitable experience of economic development for all, and most importantly, the mainstreaming of the marginalized and the oppressed. If China and India, or India and Pakistan for that matter, were to engage each other militarily, the conflict would draw out into a long and bloody war that would be further protracted because of superpower interests and the opportunity to shape a new world order from the outcome. China and India match each other in terms of modern weaponry, numbers and doctrinal development. India and Pakistan have a sufficient conventional imbalance, but a long-term incursion into Pakistani territory will bleed India if Pakistan's cruise missile technology and modernized armor and mechanized units are unable to prevent it. Over the last seven years, Indian Armed Forces have held over ten major exercises, and Pakistan has responded with a commensurate number of military exercises of its own, along with the development of new doctrines and battle orientations. Pakistan's Air Force, along with its supply and logistics formations, have undergone vast transformations especially because of the latter being in continuous service since 1999. Pakistan still has to develop its military's network-centric warfare capabilities and its national cyber-defence framework (Pakistan's networks and telecommunications infrastructure is pathetic compared to other countries, and the deployment of the Badr-1R satellite in August is not expected to cause a dent in this capacity).

In these developing countries, the military is often seen as a root of upward social mobility for the rural classes in particular. They offer a source of pride for family service to the country, and offer benefits and privileges to its officers and men. There are also some obligations in serving, or in acquiring military training, for all civilians, and in certain cases mass conscription – of all males and females above the age of 18 – also takes place. But the notion of defence spending and its consideration as a non-development budget item is a problem that needs to be addressed in economies where health, education, social safety nets, rule of law and state services are dwindling, or worse, in a state of decay.

China's military is in a stable position of deterrence and growth, and does not see any discrepancies or imbalances in the near future unless it is drawn into a confrontation with Russia or the US – which is unlikely at this stage. India and Pakistan, however, must use their militaries as forces of reintegration and not destruction. They must realize that a military can fight wars, protect security objectives, and also partake or aid in nation-building. The military offers a nation the common denominator of nationalism and civil service – military service in a country allows its citizens to forget structural differences like ethnicity, linguistic affiliation, provincial association, religious inclination, and so forth. Afghanistan, which suffers from the problem of a corrupt and non-representative yet "democratic" governing dispensation under the Presidency of Hamid Karzai, needs to transform its security forces into a more representative composite of Afghan society – one that is cognizant of the entire Afghan community's security needs, its traditions and ethos, and the measures and standards of effectiveness that are not only globally recognized, but regionally appreciated as well. The global economic recession requires the world's biggest markets to develop innovative economic policies suited to both the requirements and the conditions of the 21st century. Cooperation, collaboration, and cognizance of interdependence will help all nation-states in the South Asian region in particular, and the Asian region at large.

EXPLOSIVE POWER IN A GLOBAL NUCLEAR WAR

The nuclear bomb exploded over Hiroshima had an explosive power of about 13 kilotonnes, denoted 13kt. One kt is the equivalent of one thousand tonnes (of one thousand kilogrammes each) of chemical explosives. The Hiroshima bomb was an enriched uranium fission bomb and the Nagasaki bomb of 21kt was a plutonium fission bomb. Much greater explosive power can be obtained by using an enriched uranium fission explosion as a trigger to cause nuclear fusion in a mixture of lithium and deuterium (heavy hydrogen). This is the thermonuclear, fusion, hydrogen or H-bomb. Unenriched uranium is often put around the fusion bomb to absorb emitted neutrons and cause further fissions and thus increase explosive power. This is the standard fission-fusion-fission bomb, whose explosive power is usually measured in megatonnes (denoted Mt), with 1Mt equal to 1000kt. The largest atmospheric nuclear explosion was one by the Soviet Union in 1961, of about 60Mt yield.

A typical large-sized nuclear explosive in the 'strategic' arsenals of the United States or the Soviet Union used to be about 1Mt, and many weapons of this size are deployed today in the payloads of ballistic missiles. The trend in the United States for the past decade or so, and in the Soviet Union for a few years, has been to switch from a single large warhead to several smaller warheads in the payload of strategic ballistic missiles. For example, a single 1Mt bomb might be replaced by ten 50kt bombs, each independently targetable. In this case this change reduces total explosive power by one half, while the total surface area that potentially can be destroyed is increased by one third.

The overwhelming bulk of nuclear explosive power resides in the arsenals of the two nuclear superpowers, the United States and the Soviet Union. In 1960 this explosive power totalled perhaps 60,000Mt. But due to the trend noted above, present arsenals total about 11,000Mt: about 3,500Mt for the United States and 7,500Mt for the Soviet Union. While the trend to larger numbers of smaller warheads increases the potential area destroyed by nuclear weapons, the reduction in total megatonnage reduces the potential global effects. This is especially the case since the clouds from nuclear explosions of 1Mt or less are unlikely to rise high into the stratosphere, reducing stratospheric fallout and effects on ozone.

What fraction of the 11,000Mt would be exploded in a major nuclear war? This is hard to assess, but almost certainly much will not be exploded. Both the United States and the Soviet Union place a high priority on targeting their opponent's military forces, nuclear forces in particular. A sizable fraction of nuclear arsenals is likely to be destroyed before use (attacks on nuclear submarines, airfields, missile silos), be unavailable for use (submarines in port, missiles cut off from communications) or fail to perform properly. One estimate is that one sixth to one third of superpower arsenals will be used, depending on whether the war occurs suddenly or builds up gradually.

If these estimates are correct then about 2000Mt to 4000Mt of nuclear firepower might be exploded in a major nuclear war. The total could be much smaller in a 'limited' nuclear war. The figure of 4000Mt is used in this article in making illustrative calculations. It is assumed that half of this total is due to fission and half to fusion.

Overkill

'Overkill: the ability to exterminate a population more than once. "Both the US and the Soviet Union now possess nuclear stockpiles large enough to exterminate mankind three or four - some say ten - times over" (Philip Noel-Baker, Nobel Peace Prize winner, 1971) .'

Many people believe that the capacity of nuclear weapons for 'overkill' means that all or most of the people on earth would die in a major nuclear war. In spite of the prevalence of this idea, there is little scientific evidence to support it.

Many calculations of 'overkill' appear to be made using the nuclear attacks on Hiroshima and Nagasaki as a baseline. Estimates of the number of people killed at Hiroshima from a 13kt bomb range from 63,000 to over 200,000. Adopting a figure of 130,000 for illustrative purposes gives ten people killed for each tonne of nuclear explosive. By linear extrapolation, explosion of a third of a million times as much explosive power, 4000Mt, would kill a third of a million times as many people, namely 40,000 million, or nearly ten times the present world population.

But this factor of ten is misleading, since linear extrapolation does not apply. Suppose the bomb dropped on Hiroshima had been 1000 times as powerful, 13Mt. It could not have killed 1000 times as many people, but at most the entire population of Hiroshima perhaps 250,000. Re-doing the 'overkill' calculation using these figures gives not a figure of ten but of only 0.02. This example shows that crude linear extrapolations of this sort are unlikely to provide any useful information about the effects of nuclear war.

'Overkill' can be meaningful if applied to specific targets which will be attacked by several nuclear weapons. But applied to the entire world population the concept of 'overkill' is misleading. By the same logic it might be said that there is enough water in the oceans to drown everyone ten times.

It has been argued that if the megatonnage in nuclear arsenals were increased by ten or 100 times and used in war, the fallout would be sufficient to threaten the life of most people on earth. Since total megatonnage has been decreasing in recent years, this particular possibility remains hypothetical, at least at the moment.

PEACE MOVEMENT FOR NUCLEAR WAR

The risk of nuclear war

Unless nuclear weapons are totally eliminated, it is a virtual certainty that nuclear war will occur eventually. The likelihood of war in any given year may be small, but the cumulative effect of small probabilities can approach certainty. The likelihood is definitely not zero. For example, it is known that US policy-makers have seriously considered using nuclear weapons unilaterally on a number of occasions.

Two developments have increased the risk of nuclear war in recent years. First is the deployment of highly accurate strategic missile systems in the US and the Soviet Union, plus developments in anti-submarine warfare and communications and control systems. This is increasing the chance that one of the superpowers will launch a 'first strike' in an attempt to destroy the opponent's nuclear inventory. Second is the spread of the capability to make nuclear weapons to more and more countries, fostered by the expansion of the nuclear power industry. It seems likely that this nuclear proliferation will be aided at some stage by laser enrichment of uranium, a technique which will dramatically reduce the obstacles to obtaining nuclear weapons. The question in such circumstances is not if nuclear war will occur, but when, what kind, and on what scale.

The risk of nuclear war could be removed if all nuclear weapons were eliminated- total nuclear disarmament. How could this happen? I have argued elsewhere that convincing decision-makers or mobilising public opinion to influence decision-makers is insufficient, and that what is required is grassroots initiatives mobilising large numbers of people in activities that challenge or transform warlinked institutions and which create new institutions.

The chance that the people struggling for fundamental institutional change will succeed worldwide in 20, 50 or 100 years is much less than certainty. Indeed, any realistic assessment of the strength of the present peace movement, in terms of its ability to fundamentally affect arms races and their institutional bases, would have to admit its extreme weakness. The peace movement seems highly unlikely to bring about nuclear disarmament within the next few years, and hence it should be prepared for the possibility of nuclear war. Whether a nuclear war is limited or global, available evidence suggests that a large fraction of the world's population may be unaffected physically. A long term strategy for peace must provide the basis for transforming the war system both before and after nuclear war or nuclear wars, and at the same time minimise the chance of nuclear war occurring in the first place.

In addition to the important physical effects of nuclear war there would be important indirect political effects. It seems very likely that there would be strong moves to maintain or establish authoritarian rule as a response to crises preceding or following nuclear war. Ever since Hiroshima, the threat of nuclear destruction has been used to prop up repressive institutions, under the pretext of defending against the 'enemy'. The actuality of nuclear war could easily result in the culmination of this trend. Large segments of the population could be manipulated to support a repressive regime under the necessity to defend against further threats or to obtain revenge. A limited nuclear war might kill some hundreds of thousands or tens of millions of people, surely a major tragedy.

But another tragedy could also result: the establishment, possibly for decades, of repressive civilian or military rule in countries such as Italy, Australia and the US, even if they were not directly involved in the war. The possibility of grassroots mobilisation for disarmament and peace would be greatly reduced even from its present levels. For such developments the people and the peace movements of the world are largely unprepared.

Preparedness for crisis situations

As well as encouraging moves towards repressive rule, the political and social upheaval resulting from nuclear war could also provide major opportunities for rapid social change in progressive directions. Several factors would operate here.

(a) There would be worldwide anguish and outrage at any significant use of nuclear weapons against populations. This emotion could easily turn against established institutions.

(b) A nuclear war involving the US, Soviet Union and Europe would weaken or destroy the bases for imperialism and neocolonialism in poor countries, and stimulate widespread revolutionary action that could not be contained by local elites left without rich country support.

(c) In areas directly affected by nuclear attack, the destruction of established institutions would allow the creation of new structures.

Historically, periods of economic or military crisis often have preceded revolutionary change, though not always with desirable results. Crises provide opportunities for groups which are organised and able to take advantage of them. In the case of nuclear war, present governments have made some arrangements to preserve their type of rule after a nuclear war. By contrast, the peace movement is almost completely unprepared to respond to a crisis engendered by nuclear war.

The primary objective of national security bureaucracies in the event of nuclear war is survival of the state apparatus. This has two components: continued defence against the outside enemy, and defence against challenges raised by the native population.

The health and welfare of the general population is a secondary consideration, mainly important in its effects on the two primary goals. This emphasis is reflected in preparations for the survival of key officials, for continuity of official decision-making apparatuses and communications, and for quelling 'civil disturbances'.

In the absence of any significant countervailing force, a nuclear war will not be the end of war but the beginning of the age of many nuclear wars. Although nuclear war may lead to mass revulsion, there will also be strong government and citizen pressures for retaliation, revenge, efforts to 'do better next time' and not to be caught unprepared. The rise of Nazism after World War I should point to the danger. Scenarios for World Wars IV, V, VI and so forth may be repulsive, but cannot be discounted solely for that reason.

During World War II, several key groups in the US developed plans for the post-war world. More generally, post-war political and economic considerations played a large role in many decisions, military and otherwise, during the war. The same pattern is being and will be replayed prior to and during a nuclear war. It is not for lack of anything better to do that nuclear strategists have elaborated numerous scenarios for nuclear war, recovery and future wars. During and after a nuclear crisis or war, powerful interest groups will attempt to sway developments through management of the news, mobilisation of sympathetic groups, creating scapegoats, suppressing dissent, and using many other mechanisms familiar to us today. If these developments are to be opposed, peace activists need to be prepared to act during nuclear crisis and nuclear war and afterwards.

Preparation for nuclear war by the peace movement could increase the chances of success in struggles for social justice, especially in the poor countries, during a period of chaos in the rich countries resulting from nuclear war or nuclear crisis.

Implications for the present

But these possibilities provide relatively little consolation for the human disaster of nuclear war, and certainly would not justify any policy which significantly increased the risk of nuclear war.

It is in their implications for the present that peace movement activities relating to nuclear war must be assessed. It is my belief that preparation for nuclear war by the peace movement would reduce the chance of nuclear war by providing a visible threat to the otherwise unchallenged continuance of existing political institutions. National decision-makers may wish to avoid nuclear war to save their own lives, but they have demonstrated a continued willingness to risk nuclear war, both in crises and confrontations and through the very existence of nuclear arsenals, through the policies they have promoted and the institutions they have constructed and supported. This institutionalised risk of nuclear war will seem less acceptable if one consequence of continued preparations for war were a major challenge to the complete system of political and economic power and privilege.

Nuclear weapons states have refrained from nuclear war thus far not primarily because of their perception of the human disaster of nuclear war but because of the possible political consequences. A prepared peace movement would ensure that such political consequences are as serious as possible.

There are a number of principles which seem appropriate for peace movement planning for nuclear crisis, nuclear war and its aftermath. Peace movement planning has to be based on an open rather than a hidden agenda. A full peace movement strategy must take into account supporters and sympathisers as well as opponents in working out how to take full advantage of the crisis. But most important is the task of developing strategies, methods and organisational forms which are relevant both in the nuclear crisis, nuclear war and its aftermath, and for ongoing activities today. Just as peace group organisational structures should be designed to handle infiltrators, so these structures - and other aspects of efforts for peace - should be designed to operate in the event of nuclear war.

And, vice versa, the type of preparations for nuclear war decided upon should be compatible with current effectiveness. Only if the threat of institutional revolution in the event of nuclear war is also raised in the present is it likely that disarmament as a reform will seem to powerholders as the lesser of two evils. In spite of the attention I am giving here to preparing for nuclear war, and in spite of the optimism of some nonmilitarists for developments in the wake of massive social disaster or breakdown,[6] the prospects for a post-nuclear war world seem rather dismal to me. Aside from the massive loss of life and continuing human suffering caused by nuclear war, moral barriers against the future use of nuclear weapons in war would be greatly reduced. We need only remember the world outrage at terrorist bombings of civilian targets during the Spanish Civil War by Germany and Italy. Not long after, such bombing became standard policy for the 'enlightened democracies'. This points to the need to be prepared to fully utilise the outrage and disruption of the first nuclear war.

THE MECHANICS OF NUCLEAR EXPLOSIONS

In nuclear explosions, about 90 percent of the energy is released in less than one millionth of a second. Most of this is in the form of the heat and shock waves which produce the damage. It is this immediate and direct explosive power which could devastate the urban centers in a major nuclear war. Compared with the immediate colossal destruction suffered in target areas, the more subtle, longer term effects of the remaining 10 percent of the energy released by nuclear weapons might seem a matter of secondary concern. But the dimensions of the initial catastrophe should not overshadow the after-effects of a nuclear war.

They would be global, affecting nations remote from the fighting for many years after the holocaust, because of the way nuclear explosions behave in the atmosphere and the radioactive products released by nuclear bursts.

When a weapon is detonated at the surface of the earth or at low altitudes, the heat pulse vaporizes the bomb material, target, nearby structures, and underlying soil and rock, all of which become entrained in an expanding, fast-rising fireball. As the fireball rises, it expands and cools, producing the distinctive mushroom cloud, signature of nuclear explosions. The altitude reached by the cloud depends on the force of the explosion. When yields are in the low-kiloton range, the cloud will remain in the lower atmosphere and its effects will be entirely local. But as yields exceed 30 kilotons, part of the cloud will punch into the stratosphere, which begins about 7 miles up. With yields of 2-5 megatons or more, virtually all of the cloud of radioactive debris and fine dust will climb into the stratosphere. The heavier materials reaching the lower edge of the stratosphere will soon settle out, as did the Castle/Bravo fallout at Rongelap. But the lighter particles will penetrate high into the stratosphere, to altitudes of 12 miles and more, and remain there for months and even years. Stratospheric circulation and diffusion will spread this material around the world.

Radioactive Fallout

Both the local and worldwide fallout hazards of nuclear explosions depend on a variety of interacting factors: weapon design, explosive force, altitude and latitude of detonation, time of year, and local weather conditions.

All present nuclear weapon designs require the splitting of heavy elements like uranium and plutonium. The energy released in this fission process is many millions of times greater, pound for pound, than the most energetic chemical reactions. The smaller nuclear weapon, in the low-kiloton range, may rely solely on the energy released by the fission process, as did the first bombs which devastated Hiroshima and Nagasaki in 1945.

The larger yield nuclear weapons derive a substantial part of their explosive force from the fusion of heavy forms of hydrogen—deuterium and tritium. Since there is virtually no limitation on the volume of fusion materials in a weapon, and the materials are less costly than fissionable materials, the fusion, "thermonuclear," or "hydrogen" bomb brought a radical increase in the explosive power of weapons. However, the fission process is still necessary to achieve the high temperatures and pressures needed to trigger the hydrogen fusion reactions. Thus, all nuclear detonations produce radioactive fragments of heavy elements fission, with the larger bursts producing an additional radiation component from the fusion process.

The nuclear fragments of heavy-element fission which are of greatest concern are those radioactive atoms (also called radionuclides) which decay by emitting energetic electrons or gamma particles. (See "Radioactivity" note.) An important characteristic here is the rate of decay.

This is measured in terms of "half-life"—the time required for one-half of the original substance to decay—which ranges from days to thousands of years for the bomb-produced radionuclides of principal interest. (See "Nuclear Half-Life" note.) Another factor which is critical in determining the hazard of radionuclides is the chemistry of the atoms. This determines whether they will be taken up by the body through respiration or the food cycle and incorporated into tissue. If this occurs, the risk of biological damage from the destructive ionizing radiation (see "Radioactivity" note) is multiplied.

Probably the most serious threat is cesium-137, a gamma emitter with a half-life of 30 years. It is a major source of radiation in nuclear fallout, and since it parallels potassium chemistry, it is readily taken into the blood of animals and men and may be incorporated into tissue. Other hazards are strontium-90, an electron emitter with a half-life of 28 years, and iodine-131 with a half-life of only 8 days. Strontium-90 follows calcium chemistry, so that it is readily incorporated into the bones and teeth, particularly of young children who have received milk from cows consuming contaminated forage. Iodine-131 is a similar threat to infants and children because of its concentration in the thyroid gland. In addition, there is plutonium-239, frequently used in nuclear explosives. A bone-seeker like strontium-90, it may also become lodged in the lungs, where its intense local radiation can cause cancer or other damage.

Plutonium-239 decays through emission of an alpha particle (helium nucleus) and has a half-life of 24,000 years. To the extent that hydrogen fusion contributes to the explosive force of a weapon, two other radionuclides will be released: tritium (hydrogen-3), an electron emitter with a half-life of 12 years, and carbon-14, an electron emitter with a half-life of 5,730 years. Both are taken up through the food cycle and readily incorporated in organic matter.

Three types of radiation damage may occur: bodily damage (mainly leukemia and cancers of the thyroid, lung, breast, bone, and gastrointestinal tract); genetic damage (birth defects and constitutional and degenerative diseases due to gonodal damage suffered by parents); and development and growth damage (primarily growth and mental retardation of unborn infants and young children). Since heavy radiation doses of about 20 roentgen or more (see "Radioactivity" note) are necessary to produce developmental defects, these effects would probably be confined to areas of heavy local fallout in the nuclear combatant nations and would not become a global problem.

A. Local Fallout

Most of the radiation hazard from nuclear bursts comes from short-lived radionuclides external to the body; these are generally confined to the locality downwind of the weapon burst point. This radiation hazard comes from radioactive fission fragments with half-lives of seconds to a few months, and from soil and other materials in the vicinity of the burst made radioactive by the intense neutron flux of the fission and fusion reactions.

It has been estimated that a weapon with a fission yield of 1 million tons TNT equivalent power (1 megaton) exploded at ground level in a 15 miles-per-hour wind would produce fallout in an ellipse extending hundreds of miles downwind from the burst point. At a distance of 20-25 miles downwind, a lethal radiation dose (600 rads) would be accumulated by a person who did not find shelter within 25 minutes after the time the fallout began. At a distance of 40-45 miles, a person would have at most 3 hours after the fallout began to find shelter. Considerably smaller radiation doses will make people seriously ill. Thus, the survival prospects of persons immediately downwind of the burst point would be slim unless they could be sheltered or evacuated.

It has been estimated that an attack on U.S. population centers by 100 weapons of one-megaton fission yield would kill up to 20 percent of the population immediately through blast, heat, ground shock and instant radiation effects (neutrons and gamma rays); an attack with 1,000 such weapons would destroy immediately almost half the U.S. population. These figures do not include additional deaths from fires, lack of medical attention, starvation, or the lethal fallout showering to the ground downwind of the burst points of the weapons. Most of the bomb-produced radionuclides decay rapidly. Even so, beyond the blast radius of the exploding weapons there would be areas ("hot spots") the survivors could not enter because of radioactive contamination from long-lived radioactive isotopes like strontium-90 or cesium-137, which can be concentrated through the food chain and incorporated into the body. The damage caused would be internal, with the injurious effects appearing over many years. For the survivors of a nuclear war, this lingering radiation hazard could represent a grave threat for as long as 1 to 5 years after the attack.

B. Worldwide Effects of Fallout

Much of our knowledge of the production and distribution of radionuclides has been derived from the period of intensive nuclear testing in the atmosphere during the 1950's and early 1960's. It is estimated that more than 500 megatons of nuclear yield were detonated in the atmosphere between 1945 and 1971, about half of this yield being produced by a fission reaction. The peak occurred in 1961-62, when a total of 340 megatons were detonated in the atmosphere by the United States and Soviet Union. The limited nuclear test ban treaty of 1963 ended atmospheric testing for the United States, Britain, and the Soviet Union, but two major non-signatories, France and China, continued nuclear testing at the rate of about 5 megatons annually. (France now conducts its nuclear tests underground.)

A U.N. scientific committee has estimated that the cumulative per capita dose to the world's population up to the year 2000 as a result of atmospheric testing through 1970 (cutoff date of the study) will be the equivalent of 2 years' exposure to natural background radiation on the earth's surface. For the bulk of the world's population, internal and external radiation doses of natural origin amount to less than one-tenth rad annually. Thus nuclear testing to date does not appear to pose a severe radiation threat in global terms. But a nuclear war releasing 10 or 100 times the total yield of all previous weapons tests could pose a far greater worldwide threat. The biological effects of all forms of ionizing radiation have been calculated within broad ranges by the National Academy of Sciences. Based on these calculations, fallout from the

500-plus megatons of nuclear testing through 1970 will produce between 2 and 25 cases of genetic disease per million live births in the next generation.

This means that between 3 and 50 persons per billion births in the post-testing generation will have genetic damage for each megaton of nuclear yield exploded. With similar uncertainty, it is possible to estimate that the induction of cancers would range from 75 to 300 cases per megaton for each billion people in the post-test generation.

If we apply these very rough yardsticks to a large-scale nuclear war in which 10,000 megatons of nuclear force are detonated, the effects on a world population of 5 billion appear enormous. Allowing for uncertainties about the dynamics of a possible nuclear war, radiation-induced cancers and genetic damage together over 30 years are estimated to range from 1.5 to 30 million for the world population as a whole. This would mean one additional case for every 100 to 3,000 people or about 1/2 percent to 15 percent of the estimated peacetime cancer death rate in developed countries. As will be seen, moreover, there could be other, less well understood effects which would drastically increase suffering and death.

8

Nuclear Power Growth in India

India now envisages to increase the contribution of nuclear power to overall electricity generation capacity from 2.8% to 9% within 25 years. By 2020, India's installed nuclear power generation capacity will increase to 20,000 MW (2.0×10 Watts, which is 20 GW). As of 2009, India stands 9th in the world in terms of number of operational nuclear power reactors. Indigenous atomic reactors include TAPS-3, and -4, both of which are 540 MW reactors. India's US$717 million fast breeder reactor project is expected to be operational by 2012-13.

The Indian nuclear power industry is expected to undergo a significant expansion in the coming years, in part due to the passing of theU.S.-India Civil Nuclear Agreement.

This agreement will allow India to carry out trade of nuclear fuel and technologies with other countries and significantly enhance its power generation capacity. When the agreement goes through, India is expected to generate an additional 25,000 MW of nuclear power by 2020, bringing total estimated nuclear power generation to 45,000 MW.

India has already been using imported enriched uranium for light-water reactors that are currently under IAEA safeguards, but it has developed other aspects of the nuclear fuel cycle to support its reactors. Development of select technologies has been strongly affected by limited imports. Use of heavy water reactors has been particularly attractive for the nation because it allows Uranium to be burnt with little to no enrichment capabilities. India has also done a great amount of work in the development of a thorium centred fuel cycle. While uranium deposits in the nation are limited there are much greater reserves of thorium and it could provide hundreds of times the energy with the same mass of fuel. The fact that thorium can theoretically be utilised in heavy water reactors has tied the development of the two. A prototype reactor that would burn Uranium-Plutonium fuel while irradiating a thorium blanket is under construction at Kalpakkam by BHAVINI - another public sector enterprise like NPCIL

Uranium used for the weapons programme has been separated from the power programme, using uranium from indigenous reserves. This domestic reserve of 80,000 to 112,000 tons of uranium (approx 1% of global uranium reserves) is large enough to supply all of India's commercial and military reactors as well as supply all the needs of India's nuclear weapons arsenal.

Currently, India's nuclear power reactors consume, at most, 478 tonnes of uranium per year. Even if India were quadruple its nuclear power output (and reactor base) to 20 GW by 2020, nuclear power generation would only consume 2000 tonnes of uranium per annum.

Based on India's known commercially viable reserves of 80,000 to 112,000 tons of uranium, this represents a 40–50 years uranium supply for India's nuclear power reactors (note with reprocessing and breeder reactor technology, this supply could be stretched out many times over). Furthermore, the uranium requirements of India's Nuclear Arsenal are only a fifteenth (1/15) of that required for power generation (approx. 32 tonnes), meaning that India's domestic fissile material supply is more than enough to meet all needs for it strategic nuclear arsenal. Therefore, India has sufficient uranium resources to meet its strategic and power requirements for the foreseeable future.

Indian President A.P.J.Abdul Kalam, stated while he was in office, that "energy independence is India's first and highest priority. India has to go for nuclear power generation in a big way using thorium-based reactors. Thorium, a non fissile material is available in abundance in our country." India has vast thorium reserves and quite limited uranium reserves.

NUCLEAR POWER PLANTS

Anti-nuclear Protests

Following the March 2011 Fukushima nuclear disaster in Japan, populations around proposed Indian NPP sites have launched protests that had found resonance around the country. There have been mass protests against the French-backed 9900 MW Jaitapur Nuclear Power Project in Maharashtra and the 2000 MW Koodankulam Nuclear Power Plant in Tamil Nadu. The Government of West Bengalrefused permission to a proposed 6000 MW facility near the town of Haripur that intended to host 6 Russian reactors. But that now is disputed: it's possible for Bengal to have its first nuclear power plant at Haripur despite resistance. A Public-interest litigation (PIL) has also been filed against the government's civil nuclear programme at the Supreme Court. The PIL specifically asks for the "staying of all proposed nuclear power plants till satisfactory safety measures and cost-benefit analyses are completed by independent agencies". But the Supreme Court said it was not an expert in the nuclear field to issue a direction to the government on the nuclear liability issue.

INDIAN NUCLEAR POWER

- India has a flourishing and largely indigenous nuclear power program and expects to have 14,600 MWe nuclear capacity on line by 2020. It aims to supply 25% of electricity from nuclear power by 2050.
- Because India is outside the Nuclear Non-Proliferation Treaty due to its weapons program, it was for 34 years largely excluded from trade in nuclear plant or materials, which has hampered its development of civil nuclear energy until 2009.
- Due to these trade bans and lack of indigenous uranium, India has uniquely been developing a nuclear fuel cycle to exploit its reserves of thorium.
- Now, foreign technology and fuel are expected to boost India's nuclear power plans considerably. All plants will have high indigenous engineering content.

- India has a vision of becoming a world leader in nuclear technology due to its expertise in fast reactors and thorium fuel cycle.

India's primary energy consumption more than doubled between 1990 and 2011 to nearly 25,000 PJ. India's dependence on imported energy resources and the inconsistent reform of the energy sector are challenges to satisfying rising demand.

INDIA AS A NUCLEAR POWER: 1998-2001

The immediate aftermath of the nuclear tests conducted by India, and then by Pakistan was not an encouraging one. In the two weeks since the conclusion of testing the Indian government has been a source of both conciliatory and potentially threatening remarks. While repeated statements have been made, most notably by Principal Secretary to the Prime Minister Mr. Brajesh Mishra on 22 May, and PM Vajpayee himself on 26 May, that India has declared a unilateral moratorium on testing, and that the weapons are not intended for aggressive purposes. India has also offered to open talks with Pakistan to discuss issues of contention and a possible nuclear weapon "no first use" agreement.

On Monday 18 May, just one week after the first test, Home Minister L.K. Advani issued sharp warnings to Pakistan about interfering in Indian-controlled Kashmir. PM Sharif responded the next day with an accusation that India had threatened to attack the territory under Pakistan's control. Although sporadic exchanges of gunfire have occurred over the years along the Line-Of-Control (LoC) that intersects Kashmir and separates the Indian and Pakistani armies, in the days following Advani's warnings there was a pronounced escalation of small arms and artillery fire on a daily basis. On 22 May B. Mishra stated "Let it not be forgotten that PoK (Pakistan occupied Kashmir), including the so-called northern areas, is an integral part of India. After all the unanimous resolution of the Indian Parliament in February 1994 to this effect is absolutely clear."

Pakistan just as firmly believes that Indian controlled Kashmir is an integral part of Pakistan. Two of the three Indo-Pakistani wars have been fought over this same territory. The increasingly aggressive Indian posture, coupled with the current outbreak of armed conflict on the LoC, raised a very real possibility of war returning to the region after a 17 year absence.

Over the next year however this threat seemingly receded. On 20 February 1999 Indian PM Atal Behari Vajpayee made history when he crossed over the Pakistani border by bus to meet Pakistani President Nawaz Sharif at Lahore, raising hopes that with the nuclear arsenals now out of their closets the two powers would back away from confrontational approaches. On 21 February 1999 the two prime ministers signed the "Lahore Declaration", committing the two nations to peacefully resolving their differences.

Development continued on India's nuclear delivery systems - on 11 April 1999 India conducted a successful 14 minute test flight of the 2,500 kilometer Agni-II missile. "The entire process of achieving a minimum deterrent has been completed," Vajpayee announced following the test. "We are satisfied that we are now fully capable of defending our borders," he added. Pakistan responded with an eight-minute test flight of the Ghauri II three days later.

The promise of the Lahore Declaration proved to be stillborn. On 5 May 1999 two Indian army patrols in the snowy Yaldor area in Kargil, a border region next to Kashmir, were surprised to encounter a group of armed men, apparently from Pakistani Kashmir (known in India as "Pakistan-occupied Kashmir" or POK; in Pakistan they are called the Northern Areas or NA). This was the first contact with an infiltration operation from Pakistan to seize the mountain peaks inside India as an escalation of the long-standing Kashmir conflict, which would be become known as the Kargil War.

The "line of control", or LoC, between India and Pakistan runs across some of the harshest, most rugged, and highest territory in the world and consequently much of it consists of "unheld areas", territory so inhospitable that both sides abandon it during the brutal winters. It was because India had suspended patrol operations in the winter that made it possible for infiltrators to set up camp without being detected. The patrols that encountered them were the first of the season. Such areas had been opportunities for adventurousness in the past, as when the Siachen glacier was suddenly occupied by armed forces many years ago - becoming the highest and coldest battlefield on Earth. But this was the first time Pakistan had ever tried to exploit this particular region.It appears the infiltration operation was already underway during the signing of the Lahore Declaration. The larger of the two patrol parties went to check on the strangers, and found itself in an ambush and lost four soldiers. Firing continued for nearly a week before aerial surveillance on 12 May revealed to the army realized that the incursion was far more serious than it had assumed. Around 500 heavily armed guerillas had occupied at least 35 well-fortified positions atop the ridges facing Dras, Kargil, Batalik and the Mushko valley. Cover fire was being provided by the Pakistani artillery, which had begun a systematic bombardment of National Highway 1A that connects Leh to Srinagar in the Dras-Kargil region.

Within days the Indian army moved nearly 30,000 troops into the Kargil-Dras area along with special forces dropped on the high ridges by helicopter, and the battle was on in earnest; "Operation Vijay" (victory) to recapture the heights was launched in late May. Pakistan initially claimed not to be involved with the infiltration effort, a remarkable attempt at dissociation considering that the infiltrators were very well equipped and supplied, came from territory controlled by the Pakistani military, and were clearly in direct contact with the Pakistanis from which they were receiving direct artillery fire support. Eventually the continued direct involvement of regular Pakistani forces made the pretense an embarrassment for Pakistan, which dropped the attempt at evasion.

Over the next several weeks India outmaneuvered Pakistan both on the battlefield and in international diplomacy. Heavy Pakistani fire directed by the infiltrators from their commanding positions made the situation very difficult for India, but Pakistani positions on the Indian side were progressively captured or cut off from support as the superior weight of Indian forces made itself felt. By promising not to cross the LoC itself, India garnered nearly universal international support - and especially active

Amercian support - for its position, while at the same time by mobilizing its forces along the entire Pakistani border it signalled that India was prepared to escalate and use its full military strength if necessary to prevent a Pakistani victory.

The objective of this operation seems to have been to try to obtain a limited gain on the ground - revising the LoC several kilometers in Pakistan's favor. The LoC has after all always been defined in de facto terms - it has no recognized status, it simply marks the effective zones of control of the two nations. The operation was calculated to circumvent India's military superiority - by picking the most difficult terrain possible for India's operations, and achieving the initial gain through stealth alone. Pakistan evidently hoped that international pressure would halt the conflict before India succeeded in driving the guerillas back.

By mid June the tide was turning, and by mid July the Kargil incursion had turned into a rout for Pakistan, both militarily and diplomatically. Pakistani forces retreated behind the LoC, and Pakistan suffered another severe blow to its international credibility, and in turn boosted India's prestige. After the end of the war Pakistani Prime Minister Nawaz Sharif asserted that the operation had been instigated without his knowledge - a claim, which whether true or not, was unfortunately all too plausible in Pakistan, with its tradition of the military operating free from civilian control.

The total depth of penetration across the LoC was no more than eight or nine kilometres at most. As intended by Pakistan, the operations for retaking the occupied areas were very difficult for India and this short, sharp war resulted in 474 killed and 1109 wounded on the Indian side (as of July 26, 1999).

A crucial but at the time unreported consequence of the Kargil War, tied in with the Indian mobilization along the Pakistani border, was the apparent deployment of at least five nuclear armed missiles. "Four nuclear armed Prithvis and one Agni were deployed for retaliatory strikes" according to Dr. Sanjay Badri-Maharaj, author of*The Armageddon Factor* (Indian Express, 18 June 2000). This would have been a preproduction model of the Agni-II, the first deployable Agni version. Sharif's demurral became even more plausible three months later when a showdown occurred between

PM Sharif and army chief Gen. Pervez Musharraf on 13 October 1999. Acting while Musharraf was out of the country, Sharif fired him, but hours later Musharraf returned and overthrew Sharif in a coup (later to put Sharif on trial for his life).

Following the aggressive, destabilizing, and ill-conceived military operation of Kargil, the military coup in Pakistan did absolutely nothing to reassure India or the world regarding Pakistan's soundness and circumspection. The result was naturally even deeper isolation for Pakistan, on top of the sanctions that followed the 1998 tests, and the Kargil adventure.

Overt hostilities along the border continued to persist after the conclusion of the Kargil War. On 10 August 1999 an Indian fighter jet shot down a slow-moving Pakistani reconnaissance plane, killing all 16 aboard. The Indians said the plane had strayed across the border, though most of the wreckage landed in Pakistan.

On 17 August 1999, India took the major - though belated step - toward formalizing its declared status as a nuclear power by issuing a six-page document detailing a proposed doctrine governing its nuclear arsenal, entitled the "Draft Report of National Security Advisory Board on Indian Nuclear Doctrine". The report, which was prepared by a government-appointed advisory board, was made public Tuesday by National Security Advisor Brajesh Mishra.

The essential points of this doctrine were that India asserted a right to possess nuclear weapons, and would pursue a policy of credible "minimum" nuclear deterrence and use nuclear weapons only to retaliate against a first strike. According to the draft, "Any nuclear attack on India and its forces shall result in punitive retaliation with nuclear weapons to inflict damage unacceptable to the aggressor."

"India's peacetime posture aims at convincing any potential aggressor that any threat of use of nuclear weapons against India shall invoke measures to counter the threat," the draft said. It further stated that India would not use nuclear weapons against a state that does not have them or is not aligned with a nuclear-armed power, and that nuclear weapons would be tightly controlled and launched only with the authorization of the prime minister, or a designated successor. The draft said the size, components, deployment and employment of nuclear forces would be decided in light of the strategic environment, economic imperatives and the needs of national security. But it took an expansive view of the concept of "minimum deterrence", recommending an arsenal that is able to deliver a nuclear blast from "a triad of aircraft, mobile land-based missiles and sea-based assets," one that can respond to an attack "in the shortest possible time" and employs a space-based early warning system. To raise the threshold for the outbreak of military conflict, India also would maintain highly effective conventional warfare capabilities, the draft document said.

The draft did not mention the Comprehensive Test Ban Treaty (CTBT) but it criticized the Nuclear Nonproliferation Treaty, saying it legitimized the possession of nuclear weapons by states that already had them.

The official U.S. State Department reaction given by Spokesman James P. Rubin was that India was "moving in the wrong direction" by trying to create a credible nuclear deterrence. Rubin said "We think it would be unwise to move in the direction of developing a nuclear deterrent and encouraging the other country to develop a nuclear deterrent and thereby creating an action-reaction cycle that will increase the risks to both countries."

China also condemned the document; and Pakistan, which 15 months ago matched India's nuclear tests with its own, said it would soon be matching India's doctrine with a published doctrine of its own.

Unlike from the U.S., the initial reaction from Europe was cautious. France welcomed the draft doctrine as a logical consequence of the decision to develop nuclear weapons.

The situation was cogently summarized by Tanvir Ahmad Khan in the Pakistani newspaper *The Dawn* on 24 August 1999:

> The present draft is a landmark for three major reasons.
>
> - First, it gathers together in a forceful single document elements that had surfaced disparately and with a certain air of tentativeness since the tests.

- Secondly, it relegates to history half-way concepts like existential deterrence and recessed deterrence that had been debated in both India and Pakistan. In doing so, it delivers a mighty blow to efforts aiming at freezing Indian and Pakistani capability at a non-weaponized level.
- Third, the nuclear doctrine as set forth in the text has hardly any meaning unless the weapons are manufactured and actually deployed in large numbers, and a sizable reserve of warheads and delivery vehicles is permanently maintained.

Tanvir Khan also observed that "the draft published at the moment does not add any transparency to the Indian targeting policy. Nor does it specify Pakistan or China as the principal zones of targeting." He also made some interesting assertions about Indian strategic literature:

Some analysts define the objective as the destruction of Pakistan as a social and economic entity. The targets considered in the relevant Indian literature include six to ten Pakistani metropolitan centres, four hydroelectric and thermal power stations, flooding of Punjab, obliteration of Pakistani railway system with attacks on Gujrat, Bahawalpur, Hyderabad and Dera Ghazi Khan, and disruption of all sea communications with nuclear attacks on Karachi and Gwadar. It has been calculated that a total of seventeen nuclear strikes will achieve all the objectives. If Pakistan also draws up a similar list of countervalue targets, breakdown of deterrence and the ensuing nuclear exchange would mark the end of a civilization.

Although a the time of its announcement, it was expected that the government in place following the elections in the autumn of 1999 would enact the draft doctrine formally, by early 2001 no action had been taken and the draft remained a proposal without official weight, except to the extent it reflected the thinking of Indian government officialdom.

In May 2000 the Atomic Energy Regulatory Board (AERB) which has been set up on 15 November 1983 by order of the President of India to exercise regulatory and safety functions for atomic energy in India was split off from the Bhabha Atomic

Research Centre (BARC). According too an unnamed senior official of the Dept. of Atomic Energy (DAE) quoted by *Aviation Week & Space Technology* (19 June 2000), this split indicated that nuclear warheads for India's armed forces had entered series production. The separation "means the weaponization program at BARC is completed," explained the official. "It is a clear assertion that BARC does not want the AERB to look into its weaponization program." Instead, BARC will have an internal safety committee, which was set up by BARC Director, Anil Kakodkar.

The order for the split issued by Atomic Energy Commission (AEC) Chairman, Rajgopalan Chidambaram stated, "The regulatory and safety mechanism of BARC and its functions, hitherto exercised by the AERB, will henceforth be exercised through an internal safety committee structure to be constituted by the BARC director....

This is being done so as to ensure safety of the strategic nuclear program." Chidambaram added that the regulatory body is "always transparent" and has frequent interactions with the public. He said that BARC's internal committee will ensure compliance "wherever applicable" with the principles of good safety management as given in safety standards developed by the AERB. Despite the assertion of 'transparency' Chidambaram, speaking to a UNI reporter declined to give any details of the new committee saying that it was of strategic importance and details could not be revealed.

The DAE official said, "Most weapon laboratories have their internal checks systems, the Lawrence Livermore [Laboratories] in the U.S. being an example." However, he omitted to mention that in the U.S. the Department of Energy maintains independent oversight with the Defense Nuclear Facility Safety Board (DNFSB) which even includes reviewers outside of the DOE.

Further insight on the significance of this split was added in a *Times of India* article on 15 June 2000. S. Rajagopal, an expert on nuclear affairs and a professor of the Bangalore-based National Institute of Advanced Studies, observed that this decision effectively reclassified BARC as a nuclear weapons laboratory. "This in turn will eliminate the need to place it under the International Atomic Energy Agency (IAEA) safeguards programme," he said.

Chidambaram's eight years in office as Chairman of the Atomic Energy Commission ended on 30 November 2000 when he was replaced by Dr. Anil Kakodkar today took charge as AEC Chairman, and as Secretary to the Government of India, Department of Atomic Energy in a brief ceremony held at Anushakti Bhavan, CSM Marg, Mumbai. Kakodkar This continued the tradition since Vikram Sarabhai's death in 1971 of having the top official in Atomic Energy be a leader of India's nuclear weapon program. As BARC director, Kakodkar had been the principal scientist involved in the May 1998 nuclear tests.

INDIAN NUCLEAR POWER INDUSTRY DEVELOPMENT

Nuclear power for civil use is well established in India. Its civil nuclear strategy has been directed towards complete independence in the nuclear fuel cycle, necessary because it is excluded from the 1970 Nuclear Non-Proliferation Treaty (NPT) due to it acquiring nuclear weapons capability after 1970. (Those five countries doing so before 1970 were accorded the status of Nuclear Weapons States under the NPT.)

As a result, India's nuclear power program has proceeded largely without fuel or technological assistance from other countries . Its power reactors to the mid 1990s had some of the world's lowest capacity factors, reflecting the technical difficulties of the country's isolation, but rose impressively from 60% in 1995 to 85% in 2001-02. Then in 2008-10 the load factors dropped due to shortage of uranium fuel.

India's nuclear energy self-sufficiency extended from uranium exploration and mining through fuel fabrication, heavy water production, reactor design and construction, to reprocessing and waste management. It has a small fast breeder reactor and is building a much larger one. It is also developing technology to utilise its abundant resources of thorium as a nuclear fuel.

The Atomic Energy Establishment was set up at Trombay, near Mumbai, in 1957 and renamed as Bhabha Atomic Research Centre (BARC) ten years later. Plans for building the first Pressurised Heavy Water Reactor (PHWR) were finalised in 1964, and this prototype - Rajasthan-1, which had Canada's Douglas Point reactor as a reference unit, was built as a collaborative venture between Atomic Energy of Canada Ltd (AECL) and NPCIL. It started up in 1972 and was duplicated Subsequent indigenous PHWR development has been based on these units, though several stages of evolution can be identified: PHWRs with dousing and single containment at Rajasthan 1-2, PHWRs with suppression pool and partial double containment at Madras, and later standardized PHWRs from Narora onwards having double containment, suppression pool, and calandria filled with heavy water, housed in a water-filled calandria vault.

The two Tarapur 150 MWe Boiling Water Reactors (BWRs) built by GE on a turnkey contract before the advent of the Nuclear Non-Proliferation Treaty were originally 200 MWe. They were down-rated due to recurrent problems but have run well since. They have been using imported enriched uranium and are under International Atomic Energy Agency (IAEA) safeguards. However, late in 2004 Russia deferred to the Nuclear Suppliers' Group and declined to supply further uranium for them. They underwent six months refurbishment over 2005-06, and in March 2006 Russia agreed to resume fuel supply. In December 2008 a $700 million contract with Rosatom was announced for continued uranium supply to them.

The two small Canadian (Candu) PHWRs at Rajasthan nuclear power plant started up in 1972 & 1980, and are also under safeguards. Rajasthan-1 was down-rated early in its life and has operated very little since 2002 due to ongoing problems and has been shut down since 2004 as the government considers its future. Rajasthan-2 was restarted in September 2009 after major refurbishment, and running on imported uranium at full rated power.

The 220 MWe PHWRs (202 MWe net) were indigenously designed and constructed by NPCIL, based on a Canadian design. The only accident to an Indian nuclear plant was due to a turbine hall fire in 1993 at Narora, which resulted in a 17-hour total station blackout. There was no core damage or radiological impact and it was rated 3 on the INES scale - a 'serious incident'. The Madras (MAPS) reactors were refurbished in 2002-03 and 2004-05 and their capacity restored to 220 MWe gross (from 170). Much of the core of each reactor was replaced, and the lifespans extended to 2033/36.

Kakrapar unit 1 was fully refurbished and upgraded in 2009-10, after 16 years operation, as was Narora-2, with cooling channel (calandria tube) replacement.

Following the Fukushima accident in March 2011, four NPCIL taskforces evaluated the situation in India and in an interim report in July made recommendations for safety improvements of the Tarapur BWRs and each PHWR type. The report of a high-level committee appointed by the Atomic Energy Regulatory Board (AERB) was submitted at the end of August 2011, saying that the Tarapur and Madras plants needed some supplementary provisions to cope with major disasters. The two Tarapur BWRs have already been upgraded to ensure continuous cooling of the reactor during prolonged station blackouts and to provide nitrogen injection to containment structures, but further work is recommended. Madras needs enhanced flood defences in case of tsunamis higher than that in 2004. The prototype fast breeder reactor (PFR) under construction next door at Kalpakkam has defences which are already sufficiently high, following some flooding of the site in 2004.

MORE RECENT NUCLEAR POWER DEVELOPMENTS IN INDIA

The Tarapur 3&4 reactors of 540 MWe gross (490 MWe net) were developed indigenously from the 220 MWe (gross) model PHWR and were built by NPCIL. The first - Tarapur 4 - was connected to the grid in June 2005 and started commercial operation in September. Tarapur-4's criticality came five years after pouring first concrete and seven months ahead of schedule. Its twin - unit 3 - was about a year behind it and was connected to the grid in June 2006 with commercial operation in August, five months ahead of schedule. Tarapur 3 & 4 cost about $1200/kW, and are competitive with imported coal.

Future indigenous PHWR reactors will be 700 MWe gross (640 MWe net). The first four are being built at Kakrapar and Rajasthan.

They are due on line by 2017 after 60 months construction from first concrete to criticality. Cost is quoted at about Rs 12,000 crore (120 billion rupees) each, or $1700/kW. Up to 40% of the fuel they use will be slightly enriched uranium (SEU) - about 1.1% U-235, to achieve higher fuel burn-up - about 21,000 MWd/t instead of one third of this. Initially this fuel will be imported as SEU.

Kudankulam: Russia's Atomstroyexport is building the country's first large nuclear power plant, comprising two VVER-1000 (V-392) reactors, under a Russian-financed US$ 3 billion contract. A long-term credit facility covers about half the cost of the plant. The AES-92 units at Kudankulam in Tamil Nadu state are being built by NPCIL and will be commissioned and operated by NPCIL under IAEA safeguards. The turbines are made by Leningrad Metal Works. Unlike other Atomstroyexport projects such as in Iran, there have been only about 80 Russian supervisory staff on the job.

Russia is supplying all the enriched fuel through the life of the plant, though India will reprocess it and keep the plutonium. The first unit was due to start supplying power in March 2008 and go into commercial operation late in 2008, but this schedule has slipped by more than three years. In the latter part of 2011 and into 2012 completion and fuel loading was being delayed by public protests.

The second unit is about 8 months behind unit 1. While the first core load of fuel was delivered early in 2008 there have been delays in supply of some equipment and documentation.

Control system documentation was delivered late, and when reviewed by NPCIL it showed up the need for significant refining and even reworking some aspects. The design basis flood level is 5.44m, and the turbine hall floor is 8.1m above mean sea level. The 2004 tsunami was under 3m.

A small desalination plant is associated with the Kudankulam plant to produce 426 m^3/hr for it using 4-stage multi-vacuum compression (MVC) technology. Another RO plant is in operations to supply local township needs. Kaiga 3 started up in February, was connected to the grid in April and went into commercial operation in May 2007.

Unit 4 started up in November 2010 and was grid-connected in January 2011, but is about 30 months behind original schedule due to shortage of uranium. The Kaiga units are not under UN safeguards, so cannot use imported uranium. Rajasthan-5 started up in November 2009, using imported Russian fuel, and in December it was connected to the northern grid. RAPP-6 started up in January 2010 and was grid connected at the end of March.

A 500 MWe prototype fast breeder reactor (PFBR) is under construction at Kalpakkam near Madras by BHAVINI (Bharatiya Nabhikiya Vidyut Nigam Ltd), a government enterprise set up under DAE to focus on FBRs.

It was expected to start up about the end of 2010 and produce power in 2011, but this schedule is delayed significantly. Construction was reported 81% complete at the end of November 2011. Four further oxide-fuel fast reactors are envisaged but slightly redesigned by the Indira Gandhi Centre to reduce capital cost. One pair will be at Kalpakkam, two more elsewhere.

In contrast to the situation in the 1990s, most reactors under construction more recently have been on schedule (apart from fuel shortages 2007-09), and the first two - Tarapur 3 & 4 – were slightly increased in capacity. These and future planned ones were 450 (now 490) MWe versions of the 202 MWe domestic products. Beyond them and the last three 202 MWe units, future units will be nominal 700 MWe.

The government envisages setting up about ten PHWRs of 700 MWe capacity to about 2023, fuelled by indigenous uranium, as stage 1 of its nuclear program. Stage 2 - four 500 MWe FBRs - will be concurrent.

Construction costs of reactors as reported by AEC are about $1200 per kilowatt for Tarapur 3 & 4 (540 MWe), $1300/kW for Kaiga 3 & 4 (220 MWe) and expected $1700/kW for the 700 MWe PHWRs with 60-year life expectancy.

INDIAN NUCLEAR DOCTRINE

The nuclear doctrine of India was perhaps the first of its kind among the known nuclear weapon states of the world, and India prepared the draft nuclear doctrine document before obtaining capability mentioned in it. Since August 1999, when the doctrine was pronounced by India's national security advisor, the document had not been put before any parliamentary committees or been given a formal title. It was not clear whether the doctrine as presented was a set of recommendations or just simply a set of formulations based on reasoned judgement made by a select group of India's leading academics, bureaucrats, diplomats mostly based in the New Delhi's power corridor.

The precise timing of the release of the DND (Draft Nuclear Doctrine) has raised eyebrows due to the fact that, in August 1999, the Vajpayee government was in a caretaker capacity having lost its majority in the lower house of Indian parliament. A new election had already been called for October 1999. Some might argue that the draft doctrine was released to the media to bolster Bharatiya Janata Party's electoral advantage. It might also be suggested that the nuclear doctrine was formulated only to formalize BJP's nuclear policy declared after the nuclear tests conducted in May 1998. Yet, another view might be that it was to legitimise India's nuclear weapons through the formulation of Draft Nuclear Doctrine arising out of "the reciprocal fear of surprise attack" on the part of political leaders, military planners and strategic analysts in India. Perhaps a succinct view was put forth this way. "The bomb has many fathers. The Congress conceived it, the United Front nurtured it, The BJP delivered. Let us not give the obstetrician any more credit than is due."

INDIA AND THE INTERNATIONAL NONPROLIFERATION REGIME

India's nuclear technology is not homegrown; it was imported from the U.S. and its allies. Under the Eisenhower Administration's Atoms for Peace program, the United States assisted non-nuclear states in the development of peaceful nuclear capability. Beginning in 1955, the United States trained foreign nuclear scientists and engineers and declassified thousands of reports on plutonium processing and other nuclear-related information.

In 1955, members of the U.S. Joint Committee on Atomic Energy visited India to promote the peaceful uses of atomic energy, and Indian Prime Minister Jawaharlal Nehru succeeded in persuading the international community to make Homi Bhahba (father of India's nuclear establishment) president of the first U.N. Conference on the Peaceful Uses of Atomic Energy, held in Geneva in July and August. This conference facilitated the flow of U.S., Canadian, and British assistance to the Indian nuclear programs in the mid-1950s.

Also in 1955, Canada agreed to supply India with a powerful research reactor-the 40 megawatt Canada-India Reactor (CIR). Then, in February 1956, Washington supplied 21 tons of heavy water for this reactor, now dubbed the Canada-India Reactor, U.S. or CIRUS.

Acquisition of CIRUS was a turning point for India's nuclear weapons ambitions. The reactor's design was ideal for producing weapons-grade plutonium. CIRUS produced the plutonium used in India's first nuclear test in 1974, provided the design prototype for India's more powerful Dhruva plutonium production "research" reactor, and is directly responsible for producing nearly half of the weapons-grade plutonium currently believed to be in India's stockpile. Although U.S. cooperation on the CIRUS project was granted on the understanding that the reactor would be used only for peaceful purposes, there were no international safeguards available to regulate and verify the use of transferred technology.

After India's 1974 nuclear weapon test-which India described as a "peaceful" explosion-the United States and other countries that produced nuclear technology formed the Nuclear Supplier's Group (NSG). The goal of the NSG was to prevent exports of commercial and civilian nuclear and dual-use technologies from being diverted to the weapons programs of other countries. For 30 years, U.S. India nuclear technology transfers stopped.

Nevertheless, New Delhi did not stop its nuclear weapons programs. At the end of the Cold War, India's patron, the Soviet Union, was gone, the Indian economy was a crumbling socialist relic, and China was the new emerging power. To reassert itself on the world stage, India embarked on an effort to reform its economy in 1991, began courting a closer relationship with the United States, and tested its nuclear weapons again in 1998 as a demonstration of strength. Although the test brought another storm of international condemnation, both the Bush and Clinton Administrations soon began to seek out ways to cooperate with India as a friendly, *de facto* nuclear power that shared American values and interests.

The United States and India agreed to the Next Step for a Strategic Partnership (NSSP) in July 2005 and to a follow-up agreement in March 2006 in which the United States and India agreed to civilian nuclear and space cooperation. These agreements, if implemented, run counter to the spirit of the NPT. The NPT encourages cooperation in the civilian nuclear power field only with non-nuclear-weapon states in exchange for their clear commitments not to seek nuclear weapons.

In the past, the U.S. has withheld nuclear cooperation from and has severely limited defense cooperation with countries openly seeking nuclear weapons, including India. The new willingness of the U.S. to engage in cooperative activities in the civilian nuclear power field with a state outside of the NPT raises questions about the future of U.S. nuclear nonproliferation policy.

Despite its snub of international proliferation controls, New Delhi has many policies that serve broader U.S. interests and demonstrate a respect for nonproliferation goals, including the following:

- Although not a signatory of the NPT, India has no record of proliferating nuclear technology to other countries, while China, a *de jure* nuclear-weapon state, is suspected of sharing nuclear weapons technology with both Pakistan and North Korea. Pakistan has admitted to sharing nuclear technology with North Korea, Libya, and Iran. Russia is also bargaining to sell nuclear technology to Iran, a country that is known to be violating its NPT safeguards agreement.
- India is a democracy. While the governments of other *de jure* and *de facto* nuclear-weapon states (e.g., China, Pakistan, and North Korea) are less than democratic, there is a high correlation between the quality of democracy and a country's proliferation record.
- India and the United States have a sophisticated and mutually beneficial defense relationship. India generally

shares American and Western concerns about regional security issues.

- India has agreed to separate its civilian and military nuclear facilities and to place its civilian reactors under International Atomic Energy Agency (IAEA) safeguards-a move warmly approved by IAEA Director General Mohammed ElBaradei, who called India "an important partner in the nonproliferation regime." North Korea and Iran have withdrawn from or have violated their IAEA safeguard agreements.
- While India has not signed the Comprehensive Test Ban Treaty (CTBT), it has declared a unilateral moratorium on testing nuclear weapons.

India and Pakistan

Despite India's appearance as a model of moderation and stability, there are perceptions of India's nuclear weapons programs that, if not properly addressed, could ignite a regional arms race. Most important is the perception of India in Pakistan.

The primary purpose of Pakistan's nuclear deterrent is India. Islamabad has largely accepted that New Delhi needs a minimum nuclear arsenal, but Islamabad asserts that India should not substantially exceed Pakistan's deterrent in size or capability.

There are also three U.S. policies toward India that unfavorably affect Islamabad's security perceptions.

First, India and the United States are cooperating on regional missile defense, which could someday counter Pakistan's missile delivery capability.

Second, the proposed U.S.-India nuclear deal excludes eight of India's nuclear reactors, including its fast breeder reactor. Fast breeder reactors are known to be very efficient at creating weapons-grade fuel. Islamabad is afraid that without international controls, India will continue to produce nuclear weapons until it has an overwhelming advantage.

Finally, the United States is not including Pakistan in a civilian nuclear deal. Islamabad feels that it needs a conventional military deterrent against India to avoid escalation in the event of war or border confrontation. Pakistan is already insecure about India's much greater size, and Islamabad worries about an American alliance with its greatest enemy.

That said, there is little motivation in Washington to change policies. Specifically:

- Pakistan has an extensive nuclear proliferation network, and its belated efforts to stop proliferating nuclear weapons technology are incomplete and will not recall technology that is already spread to North Korea and Iran.
- Pakistan is not a democracy. President Pervez Musharraf's claim that only continued army control can keep Pakistan together is a self-serving sham.
- The United States and Pakistan have a long and mutually beneficial defense relationship, but Pakistan's past support of terrorist groups and current ineffectual attacks on the same groups are the reasons the United States does not want to extend civil nuclear cooperation to Pakistan.

Nevertheless, it is in America's interests to reassure Pakistan and the international community that a criteria-based second-track policy does not present open-ended exceptions to qualifying non- nuclear-weapon states. Indeed, reassuring Pakistan is a central goal of the second track of the two-track policy proposed in this paper.

While properly crafted legislation and international agreements should establish criteria that permit only qualifying *de facto* nuclear-weapon states to benefit from civil nuclear cooperation, second-track negotiations should reassure Islamabad that Washington will not permit New Delhi to use its nuclear deal with the U.S. to dominate Pakistan or accelerate the arms race in Asia. In fact, the U.S. should press for the resolution of regional disputes in the second track with the ultimate goal of convincing both India and Pakistan that neither country needs nuclear weapons. Success in the second track, therefore, will serve the purpose of the NPT, which is to limit nuclear weapons to the five *de jure* nuclear-weapon states identified by the treaty.

What the U.S. Should Do

The United States should develop a criteria-based policy rather than an exception-based policy for engaging *de facto* nuclear states in civil nuclear cooperation and other forms of cooperation. Engagement with *de facto* nuclear states that meet American criteria could include military-to-military contacts, conventional arms sales, space cooperation, missile defense cooperation, and joint military exercises. In deference to the nuclear nonproliferation goals and treaty obligations of the United States, however, under no circumstances should cooperation extend to nuclear weapons and delivery systems designed for nuclear weapons. The criteria for nuclear power technology transfers should include:

- A stable democracy and rule of law. Democracy is not a shallow political ideology; it is a necessity for any effective nonproliferation regime. Of the current 10 *de jure* and *de facto* nuclear-weapon states, the ones with the best nonproliferation records are the democracies. The United States and its allies did assist India in developing its nuclear industry, indirectly assisting its weapons program; but when India tested a nuclear weapon in 1974, cooperation halted, and the democracies moved to block further technology transfers. Furthermore, India has no record of passing nuclear technology to other countries. On the other hand, all the non-democratic nuclear-weapon states are aggressive and indiscriminate proliferators.
- A record of not proliferating nuclear technology "to other states" and a demonstrated respect for the international nuclear nonproliferation regime's obligations for nuclear-weapon states.India has no record of transferring nuclear technology to any other country- consistent with the NPT. India has also declared a unilateral moratorium on testing nuclear weapons-consistent with the Comprehensive Test Ban Treaty (CTBT)-and has demonstrated an interest in participating in the Proliferation Security Initiative (PSI). It is American reluctance to accept a country that is not an NPT member that has delayed India's participation in PSI activities.

- Not being a state sponsor of terrorism. The nexus of state-sponsored terrorism and nuclear weapons is America's greatest nightmare.
- Firm separation between civilian and military nuclear programs. Commercial power reactors are an area in which the United States can accomplish multiple goals with *de facto* nuclear powers. For example, an energy trade deal with India should include provisions that prevent India from subsidizing civilian reactors and prevent the United States and other nuclear suppliers from providing nuclear technologies or facilities at prices below the cost of production. Without government assistance, a nuclear power plant would not be economically viable if it was diverting resources to expensive military projects, such as building bombs. At the same time, a trade agreement that eliminated government subsidies and allowed India's power plants to operate for profit would force substantial reform in India's energy sector and contribute to the country's economic development.
- Non-aggressive security policies. This criterion addresses the fundamental security pretexts for developing nuclear weapons in ways that will encourage *de facto* nuclear states to abandon or reduce their nuclear weapons programs. For example, the threat posed by Pakistan is one of many reasons for India to possess nuclear weapons, but India is Pakistan's only reason for possessing nuclear weapons. This criterion would require India to engage in substantive negotiations to resolve disputes.

India, however, does meet this criterion. The ongoing armistice at the Line of Control and the Kashmir border talks between Pakistan and India are making remarkable progress. Although neither country is close to making a fundamental compromise on Kashmir, they have reached a range of agreements on other matters, particularly on controls for their nuclear weapons.

- A willingness to consider limits on the number of nuclear weapons. Arms control advocates assert that this agreement, when implemented, would free India's domestic capacity to produce the fissile material (highly enriched uranium and plutonium) needed to build nuclear weapons and would set a bad precedent for other *de facto* nuclear-weapon states. The Bush Administration's proposed legislation to implement the agreement with India addresses this issue by conditioning U.S. support for India's civil nuclear program on India's assistance to the U.S. in concluding a multilateral Fissile Material Cut-off Treaty.

Ultimately, the size of a state's nuclear arsenal depends on more than just the volume of fissile material that it can produce. Perceived threats and military doctrine regarding the use of nuclear weapons are at least as important. This issue is best addressed in the second track of the two-track nonproliferation policy, which focuses on regional security issues. The broader purpose of the second track is to address the underlying security concerns that prompted India to obtain nuclear weapons in such a way that India concludes that it no longer needs nuclear weapons. Clearly, the second-track agenda should address the threat and doctrinal issues in ways that, among other issues, lessen the threats that the state faces.

THE EVOLUTION OF INDIAN NUCLEAR POLICY

The slow process of Indian nuclearization reflects the interplay between the structural reality of the international system (emerging threats) and domestic preferences about security (unease with nuclear weapons). After Independence, India's first Prime Minister, Jawaharlal Nehru, laid the foundation of nuclear policy. On the one hand, he strongly rejected nuclear weapons because of their capacity for great and indiscriminate destruction, and on the other, he was reluctant to close the door to them entirely, acknowledging that "there is always a built-in advantage of defence use if the need should arise." This mix of idealism and realism set the tenor for future nuclear policy. In 1964, when China demonstrated its nuclear capability just two years after defeating India in a border war, Prime Minister Lal Bahadur Shastri approved advanced research on an underground test, but did not approve an actual test. A decade later, amidst an increasing sense of isolation as the Cold War appeared to be fading, Indira Gandhi did approve the 1974 test, but did not follow it up with a weapons programme. She did, however, initiate the Integrated Guided Missile Programme, which led to the development of India's present crop of nuclear-capable and conventional missiles.

For the reasons briefly outlined above, the nuclear weapons programme was revived in the late 1980s. Successive prime ministers – Rajiv Gandhi and P. V. Narasimha Rao of the Congress, and H. D. Deve Gowda and I. K. Gujral of the United Front coalition – sustained the incremental shift to weaponization during the 1990s, until Atal Behari Vajpayee's BJP-led coalition took the fateful decision to test in 1998. No doubt India's reluctant nuclearization was in part due to the concern that it would invite sanctions. But there had been no such apprehension before the 1974 test. More importantly, having gone nuclear and having overcome the sanctions problem, India has not felt it necessary to deploy its weapons, let alone undertaken a major weaponization programme. Though it is still developing its nuclear delivery capability, especially vis-à-vis China, there is no sign of urgency. There is a consistence in the observance of restraint rather than a headlong rush into nuclearization despite the emergence of significant threats, notably the Chinese threat in 1964, and the Sino-Pakistani nexus during the 1980s. Despite high levels of tension with Pakistan, India has not deployed nuclear weapons, but instead has kept delivery vehicles separate from warheads, and maintained the warheads themselves in disaggregated condition. The contrast with the Cold War could not be greater. To understand the essential character of the Indian approach to deterrence, it is useful to comprehend the main features of India's distinctive strategic culture with respect to nuclear weapons.

STRATEGIC CULTURE AND INDIAN NUCLEAR POLICY

Indian strategic culture – defined as a set pattern of thought and behaviour – with respect to nuclear weapons may be described as nuclear minimalism. Its chief characteristics are:

Low level of importance accorded to nuclear weapons. Nuclear weapons are viewed as dangerous and deeply problematic, and hence not central to the attainment of national security. Though potential nuclear threats have existed since China, soon after its war with India, became a nuclear power in 1964, there has never been a sense of urgency in India's nuclearization. The fact that India did not build an arsenal after the 1974 test and the absence of deployment after 1998 show that India remains a reluctant nuclearizer.

A political rather than a military approach to nuclear weapons. Such a view treats nuclear weapons as political instruments that are unusable for purposes other than deterrence, as opposed to an operational view, which would tend to regard them as extensions of conventional weapons. There is little interest in the concept of nuclear warfighting, even among military officers. Defence strategy as a whole, and nuclear strategy in particular, are completely civilian-dominated.

Emphasis on minimum deterrence. This involves the conviction that it does not take large numbers or a high degree of sophistication to deter an adversary. Immediately after the 1998 tests, the Indian government, backed by its nuclear scientists, announced that more tests were not needed. Moreover, from this standpoint, nuclear balances are of no consequence. Hence, India need not worry about China's far larger nuclear arsenal. This precludes arms racing, which is both costly and risky. It restrains unnecessary spending on a nuclear build-up and prevents the diversion of resources from the more pressing needs of economic development.

Strong commitment to arms control. This is a logical extension of the long-held apprehension that nuclear weapons are as much a source of insecurity as of security. India's preference is for comprehensive, non-discriminatory and multilateral disarmament, but the earlier unrealistic expectations of its feasibility have been toned down. Today, bilateral as well as multilateral (non-discriminatory) arms control is considered acceptable. India has agreed on a number of pre-nuclear confidence building measures (CBMs) with China and Pakistan. In contrast with the United States and the Soviet Union, India and Pakistan agreed on a nuclear CBM even *before* they officially declared their nuclear weapons status when they signed in December 1988 an agreement not to attack each other's nuclear facilities. In the wake of the 1998 tests, the Lahore Memorandum of Understanding (February 1999) provided for mutual notification of impending missile tests. Currently, follow-up negotiations with Pakistan are being taken up.

However, there are some problems that appear to be inadequately resolved. Two significant ones – a failure to comprehend fully the relationship between different levels of conflict, and a lack of doctrinal clarity – are discussed below.

The Nuclear-Sub nuclear Linkage

A major problem with Indian thinking about nuclear weapons is its lack of clarity in relating the different levels of armed conflict, i.e., the relationships between subconventional, conventional and nuclear conflict. Initially, the advent of nuclear deterrence was regarded as having brought to an end *all* forms of physical conflict between India and its adversaries. Notably, it was expected by the leadership that Pakistan could no longer attempt to pursue its long-standing objective of obtaining full control over the disputed state of Jammu and Kashmir through military means.

Once India and Pakistan had established mutual deterrence, prudence would be the order of the day. Pakistan could no longer risk a conflict in Kashmir, the strategic status quo would be permanently frozen, and India would be able to deal with its Kashmir insurgency as an internal problem. This crucial error in Indian strategic thinking was exposed by the Kargil conflict of 1999. Accompanied by insurgents, Pakistani forces dressed in civilian garb occupied territory on the Indian side of the mutually agreed Line of Control (LoC) in Kashmir. The aim was to create a crisis without officially crossing the LoC, i.e., to obtain a military advantage while retaining official deniability. This would evoke a general fear of escalation from subconventional to conventional to nuclear conflict and thereby induce international intervention, compelling India to negotiate.

The attempt backfired for two reasons. First, India was able to use massive conventional firepower and throw out the occupying forces, whereas Pakistan could not overtly cross into Indian territory in response for fear of raising the conflict to a full-scale conventional war. Second, Pakistan's actions evoked a strongly critical international response, particularly from the United States, forcing it to announce a humiliating withdrawal of its campaign. However, the Kargil conflict did demonstrate to Indian leaders the problem of the "stability-instability paradox": that the standoff between nuclear rivals permits lowintensity or subconventional conflicts to occur between them. The working of the stability-instability paradox imposed on India a kind of strategic paralysis which Indian leaders found frustrating in the extreme. Though Kargil had failed, Pakistan was able to sustain its low-cost strategy of backing terrorist groups such as the Hizbul Mujahideen, the Lashkar-e-Taiba, and the Jaish-e-Muhammad in striking at will within India. Indian leaders struggled to devise a suitable response. The discourse among policy makers steadily shifted away from a search for political solutions to a quest for appropriate modes of force projection against Pakistan.

The options aired included hot pursuit of terrorists into Pakistani territory, limited strikes or special operations missions against terrorist camps in Pakistan, and a vague and undefined conception of "limited war." In January 2000, Defence Minister George Fernandes asserted that nuclear weapons "can deter only the use of nuclear weapons, but not all and any war," and that Kargil had demonstrated that Indian forces "can fight and win a limited war, at a time and place chosen by the aggressor." While admitting that under the nuclear shadow, there were "definite limitations if escalation across the nuclear threshold was to be avoided," Fernandes claimed that conventional war "has not been made obsolete by nuclear weapons." However, the likelihood that a resort to armed conflict might invite an adverse international response prevented action.

The terrorist attacks of September 11, 2001 in the US altered the situation. The American intervention in Afghanistan created a favourable climate for a strong Indian response to Pakistan's support for cross-border terrorism. Furthermore, major terrorist attacks on the Jammu and Kashmir legislature in October, and on the Indian Parliament in December, sharply increased pressure on the Indian government to act. Indian leaders sought to break out of their straitjacket of inaction and turn the stability-instability paradox against Pakistan through the exercise of coercive diplomacy. They initiated a massive conventional build-up along the Pakistan border and threatened to launch an unspecified form of limited war unless Pakistan stopped abetting terrorism in India. Though nuclear weapons did not enter the picture directly (there is no evidence so far of nuclear weapons being readied by either side), the mobilization did have a strong nuclear-strategic component. India's strategy was a two-pronged one. It attempted *direct compellence* in pressurizing Pakistan to back off in the face of a looming full-scale conventional and possibly nuclear conflict. It simultaneously attempted *indirect compellence* by causing the United States, fearful of a regional holocaust, to pressurize Pakistan to reverse its strategy of supporting cross-border terrorism.

Thus, a linkage was established between subconventional and nuclear conflict through conventional mobilization. India warned that if Pakistan chose to bring nuclear weapons into the fray, it (Pakistan) would suffer far more than India. On December 29, 2001, Fernandes warned:

Pakistan can't think of using nuclear weapons despite the fact that they are not committed to the doctrine of no first use like we are. We could take a strike, survive, and then hit back. Pakistan would be finished. I do not really fear that the nuclear issue would figure in a conflict.

In effect, what the Minister was saying was that nuclear balances do matter. This was in direct contravention of his government's doctrine of minimum deterrence, which rests on the belief that they do not. Besides, the idea that India could tolerate some damage from nuclear weapons seriously undercut its deterrence philosophy.

In the end, the whole exercise was fruitless. Despite considerable US pressure, Pakistan's promises to end support for terrorists operating in Kashmir were tactical and temporary, and, in the face of Pakistani counter-mobilization, India had to withdraw its forces in October 2002 after a ten-month-long deployment. It could not take the risk of treating a smaller quantum of nuclear damage as acceptable in practice, as opposed to its rhetorical argument. Deterrence overrode compellence. While the Indian government has not abandoned the possibility of other forms of limited conventional action, it is evident that the experience has taught a lesson. The episode revealed the difficulty involved in attempting to create strategic space for limited armed conflict in a nuclear environment. This explains the BJP-led government's October 2003 decision to resume negotiations with Pakistan.

Lack of Clarity on Minimum Deterrence

Where does India stand today? The picture is not yet clear. Its doctrine of "credible minimum deterrence" has yet to be articulated fully, and has undergone significant changes between 1999 and 2003. After the 1998 tests, Prime Minister Vajpayee made a brief announcement in Parliament on the elements of his government's nuclear doctrine. He stated that further testing was not necessary for credibility, affirmed India's commitment to the principle of no first use (NFU), and declared that arms control and disarmament remained central to the national agenda. But he said nothing about the sources of threat, the nature of deployment, the types and number of weapons desired, targeting, and other details which are normally considered the primary components of a deterrence strategy. Much of the public understanding of India's minimum deterrence doctrine till recently was based on the Draft Nuclear Doctrine (DND) released by the National Security Advisory Board (NSAB) in August 1999. The DND envisages "credible minimum deterrence" based on a capacity for "punitive retaliation with nuclear weapons to inflict damage unacceptable to the [nuclear] aggressor." For this, the requirements are "sufficient, survivable and operationally prepared nuclear forces" and the organization and will to employ nuclear weapons in the event deterrence fails. It proclaims NFU as well as non-use against countries which are not nuclear and are not allied with nuclear powers. It also calls for robust conventional forces in order to raise the nuclear threshold.

The DND supports a triad of air, land and sea-based delivery systems whose "survivability will be enhanced by a combination of multiple redundant systems, mobility, dispersion and deception." It distinguishes between an unspecified mode of "peacetime deployment" and a shift to "fully employable forces" in the event of a conflict arising. There is an emphasis on credibility – "any adversary must know that India can and will retaliate" – and on effectiveness based on "reliability, timeliness, accuracy and weight of attack." The document goes on to outline the requirements for command and control, security and safety, and research and development, and concludes by focusing on disarmament and arms control. The DND has been criticized for its lack of clarity and its open-endedness. Its call for a triad of delivery systems, and its emphasis on effectiveness and survivability go against the grain of a minimum deterrence posture since they reflect the typical Cold War approach used by the United States and the Soviet Union, both of which built needlessly large forces on the basis of such arguments. In short, the DND reveals a distinct preference for the operational rather than the political aspect of deterrence.

However, as Minister of External Affairs Jaswant Singh told an interviewer subsequently, the report was released in order to generate a national debate and was "not a policy document of the Government of India." Singh's interview provides a much more political exposition of Indian nuclear thinking. There are, certainly, a number of common elements in the DND and the interview. Both declare that India will not be the first to use nuclear weapons; that its retaliation-only posture will be based on the mobility and dispersal of assets as well as on an unspecified level of redundancy; that a distinction has to be made between peacetime and active deployment, implying the possibility of a normally de-mated disposition of warheads and launch vehicles; and that ultimate authority over the arsenal must be civilian.

But Singh's enunciation of nuclear doctrine differs from the DND in important respects. While noting that nuclear assets must be survivable, he does not endorse the DND's stress on India's need for "multiple redundant systems" as necessary for survivability. The latter implies a discomfort with imbalance and a penchant for arms racing because its points of reference are the operational characteristics of an adversary's inventory. Singh explicitly states that "parity is not essential for deterrence," that

India will not engage in arms racing, and that minimum deterrence is only a question of "adequacy," not specific numbers – a point not made clear in the DND. Singh also makes the crucial point that retaliation need not be instantaneous. The implication for stability is clear: there is no need for Indian nuclear forces to be on high alert status, ready for instant retaliation. This facilitates a relatively stable nuclear posture. This is a question that is not addressed in the DND.

Further, whereas the DND does not focus on the question of targeting, Singh observes that "we have discarded the Cold War reference frame of nuclear war fighting," and that "we do not see nuclear weapons as weapons of war fighting," which is an unambiguous rejection of counterforce doctrine. Another difference is with regard to the development of a nuclear triad. While the DND calls for a triad, Singh's position is that though development of diverse capabilities will go on, it is "premature" to talk of a triad and, more important, that a triad is not a "pre-requisite for credibility." The overall effect of the interview is to convey a relatively strong sense of commitment to nuclear minimalism based on a restrained posture with few weapons. In this respect, Singh is more reassuring than the DND. His delineation of nuclear doctrine is in keeping with a pattern of strategic preferences that treats nuclear weapons with circumspection. This helps explain the early initiative taken by Prime Minister Vajpayee in February 1999 (less than a year after the nuclear tests of 1998) to travel to Lahore in an attempt to establish regional strategic stability.

Though these commitments do tell us something about India's deterrence posture, none of them has a direct bearing on the central character of *minimum* deterrence. NFU is a promise rather than a guarantee, and adversaries are unlikely to take it seriously in their calculations of risk. Besides, in comparison with earlier statements, it is diluted by the exceptions made with regard to chemical and biological weapons.

Massive retaliation is a threat that will in any case be expected by an adversary, for nuclear weapons, inevitably, are conducive to worst-case assumptions. Perhaps the pronouncement nearest to conveying a commitment to minimum deterrence is the pledge not to test, since a sophisticated arsenal of diverse and "reliable" weapons would require testing. The critical aspects of minimum deterrence are *not* mentioned in the announcement: the perception that deterrence can be achieved with a small number of weapons, with weapons of relatively little variety and sophistication, and with weapons that are not deployed or even assembled. If these aspects of minimum deterrence were to be spelt out, then a truly minimalist doctrine would have been articulated. That they have not been officially declared does not mean that a minimum deterrence doctrine does not exist. Quite clearly, it does. That is evident in its practice. However, the continuing search for diverse capabilities – land, air and sea-based – shows that the concept of minimum deterrence is not consistent. The only argument in favour of a triad is that it will reduce vulnerability, which is a standard Cold War argument. Sufficiency has to be defined in terms of the risk of retaliation faced by the adversary in contemplating the use of nuclear weapons, not one's own risk in being devastated by a first strike.

This brief review shows the lack of clarity and consistency in India's understanding of minimum deterrence. If ambivalence is allowed to persist, the possibility of nuclear thinking and practice drifting toward an open-ended operational conception of deterrence will increase. As India's nuclear infrastructure grows and takes shape, operational pressures led by military personnel, whose job, after all, is to treat nuclear weapons as usable weapons, will also grow.

Questions about vulnerability and reliability – and above all "credibility" – will be raised in the quest for more and "better" weapons. Unless minimum deterrence is clearly and thoroughly understood, there is always the possibility that some combination of intellectual drift, organizational pressures, and sustained threats will push doctrine toward open-ended expansion.

Bibliography

Allison, Graham: *Nuclear Terrorism: The Ultimate Preventable Catastrophe*, New York: Times Books, 2004.

Basrur, Rajesh M., and Hasan-Askari Rizvi, *Nuclear Terrorism and South Asia*, Albuquerque, NM: Sandia National Laboratories, February 2003.

Bhatia, Shyam: *India's Nuclear Bomb*, Ghaziabad: Vikas Publishing House, 1979.

Bradley, John. Learning to Glow: *A Nuclear Reader*. Tucson: University of Arizona Press, 2000.

Bukharin, Oleg: *The Threat of Nuclear Terrorism and the Physical Security of Nuclear Installations and Materials in the former Soviet Union*, Monterey, CA: Center for Russian and Eurasian Studies, Monterey Institute of International Studies, 1992.

Buzan, Barry & Eric Herring: *The Arms Dynamic in World Politics*, London: Lynne Rienner Publishers, 1998.

Cochran, Thomas B. *Nuclear Weapons Databook*. Cambridge, MA: Ballinger Publishing Company, 1987.

Dunn, Lewis A., *'India, Pakistan, Iran: A Nuclear Proliferation Chain'*, Colorado: Westview Press, 1977.

Fernlund, Kevin J. *The Cold War American West, 1945–1989*. Albuquerque: University of New Mexico Press, 1998.

Friedman, G.: *The Future of War of Cyber Crimes*, N.Y., Random House, 1996.

George Perkovich: *India's Nuclear Bomb: The Impact on Global Proliferation*, University of California Press: Berkeley, 1991.

Herken, Gregg. *The Winning Weapon: The Atomic Bomb in the Cold War, 1945-1950*. Princeton: Princeton University Press, 1988.

Kapur, Ashok: *Pakistan's Nuclear Development*, New York: Croom Helm, 1987.

Kaufmann, Albert R. *Nuclear Reactor Fuel Elements: Metallurgy and Fabrication.* New York: Interscience Publishers, Inc., 1962.

Kegley, C. W.: *The new global terrorism: Characteristics, causes, and controls,* Upper Saddle Creek, NJ: Prentice Hall, 2003.

Leo Tansky, *US and USSR Aid to Developing Countries: A Comparative Study of India, Turkey, and the UAR,* New York, 1967.

Lifton, Robert Jay and Mitchell, Greg. *Hiroshima in America: A Half Century of Denial.* New York: Avon Books, 1995.

Qureshi, A. Iqbal : *Islam and the Theory of Interest,* Kitab Bhavan, New Delhi, 1994.

Rhodes, Richard, *The Making of the Atomic Bomb,* New York: Simon and Schuster, 1988.

Schroeer, Dietrich, *Science, Technology, and the Nuclear Arms Race,* Ontario: John Wiley & Sons, 1984.

Sherwin, Martin J. A World Destroyed: *The Atomic Bomb and the Grand Alliance.* New York: Vintage Books, 1977.

Sidney Fox: *Klaus Dose, Molecular Evolution and The Origin of Life,* New York: Marcel Dekker, 1977.

Spector, Leonard S., *Going Nuclear,* Cambridge, MA: Ballinger Publishing Company, 1987.

Stephen Reyna : *The Political Economy of African Famine,* Philadelphia, Gordon and Breach Science Publishers, 1991

Stout, C.: *The psychology of terrorism,* Westport, CT: Praeger, 2002.

Teller, Edward. *The Legacy of Hiroshima.* New York: Doubleday, 1962.

Whitaker, D. J.: *The Terrorism Reader,* New York: Routledge, 2001.

White, J. R.: *Terrorism: An introduction: 2002 update,* Belmont, CA: Wadsworth, 2002.

Winkler, Allan M. *Life Under A Cloud: American Anxiety About the Atom.* New York: Oxford University Press, 1993.

Winston, Mark L.: *Travels in the Genetically Modified Zone,* Cambridge, Harvard University, 2004.

Index

D

Defence Economy, 35, 36, 38, 39.

Dynamic Pressure, 202, 224, 225, 227.

E

Energy Policy, 52, 132, 133, 138, 139.

Explosive Power, 36, 216, 246, 247, 248, 254, 255.

G

Global Nuclear War, 246.

H

Horizontal Proliferation, 1, 9, 10, 19, 26, 69.

I

Indian Nuclear Doctrine, 267, 275.

Indian Nuclear Policy, 283, 284.

Indian Nuclear Power, 262, 271.

K

Kashmir Conflict, 124, 264.

M

Military Scientific Theory, 44.

N

National Defence Economy, 35, 36, 38, 39.

Nuclear Attack, 32, 59, 60, 68, 69, 70, 71, 72, 79, 104, 117, 145, 157, 162, 187, 195, 214, 251, 267.

Nuclear Command, 97, 102, 104.

Nuclear Deterrence, 59, 65, 68, 69, 70, 71, 72, 73, 78, 79, 81, 82, 93, 98, 161, 267, 268, 286.

Nuclear Doctrine, 5, 63, 98, 106, 269, 275, 276, 289, 290, 291.

Nuclear Explosions, 206, 208, 216, 220, 233, 247, 254, 255.

Nuclear Implications, 61.

Nuclear Power, 15, 18, 25, 30, 51, 52, 53, 54, 55, 56, 57, 67, 78, 83, 84, 85, 86, 87, 88, 89, 90, 91, 92, 94, 96, 99, 134, 135, 159, 169, 197, 249, 260, 261, 262, 267, 268, 271, 272, 274, 278, 281, 282, 285.

Nuclear Proliferation, 1, 4, 10, 19, 26, 29, 30, 54, 60, 69, 77, 84, 85, 88, 89, 92, 94, 96, 115, 118, 249, 280.

Nuclear Radiation, 78, 208, 209, 217, 218, 220, 221, 229.

Nuclear Strategy, 5, 60, 61, 65, 67, 106, 107, 114, 160, 170, 271, 285.
Nuclear Threshold, 46, 63, 69, 287, 289.
Nuclear War, 35, 59, 60, 64, 69, 82, 93, 105, 106, 130, 157, 161, 163, 164, 168, 213, 217, 246, 247, 248, 249, 250, 251, 252, 253, 254, 258, 259, 291.
Nuclear Weapons, 2, 3, 4, 5, 8, 9, 10, 11, 14, 16, 18, 20, 24, 27, 29, 32, 33, 34, 41, 42, 46, 49, 50, 54, 60, 62, 63, 65, 67, 68, 69, 70, 71, 72, 73, 74, 75, 76, 77, 78, 79, 80, 81, 82, 83, 84, 85, 86, 87, 88, 89, 90, 91, 93, 94, 95, 96, 97, 98, 99, 100, 101, 102, 103, 104, 105, 106, 107, 108, 109, 110, 111, 112, 114, 116, 117, 128, 129, 131, 143, 144, 145, 153, 158, 159, 161, 162, 165, 166, 167, 168, 169, 170, 171, 174, 175, 176, 178, 179, 180, 181, 182, 183, 184, 185, 186, 187, 188, 189, 190, 191, 192, 193, 194, 195, 196, 197, 198, 200, 209, 236, 244, 247, 254, 255, 256, 257, 258, 261, 262, 263, 268, 275, 276, 278, 283, 284, 285, 286, 287, 288, 289, 290, 291, 292.

P

Policy, 3, 5, 8, 13, 14, 22, 23, 40, 45, 49, 52, 59, 67, 70, 71, 72, 73, 87, 91, 94, 95, 96, 101, 102, 111, 113, 114, 115, 116, 117, 119, 121, 122, 123, 124, 129, 132, 133, 138, 139, 147, 151, 161, 162, 164, 170, 179, 182, 188, 189, 193, 197, 237, 243, 249, 252, 254, 267, 269, 276, 278, 280, 281, 283, 284, 287, 290.
Proliferation Trends, 9.

S

Security, 1, 2, 3, 5, 7, 8, 9, 10, 11, 12, 13, 14, 17, 20, 24, 36, 50, 65, 73, 81, 92, 96, 98, 99, 100, 102, 105, 112, 115, 116, 118, 119, 120, 122, 123, 127, 128, 131, 136, 142, 149, 150, 151, 152, 153, 157, 158, 160, 161, 163, 170, 179, 197, 201, 216, 221, 222, 225, 244, 245, 246, 247, 250, 251, 286, 288, 290, 291, 292.
Security Disputes, 1, 5, 10, 13.
Strategy Research, 39.

T

Thermal Radiation, 203, 204, 206, 207, 217, 219, 220, 229, 230, 231, 232, 233.

W

Weapons Development, 3, 36, 39, 40, 43, 44, 49, 116, 151, 165, 169, 197.

❑❑❑